TREASURY OF CELEBRATIONS

ALTERNATIVES

TREASURY OF CELEBRATIONS

Edited by Carolyn Pogue

Northstone

Editor: Michael Schwartzentruber
Cover design: Lois Huey-Heck
Consulting art director: Robert MacDonald

Northstone Publishing Inc. is an employee-owned company, committed to caring for the environment and all creation. Northstone recycles, reuses and composts, and encourages readers to do the same. Resources are printed on recycled paper and more environmentally friendly ground-wood papers (newsprint), whenever possible. The trees used are replaced through donations to the Scoutrees For Canada Program. Ten percent of all profit is donated to charitable organizations.

Canadian Cataloguing in Publication Data

Main entry under title:
Treasury of celebrations
ISBN 1-55145-088-7
1. Holidays. 2. Anniversaries.
3. Simplicity. 4. Conduct of life. I. Pogue,
Carolyn, 1948-
GT3930.T73 1996   394.2 C96-910435-9

Published by Northstone Publishing Inc.

Northstone

Printed in Canada by Best Book Manufacturers

Printed on Recycled Paper

Table of Contents

Part 1: Making Choices

Part 2: Gifts

Part 3: The Celebrations

January, February, March, April

May, June, July, August

Part 4: Rites of Passage

Preface

A Word from Alternatives for Simple Living

Alternatives for Simple Living – generally known as Alternatives – is a nonprofit organization whose mission is to "equip people of faith to challenge consumerism, live justly, and celebrate responsibly." Started in 1973 as a protest against the commercialization of Christmas, it encourages celebrations year-round that reflect conscientious ways of living. Throughout its 23-year history, Alternatives has led the movement to live more simply and faithfully. Alternatives emphasizes relationships and traditions over things, hoping to avoid stress and debt, and promoting alternative giving – helping the truly needy instead of splurging on ourselves.

Alternatives has developed a wide variety of resources (some in Spanish), led workshops, published six editions of the *Alternative Celebrations Catalogue,* and a quarterly magazine. Their most recent video, *Break Forth into Joy! Beyond a Consumer Lifestyle,* won a gold medal at the Houston International Film Festival (religion and ethics division).

Alternatives' annual booklet, *Whose Birthday Is It, Anyway?* has been published since 1988 and is available in 20 different editions for various denominations. It contains an Advent calendar, biblical reflections for Advent and Christmas, activities, and articles.

Alternatives' current catalogue of resources includes material produced by Alternatives, and also books and resources from other publishers on simple living and related subjects such as hunger, the environment, and media literacy. Because Alternatives provides resources for celebrations, they have adopted the motto, "Resources for responsibly living and celebrating since 1973."

Alternatives is funded by grants, memberships, and sales of resources. The regular business line is 712–274–8875; or call anytime to order or query membership at 1–800–821–6153. To send a fax, call first during business hours. The new address is 3617 Old Lakeport Road, PO Box 2857, Sioux City, Iowa 51106.

A Word from the Editor

It has been a pleasure to work with Alternatives material, and to work with Michael Schwartzentruber at one of Canada's newest publishers, Northstone Publishing, Inc.

Most of the articles in this book have been previously published in one of the six editions of the *Alternative Celebrations Catalogue*. Although some editorial work was required to update statistics, and a few articles and ideas have been added, it was a surprise to see how the thinking behind creative simplicity needs little change and no apology in 1996. Creative simplicity in the '70s and '80s, perhaps, was ahead of its time. There is no question that as we approach the end of the millennium the lifestyles described in this book are necessary and welcome.

I dedicate this book to children everywhere. Children deserve the best life can offer – a peaceful, clean, just, and safe world. May readers find encouragement and practical ideas on these pages to help bring that about.

– Carolyn Pogue

Introduction

Reshaping Our Celebrations

This is a book about joy, spontaneity, caring, justice, and concern for nature. It is a book about celebrating, a book for those who are not satisfied with the models of celebration offered by a consumer society. This book includes the experiences of people with widely varying backgrounds and perspectives, people whose celebrations give voice to the ideals by which they are trying to live.

There is a tradition which holds that the most rewarding life is one shaped around our highest civic and religious ideals, and that the arena for practicing these ideals is in the routine of daily life. It is, to be sure, a minority tradition and it stands in stark contrast to the traditions of the majority – a life of self-gratification through consumption regardless of the adverse effects on other people, on the environment, and even on our own spirits.

In her book, *Living More with Less*, Doris Janzen Longacre gave voice to the minority tradition. She proposed five "life standards" as guides for living according to our highest ideals. While neither new nor unique, these simple life standards are an important framework for thinking about what it means to live responsibly today:

- **Do justice.** From the Hebrew prophets to our ancestors, the important ideals of fair play and "the common good" are deeply imbedded in our religious and national traditions. Although injustices in our history, in our society, and throughout the world tempt us to be cynical, we are called to be attentive to the way our patterns of living affect other people, especially the poor in our country and in the developing world.

- **Learn from the world community.** The notion that North America is a cultural melting pot, no matter how flawed, carries with it the insight that we are enriched by an infusion of knowledge and spirit of people from all over the world. To continue this learning in daily life is more than enriching. It may be necessary for our survival.

- **Nurture people.** The intrinsic worth of all individuals – the importance of their rights and needs – should be the basis of all human interaction. How do we care for each other in ways that neither manipulate nor exploit, but are fair, loving, and humane?

- **Cherish the natural order.** Rather than seeing nature as a commodity to be exploited or as an obstacle to be overcome, we must learn to respect our environment as a wonderful but finite gift. We must live in harmony with nature if, in the long run, we are to live at all.

- **Nonconform freely.** Do not let the world squeeze you into its mold, St. Paul admonished the Christians at Rome. Many European immigrants viewed North America as a place where individuals were not forced into rigid social, economic, and religious patterns of behavior. Now, in the era of "mass culture" with its high-powered advertising and peer pressure, reclaiming the ideal of non-conformity may be more important than ever.

Celebrations: Regaining Perspective

While preoccupation with the details of living makes these ideals seem remote, celebrations are opportunities to regain perspective. Celebrations are ritualized interruptions in daily life that give focus to life's meaning and purpose. Whether in public or private worship or in observing a birthday or a national holiday, celebrations remind us of who we are, where we have been, and where we want to go. For people committed to living by ideals, celebrations are indispensable.

The experiences which make up the heart of this book are like a symphony with many moods and tempos: certain themes recur again and again to undergird and give coherence to the whole.

- Celebrations are rooted deeply in what it means to be human. Without celebrations we lose important ways of nourishing the human spirit.
- Celebrations in our culture tend to be commercialized, making them impersonal, over-consumptive, and destructive to the environment.
- Celebrations are more than entertainment; they are occasions for nourishing relationships and the human spirit.
- Celebrations are times to forget daily cares in order to remember what is true and abiding. Regaining perspective requires that we "forget" in order to "remember."
- Celebrations are more than personal and family occasions; they are occasions for remembering

and celebrating our kinship with the whole human family.

- Celebrations are ways to anticipate the future; they are manageable times in our lives when the future envisioned in our ideals can be practiced in the present.

While these themes recur throughout the many celebration experiences in this book, readers may not find the "ideal" celebration for each holiday or rite of passage. Our intent is to offer possibilities for breaking the tyranny imposed by society (and family) on celebrations, not to impose new ones. We know how far our celebrations are from our ideals. How we go about breaking free of these restrictions and creating new ways of celebrating are matters for individuals and their celebrating communities to decide.

Celebrations as Identification

"Let all who are hungry enter and eat," is the way the Jewish Passover Seder begins. It catches that essential element in all genuine celebration: reaffirming our kinship with all humankind. This identification in celebration occurs in three ways:

1. The **content** of the celebration: When we observe Martin Luther King, Jr.'s birthday, we identify with the struggles of Afro-Americans. In Advent, we experience the fears and hopes of a minority people in the first century. At a funeral, we hurt with those who suffer the loss of a loved one. At a wedding, we rejoice with two people who publicly declare their joy in a new covenant relationship.

2. The **manner** of the celebration: While celebrations often revolve around family and community, they can be enriched by including those who would otherwise be left without community at times of celebration.

3. The **outcome** of the celebration: To identify with others in our celebrating means more than remembering our ties to the whole of humanity, and more than occasions to practice inclusiveness in our households. Celebrations are also occasions to identify with others by diverting resources of time, energy, and money to those who are in need. Although celebrations are symbolic acts, resources diverted from celebrations are concrete ways to identify with others.

Welcome to a new/old way of viewing and celebrating Earth and our fellow travelers on the planet!

Part 1

Making Choices

Simple Living

From the Beginning...

There is a spirit movement among the peoples of this land: born of a longing for more integrity between our spiritual and economic values; born of a resentment that national and international issues, as well as the most personal aspects of our lives, are the objects of manipulation by a society whose values are closely interlocked with consumption; born of an anger that our most sacred celebrations are spiritually bankrupt, their meanings prostituted by the notion that the only vehicle for expressing joy, gratitude, love, or sorrow is purchased with money; born of a sense of estrangement among families, friends, and communities because the values of human relationships have been replaced by crass materialism; born of a sense of alienation from the land, and a fear that our world is well on the way to committing ecological suicide; born under the judgment that the precious limited resources of Earth have been exploited for the sake of the few privileged at the expense of the many without privileges.

These are not new ideas or new complaints, of course. Amos, a biblical prophet in the seventh century BCE, raged against the empty ritualism and materialism of his time:

I hate, I despise your festivals,
    and I take no delight in your
      solemn assemblies.
Even though you offer me your
    burnt offerings and grain
    offerings,
    I will not accept them; and the
      offerings of well-being of
      your fatted animals
    I will not look upon.
    Take away from me the noise of
      your songs;
    I will not listen to the melody of
      your harps.
But let justice roll down like waters,
    and righteousness like an
      everflowing stream.
      (Amos 5:21–24)

Throughout the ages, prophets have spoken similarly. They demand that we protect Earth and all Earth's peoples. Chief Seattle, speaking in his Native Duwarmish, delivered the following oration in 1854:

If We Sell You Our Land, Love It
Attributed to Chief Seattle

The Great Chief in Washington sends word that he wishes to buy our land. The Great Chief also sends us words of friendship and goodwill. This is kind of him, since we know he has little need of our friendship in return. But we will consider your offer. For we know that if we do not sell, the white man may come with guns and take our land.

Every part sacred

Every part of this Earth is sacred to my people. Every shining pine needle, every sandy shore, every mist in the dark woods, every clearing and humming insect is holy in the memory and experience of my people.

So, when the Great Chief in Washington sends word that he wishes to buy our land, he asks much of us.

The red man has always retreated before the advancing white man, as the mist of the mountains runs before the morning sun. But the ashes of our fathers are sacred. Their graves are holy ground, and so these hills, these trees, this portion of the earth is consecrated to us.

Plundering stranger

We know that the white man does not understand our ways. One portion of land is the same to him as the next, for he is a stranger who comes in the night and takes from the land whatever he needs. The Earth is not his brother, but his enemy, and when he has conquered it, he moves on... He treats his mother, the Earth, and his brother, the Sky, as things to be bought, plundered, sold like sheep or bright beads. His appetite will devour the earth and leave behind only a desert.

I do not know. Our ways are different from your ways. The sight of your cities pains the eyes of the red man. There is no quiet place in the white man's cities. No place to hear the unfurling of leaves in spring or the rustle of insects' wings... What is there to life if a man cannot hear the lonely cry of the whippoorwill or the arguments of the frogs around a pond at night?

The air is precious to the red man, for all things share the same breath – the beast, the tree, the man, they all share the same breath. The white man does not seem to notice the air he breathes. Like a man dying for many days, he is numb to the stench.

Precious air

If we sell you our land, you must remember that the air is precious to us, that the air shares its spirit with all the life it supports. The wind that gave our grandfather his first breath also receives his last sigh. And the wind must also give our children the spirit of life...

We will consider your offer to buy our land. If we decide to accept, I will make one condition. The white man must treat the beasts of this land as his brothers.

I have seen a thousand rotting buffalos on the prairie, left by the white man who shot them from a passing train. [But] I do not understand how the smoking iron horse can be more important than the buffalo that we kill only to stay alive.

You must teach your children that the ground beneath your feet is the ashes of our grandfathers. So that they will respect the land, tell your children what we have taught our children, that the Earth is our mother. Whatever befalls the Earth befalls the sons of the Earth.

All things connected

This we know. The Earth does not belong to man; man belongs to the Earth. This we know. All things are connected like the blood which unites one family. All things are connected.

Whatever befalls the Earth befalls the sons of the earth. Man did not weave the web of life, he is merely a strand in it. Whatever he does to the web, he does to himself.

But we consider your offer to go to the reservation you have for my people. We will live apart, and in peace. It matters little where we spend the rest of our days. Our children have seen their fathers humbled in defeat; they turn their days into idleness and contaminate their bodies with sweet foods and strong drink.

It matters little where we pass the rest of our days. They are not many. A few more horses, a few more winters, and none of the children of the great tribes that once lived on this Earth or that roam now in small bands in the woods will be left to mourn the graves of a people once as powerful and hopeful as yours. Men come and go, like the waves of the sea.

Even the white man, whose God walks and talks with him as friend to friend, cannot be exempt from the common destiny. We may be brothers after all; we shall see.

One thing we know, which the white man may one day discover – our God is the same God. You may think now that you own him as you wish to own our land, but you cannot. He is the God of man and his compassion is equal for the red man and the white. This Earth is precious to him and to harm the Earth is to heap contempt on its Creator.

Whites shall pass

The whites too shall pass; perhaps sooner than all other tribes. Continue to contaminate your bed, and you will one night suffocate in your own water. But in your perishing you will shine brightly, fired by the strength of the god who brought you to this land and, for some special purpose, gave you dominion over this land and over the red man. That destiny is a mystery to us, for we do not understand when the buffalo are all slaughtered, the wild horses are tamed, the secret corners of the forest [are] heavy with the scent of many men and the view of the ripe hills [is] blotted...

Where is the thicket? Gone. Where is the eagle? Gone. And what is it to say good-bye to the swift pony and the hunt? The end of living and the beginning of survival.

If we sell you our land, love it as we have loved it. Care for it as we have cared for it. Hold in your mind the memory of the land as it is when you take it. And with all your strength, with all your mind, with all your heart, preserve it for your children and love it... as God loves us all.

Almost 100 years after Chief Seattle spoke those words, *Akwesasne Notes* published the following article:

Reverence of Life: A View from the First Nations
Gayle High Pine

Our entire existence is reverence. Our rituals renew the sacred harmony within us. Our every act – eating, sleeping, breathing, making love – is a ceremony reaffirming our dependence on Mother Earth and our kinship with her every child. All of existence flows through us, and so we know the sacredness of all being. It is knowledge that cannot be grasped or defined, absolute in itself, with no meaning beyond itself.

All that is given us of the Great Spirit is sacred – life, death, the wish to avoid death and the wish to receive it, pain, hunger, anger, growth. To live in harmony with the Earth and all life, one does not use Western value judgment, isolating what might be labeled "good" (such as life, love, or pleasantness) and avoiding the "bad" or harsh (darkness, anger, discomfort, pain, or death). To be in harmony with the death of a loved one, for example, is to know grief – not to suppress, deny, or escape from it, but to flow with it, grow with it, plunge into it, celebrate it.

Technology is a superficial form of growth. A tribal people, among whom the spiritual is the first consideration, constantly tests everything new and old against its spiritual and social harmony; at its own pace it absorbs into and discards from its spiritual rhythm.

Our time perception is spherical – there is no past or future, for they are one with the present. Each point in time is itself – the unique interaction of infinite happenings since the beginning of time – with infinite consequences. As every spatial point is the center of the universe, so every point in time is the center of time – the unique and precious instant the Earth has been preparing for since her beginning.

No matter how many millenniums old a nation is, it is new, being created, growing. Language, myth, legend, song, ceremony, art are at once manifestations of tribal consciousness and instruments of its creation. Through the song we resonate with the pulse of the Earth. The song is forever, but like a flat surface – so the ceremony is given us, given of the sacredness that surrounds us, extending forever, on all sides. Through the ceremony, the sacredness is given shape. But the ceremony is not forever in time – for that we are given our individual consciousness, through which we experience and feel and know – as individuals, we are all earth and all time. The richer the culture – the myths, songs, ceremonies, customs, etc. – the more life and consciousness is created and the more joy and immersion in existence.

– Reprinted with permission of War Resistors League, New York, NY 10012

We know, from the voices of our forebears, from the distressed voices of Creation calling to us, and from the voices within our hearts, that it is time for the human race to begin to walk again. It is time to walk slowly. The Secretary for Peace, Justice and Human Rights for the Lutheran World Federation offers the following encouragement:

Ten Reasons for Choosing A Simpler Lifestyle
Jorgen Lissner

1. As an **act of faith** performed for the sake of personal integrity and as an expression of a personal commitment to a more equitable distribution of the world's resources.

2. As an **act of self-defense** against the mind- and body-polluting effects of over-consumption.

3. As an **act of withdrawal** from the achievement neurosis of our high-pressure, materialist societies.

4. As an **act of solidarity** with the majority of humankind, which has no choice about lifestyle.

5. As an **act of sharing** with others what has been given to us, or of returning what was usurped by us through unjust social and economic structures.

6. As an **act of celebration** of the riches found in creativity, spirituality, and community with others, rather than in mindless materialism.

7. As an **act of provocation** (ostentatious under-consumption) to arouse curiosity leading to dialog with others about affluence, alienation, poverty, and social injustice.

8. As an **act of anticipation** of the era when the self-confidence and assertiveness of the underprivileged forces new power relationships and new patterns of resource allocation upon us.

9. As an **act of advocacy** of legislative changes in present patterns of production and consumption, in the direction of a new international economic order.

10. As an **exercise of purchasing power** to redirect production away from the satisfaction of artificially created wants, toward the supplying of goods and services that meet genuine social needs.

Voluntary Simplicity

In the years ahead, millions of North Americans may move beyond materialistic values and choose an outwardly more simple and inwardly more rich lifestyle. The phenomenon could foreshadow a major transformation in Western values, with wide implications for future developments in business, technology, and society at large. Some of these moves come about from an inner longing for something more. Other moves are made as companies downsize, forcing employees to rethink their futures.

Voluntary Simplicity: Lifestyle of the Future?
Duane S. Elgin and Arnold Mitchell

Newspapers and magazines publish occasional articles about people abandoning the "rat race" pursuits of Western society and seeking a simpler lifestyle, less frenetic in its demands and less tied to today's high-consumption, money-orientated civilization.

We believe that these press reports reflect a social movement which has the potential of touching the United States and other developed nations to their cores. This movement is toward what Richard Gregg, many years ago, described as "voluntary simplicity" – a way of life marked by a new balance between inner and outer growth. We also believe that voluntary simplicity may prove an increasingly powerful economic, social, and political force. It could represent a major transformation of Western values and signal shifts not only in values, but in consumption patterns, institutional operations, and national policies.

Although there are many precursors and contributing streams to this social flow (environmentalism, consumerism, consciousness movement, etc.), there is little direct evidence to measure the magnitude of this way of life. This discussion, then, is not intended to be predictive or definitive; rather, as social conjecture and pattern recognition, it is inherently speculative and intended to provoke further thought and comment regarding voluntary simplicity.

What is voluntary simplicity?

The essence of voluntary simplicity is living in a way that is outwardly simple and inwardly rich. This way of life embraces frugality of consumption, a strong sense of environmental urgency, a desire to return to living and working environments which are of a more human scale, and an intention to realize our higher human potential – both psychological and spiritual – in community with others. The driving forces behind voluntary simplicity range from acutely personal concerns to critical national problems. The appeal of simple living appears to be extraordinarily widespread, even gathering sympathy among those who are not presently attempting to simplify their own life patterns.

Voluntary simplicity is not new, but the conditions and trends which appear to be driving its contemporary emergence do seem new in their magnitude and intensity. Historically, voluntary simplicity has its roots in the legendary frugality and self-reliance of the Puritans; in Thoreau's naturalistic vision at Walden Pond, in Emerson's spiritual and practical plea for "plain living and high thinking," in the teachings and social philosophy of a number of spiritual leaders such as Jesus and Gandhi.

A uniquely modern aspect of voluntary simplicity is that it seems to be driven by a sense of urgency and social responsibility that scarcely existed 40 years ago. This sense of urgency appears to derive from many serious societal problems, including: the prospects of a chronic energy shortage, growing terrorist activities at the same time that nations seem increasingly vulnerable to disruption;

growing demands of the developing nations for a more equitable share of the world's resources; the prospect that before we run out of resources on any absolute basis we may poison ourselves to death with environmental contaminants; a growing social malaise and purposelessness which causes us to drift in our social evolution; and so on. These are but a few of the elements which converge to make voluntary simplicity a seemingly rational response to the current world situation.

Values central to voluntary simplicity

The social movement toward voluntary simplicity is very rich and highly diverse. Yet there seems to be an underlying coherence to the rich diversity of expression of this way of life. Among the values which seem to lie at the heart of this emerging way of life are material simplicity, human scale, self-determination, ecological awareness, and personal growth. Let us examine each of these in turn.

Material simplicity: Simplification of the material aspects of life is one of the core values of voluntary simplicity. The American Friends Service Committee, long a leader in exploring a way of life of creative simplicity, defines simple living as a "nonconsumerist lifestyle based upon being and becoming, not having."

Living simply implies consuming quantitatively less (particularly items that are energy-inefficient, non-biodegradable, nonessential luxuries, etc.), but it does not mean that the overall cost of consumption will go down drastically. Living simply need not be equated with living cheaply. The hand-crafted, durable, aesthetically enduring products that appeal to frugal consumers are oftentimes purchased at a considerable premium over mass-produced items. Therefore, although the quantity of consumption may decrease and the environmental costs of consumption may be considerably moderated, the overall cost of consumption may remain relatively high since our economy is not oriented to producing the kinds of products which fit these criteria. Material simplicity will thus likely be manifest in consumption styles that are less ascetic than aesthetic, that is, the emphasis will not be on a strictly enforced austerity (doing without material goods) but rather on creating a pattern of consumption that will fit, with grace and integrity, into the practical art of daily living.

Human scale: A preference for human-sized living and working environments is a central feature of voluntary simplicity. Adherents of this "values constellation" tend to equate the gigantic scale of institutions and living environments with anonymity, incomprehensibility, and artificiality. The preference for smallness implies that living and working environments (which have grown to enormous levels of scale and complexity) should be decentralized into more comprehensible and manageable entities. Each person should be able to see what he or she contributes to the whole and, hence, have a sense of shared rewards and shared responsibility. Reduction of scale is seen as a means of getting back to basics by restoring to life a more human sense of proportion and perspective.

Self-determination: Voluntary simplicity embraces an intention to be more self-determining and less dependent upon large, complex institutions. Self-determination manifests itself as a desire to assume greater control over one's personal destiny and not lead a life tied to installment payments, maintenance costs, and the expectations of others. To counterbalance the trend toward increasing material dependency, people may seek to become more materially self-sufficient – to grow their own, to make their own, to do without, and to exercise self-discipline in their pattern and level of consumption so that the degree of dependency (both physical and psychological) is reduced. Personal responsibility and interdependence increase.

Self-determination shows up in production as a counterbalancing force to combat excessive division of labor. Instead of embracing specialization, a voluntary simplicity adherent may seek greater work integration and synthesis so that the contribution of their work to the whole enterprise is more evident.

In the public sector, the drive for greater self-determination is revealed by a growing distrust of, and sense of alienation from, large and complex social bureaucracies. Adherents seem to want to take charge of their lives more fully and to manage their own affairs without the undue or unnecessary intrusion of a remote bureaucracy.

This dimension of voluntary simplicity may explain some of the unusual political coalitions that seem to be emerging between the right and left, coalitions that oppose the further intrusion of big institutions into people's lives, and seek greater local self-determination and grassroots political action. The aversion to being controlled by increasingly distant bureaucracies is reminiscent of the stubborn independence which birthed the American revolution.

Ecological awareness: A sense of ecological awareness which acknowledges the interconnectedness of people and resources is central to voluntary simplicity. From this awareness emerges a number of themes that are hallmarks of this way of life. For example, ecological awareness prompts recognition that Earth is indeed limited, with all that implies for conservation of physical resources, reduction of environmental pollution, and maintenance of the beauty and integrity of the natural environment. Importantly, this concern often extends beyond purely physical resources to include other human beings as well. The philosophy of "welfare" espoused by Gandhi – *sarvodaya*, or not wanting what the least of the inhabitants of Earth cannot have – seems to spring, in large measure, from this intimate sense of felt connection with others. The growth of an ecological awareness expands the vision of voluntary simplicity outward and brings with it a strong sense of social responsibility and worldly involvement to what otherwise could be a relatively isolated and self-centered way of life.

Some of the more concrete expressions of this awareness might include: a willingness to share resources with those who are disadvantaged; a sense of global citizenship with commensurate adjustments in lifestyle, social vision, and political commitments; a preference for living where there is ready access to nature; and a desire to foster human and institutional diversity at a grassroots level.

Personal growth: For many persons taking up a materially simple way of life, the primary goal is to clear away external clutter so as to be freer to explore the "inner life." The themes of material simplicity, self-sufficiency, a more human scale to living and working, and an ecological awareness are, in a way, devices to sweep away impediments to inner growth. The goal, then, is to free oneself of the overwhelming externals so as to provide the space in which to grow both psychologically and spiritually.

Simone de Beauvoir succinctly stated the rationale for this desire for self-realization when she said: "Life is occupied in both perpetuating itself and in surpassing itself; if all it does is maintain itself, then living is only not dying." In the view of many adherents to voluntary simplicity, contemporary society is primarily occupied in perpetuating itself and living has become "only not dying." They seek an outlet for their growth potential.

A concern for the subjective aspect of experience and for the quality of human relationships has been reflected in a number of developments over the past 30 years: the emergence and proliferation of the "human potential movement"; the emergence of "transpersonal psychology" coupled with a rapid increase of interest and involvement in many Eastern meditative traditions; the growth of feminism; a cultural fascination with psychic phenomena; developments in brain research that confirm a biological basis for both the rational and the intuitive side to human nature; a growing interest in sports as both a physical and spiritual process, and more.

Without the compelling goal of exploring inner potentials, it seems unlikely that there will be sufficient motivation to adopt voluntarily a lifestyle of material simplicity. Without greater simplicity, we probably will not be able to cope successfully with scarcity and other problems. Finally, unless inner learning expands, it seems unlikely that we will develop the degree of internal maturation necessary for the human species to act as wise trustees of conscious evolution on Earth.

Our analysis still has not penetrated to the roots of the connection between personal growth and voluntary simplicity. For an adequate explanation of that connection, we must look to a deeper underlying vision. It is an old vision – perhaps as old as humanity – but an enduring one that seems destined to be rediscovered again and again. The nature of this vision is succinctly summed up by historian Arnold Toynbee:

"...Jesus, Buddha, and Lao Tse... agreed in their ethical precepts. They all agreed that the pursuit of material wealth is a wrong aim. We should aim only at the minimum wealth needed to maintain life; and our main aim should be spiritual. They all said with one voice that if we made material wealth our paramount aim, this would lead to disaster. They all spoke in favor of unselfishness and of love for other people as the key to happiness and to success in human affairs."

The foregoing five themes do not exhaust the range of basic values that may emerge as hallmarks of the way of life termed voluntary simplicity. Moreover, these values will surely be held to differing degrees and in differing combinations by different people. Nonetheless, these values possess an underlying coherence which suggests that they have not arisen randomly, but rather as a mutually supporting set or pattern. Just a few moments of reflection reveal how powerfully reinforcing these values are; for example, personal growth may foster an ecological awareness which may prompt greater material simplicity and thereby allow greater opportunity for living and working at a smaller, more human scale which, in turn, may allow greater opportunity for local self-determination. No one value theme alone could create the vitality and coherence that emerges from the synergistic interaction of these values. These values combine to form a practical "world view" – a coherent pattern of perception, belief, and behavior which could provide an important bridge between the traditional industrial world view and an uncertain and difficult social future.

What voluntary simplicity is not

We have been trying to define what voluntary simplicity is. We can also get a sense of voluntary simplicity by suggesting what it is not.

- **Voluntary simplicity should not be equated with a back-to-nature movement.** Voluntary simplicity seems perhaps as compelling for the urban majority as it does for the rural minority. An urban existence need not be incompatible with voluntary simplicity. Indeed, many of the experiments with appropriate technology, intensive gardening and such have been conducted in urban contexts.
- **Voluntary simplicity should not be equated with living in poverty.** Indeed, impoverishment is in many ways the opposite of simple living in that poverty tends to make life a struggle to maintain oneself and provides little opportunity to surpass oneself.
- **Voluntary simplicity is not confined to the United States and Canada.** Virtually all of the developed Western nations seem to be moving in a somewhat similar

direction. Many European nations, with more limited land and resources, have been learning how to cope with scarcity for far longer than North America has. And there is evidence that other nations may opt for voluntary simplicity rather than endure the stress of striving for affluence.

- **Voluntary simplicity is not a fad.** Its roots reach far too deeply into the needs and ideals of people everywhere to be regarded as a transitory response to a passing societal condition.

The push toward voluntary simplicity

Despite the strength of the pull to voluntary simplicity, there is little reason to think that this way of life will grow to embrace substantial proportions of the population unless the pull is matched by substantial pushes. The twin elements of push and pull need to be considered if we are to assess the likelihood that voluntary simplicity will gather social momentum in the future. Let us therefore consider whether societal problems will push us in a direction similar to that exerted by the pull toward voluntary simplicity.

The range and diversity of contemporary societal problems are enormous. Space does not allow more than a cursory glance at some of the more prominent problems which may, in their eventual resolution, push us toward a simple way of life. These problems include:

- the prospect of running out of cheaply available, critical industrial raw materials;
- the prospect of chronic energy shortages and a difficult transition to a much more energy-efficient economy;
- the growing threat that we will pollute ourselves to death with the intrusion of many thousands of hazardous substances into our living environments and food chains;
- rising material demands of the developing world, coupled with climatic changes which may induce periodic but massive famine in certain areas; the growing threat of terrorism (nuclear and biological as well as conventional), coupled with the growing vulnerability of the highly complex and interdependent technology (e.g., communications, energy, and transportation systems) common to the Western nations;
- the poverty of abundance: a growing dissatisfaction with the output of our industrial society as the sole or even primary reward and reason for our individual existences;
- apparent loss of social purpose and direction coupled with rising levels of individual alienation;
- chronic and pervasive fiscal crisis of many of our largest cities;
- decline in the expected number

of meaningful work roles, growing levels of automation, and chronic underemployment and unemployment;

- the prospect that we have created social bureaucracies of such extreme levels of scale, complexity, and interdependence that they now exceed our capacity to comprehend and, therefore, to manage them; coupled with growing demands upon government at all levels;
- growing demands that domestic economic inequities be moderated, coupled with the prospect of a little or no-growth economy in the foreseeable future, yielding the specter of intense competition for a fixed or slowly growing pie.

Resolution of the foregoing problems will likely push our society in a direction which is more ecologically conscious, more frugal in its consumption, more globally-oriented, more decentralized, more allowing of local self-determination, and so on.

Solving these increasingly serious problems will probably push us in a direction at least similar to that implied by the pull toward voluntary simplicity.

Two groups

We think there are at least two very distinct kinds of people living a life of voluntary simplicity. The first consists of families and individuals who have voluntarily taken up simple living after years or decades of active involvement in the mainstream. The motivations of such people tend to be highly private and specific – a desire to escape the "rat race," personal disillusionment, boredom with their jobs, a wish to live a more "meaningful," less artificial life, and so on. Such changes in lifestyle make good copy and hence this type of phenomenon gets much publicity. In terms of numbers, this group does not appear very significant, but, as a model for others to emulate, it may be profoundly important.

The other type tends to be younger, more motivated by philosophical concerns, and more activistic.

Criteria for simplicity

A group of Quakers have identified four consumption criteria which evoke the essence of voluntary simplicity:

- Does what I own or buy promote activity, self-reliance, and involvement, or does it induce passivity and dependence?
- Are my consumption patterns basically satisfying, or do I buy much that serves no real need?
- How tied is my present job and lifestyle to installment payments, maintenance and repair costs, and the expectations of others?
- Do I consider the impact of my consumption patterns on other people and on Earth?

Fundamental Change in Values
Milo Thornberry

The long-term social ramifications of voluntary simplicity – if it develops into a major social movement – are enormous. The eventual result could be the creation of a social order that is as different from the present as the industrial era was different from the Middle Ages.

The reason that the potential social implications are so vast is that voluntary simplicity does not represent merely an internal readjustment of the prevailing values pattern, but rather constitutes a fundamental shift in that pattern. Widespread adoption of this way of life could launch our society on a new developmental trajectory.

We are by no means suggesting that voluntary simplicity offers the only approach to a viable culture and economic future. However, the Western world seems to be in a period of social drift. We appear to be losing both momentum and a sense of direction. People seem to be waiting for some leader or chain of events to make clear the nature of an alternative social vision. The uncertainty, indecision, and growing anxiety over appropriate social direction has prompted a new willingness to "think the unthinkable," to deeply consider what life means and where we wish to go. Voluntary simplicity as a co-

herent, broadly relevant, practical, and purposeful world view could provide an important point of reference or anchoring point as we search for and experiment with new social forms.

Alternative futures

Although voluntary simplicity as a way of life may have great and obvious long-term significance, it seems at present to be struggling to achieve a critical mass of social awareness and acceptance. If we are to understand the prospects of voluntary simplicity, we must attempt to understand the nature and dynamics of the large social context out of which this way of life could emerge.

There is a great uncertainty regarding the future course of social evolution in North America, but we have identified four alternative futures which suggest the range of social possibility over the next several decades:

- **Technological salvation:** This is a future where, with good luck and great ingenuity, we find the social will and technological know-how to cope with critical national problems and continue along a trajectory of relatively high material growth. This future assumes that the value premises of the industrial era (rugged individualism, rationalism, material growth, etc.) will withstand current challenges and provide people with meaningful and workable living environments.

- **Descent into social chaos:** This is a future in which society is torn by divisions and tensions among competing interest groups. There is no cataclysmic demise – just the grinding, unrelenting deterioration of the social fabric as crisis is compounded by crisis amidst diminishing public consensus as to how to cope with it all. Inept bureaucratic regulation and unforeseen events (such as severe climatic changes) could change the drift toward social chaos into a rush.

- **Benign authoritarianism:** Despite the growing public pressure for, and acceptance of, the need for fundamental social change, the large, complex, and highly interdependent bureaucracies in both public and private sectors could thicken and, like slowly hardening concrete, lock people into an inescapable net of regulations and institutions. The new order could be a benign authoritarianism which emerges from the unstoppable logic of well-intended bureaucratic regulation which seeps into nearly every facet of life.

- **Humanistic transformation:** One expression of this alternative could be a future in which the underlying value premises shift and two closely related ethics emerge. The first is an ecological ethic that accepts Earth as limited, recognizes the underlying unity of the human race, and perceives humans as an integral part of the natural environment; the second is a self-realization ethic which asserts that each person's proper goal is the evolutionary development of his or her fullest human potential in community with others. Each ethic could serve as a corrective for possible excesses in the other. A humanistic transformation might substantially embrace voluntary simplicity or some similar way of life that, though materially more modest than current lifestyles, is more satisfying overall.

These thumbnail sketches of alternative futures present an enormous range of social possibility. Yet, to the extent that each of these is a plausible future, its seeds must exist in the present. Therefore, they need not be mutually exclusive social futures. For example, we can imagine a plausible future marked by both a humanistic transformation and by technological success.

One way to test the viability of voluntary simplicity as an emergent way of life is to assess the extent to which it could assume a significant role in all four of these futures. In other words, is voluntary simplicity a social movement that has relevance only in the context of a future humanistic transformation, or could it plausibly play a major role in the other three futures as well?

A future marked by "technological success" would probably still require people to attack the problems of resource scarcity, environmental pollution, and global economic inequities by consuming less. To the extent that there is a continuing need to approach these and related problems from the demand side, there will be a corresponding role for voluntary simplicity even in this materially successful scenario.

In a society of growing internal strife and tension, voluntary simplicity could, in the short run, exacerbate that conflict. In the longer run, however, voluntary simplicity might help to alleviate social tensions. To the extent that voluntary simplicity provides a way of life that transcends traditional interest group conflicts and provides a meaningful and workable response to a worsening social condition, it might alleviate tensions by directing social energy in a more coherent and harmonious direction.

In a society marked by changing bureaucratic regulation and democratic processes, voluntary simplicity (with its emphasis on local self-determination, human scale, and self-sufficiency) could provide a

healthy corrective and counterbalancing force. Voluntary simplicity could provide an important source of grassroots innovation and vitality to what otherwise could be an increasingly rigid and somber society.

The important point is that voluntary simplicity fits into many alternative futures and therefore it is unlikely to disappear soon from the social landscape.

Social impacts

What kind of society would emerge if voluntary simplicity were to become the predominant way of life? A partial answer to this question can be found by examining stereotypical contrasts between the value premises and social characteristics of the industrial "world view" and the voluntary simplicity "world view."

If this way of life were adopted by a majority of the population, we could anticipate certain long-term directions of social change that seem congruent with voluntary simplicity, including:

National tenor: A society in which a large proportion of the population adopts voluntary simplicity would probably have a uniquely different "feel" to it. Such a society might possess a greater sense of frontier spirit, a feeling of continuing challenge at the prospects of forging new, evolving relationships among individuals, societies, nature, and the cosmos. It could have a higher degree of cultural cohesion, social maturity, and social consensus. People would likely have a greater sense of future destiny and the conviction they were working on behalf of future generations as well as for themselves.

Material growth: Society would tend to move from a goal of material abundance to a goal of material sufficiency. What level of material sufficiency is appropriate would largely be decided by individual choice constrained by resource availability and prevailing cultural norms. Clearly, this presumes a strongly cultural context with widely shared beliefs as to what constitutes appropriate levels of material sufficiency. Although material growth may tend toward a steady-state condition, this need not imply a materially static society. With selective growth, some sectors of the economy would grow rapidly while others would contract. For example, growth in appropriate technology might be rapid while production of items of conspicuous consumption declines.

Human growth: The society would tend to transfer its growth potential and aspirations from a material dimension to an increasingly nonmaterial dimension. This shift would be of the highest import if, as many suggest, our present problems arise in part from a gross disparity between the relatively underdeveloped internal faculties of humans and the extremely powerful external technologies at their disposal. Society would attempt to achieve greater balance by fostering a degree of interior human growth that is at least commensurate with the enormous exterior growth that has occurred over the last several hundred years.

Life environment: Society could tend to shift from living and working in large, complex environments to living and working in smaller, less complex environments. Accompanying this could be migration from large cities to small cities, towns, and the country.

Identity: The voluntary simplicity society would tend to define personal identity less in terms of consumption than in terms of one's awareness – psychological, social, spiritual. For many North Americans, consumption is not only an expression of identity but is basic to their sense of identity. The growth of voluntary simplicity would tend to produce a cultural perspective in which identity could be expressed in many other ways, such as experimenting with various forms of voluntary simplicity; developing vital communities through new forms of groups and extended family relationships; exploring human consciousness through the hundreds of consciousness-expanding disciplines, ranging from meditation, biofeedback, hypnosis, encounter, bioenergetics, and so on.

Technology: Society would tend to move from "high" or "space age" technology to the careful application of "intermediate" or "appropriate" technology. Just as the industrial era was built on high technology, the voluntary simplicity era would likely rely on technology that is explicitly designed to be ecologically sound, energy-conserving, comprehensible by humans, integrated with nature, and efficient when used on a small scale.

Politics: If voluntary simplicity were to emerge as a dominant way of life, much of its growth could be driven by political activism at a grassroots level. Extensive decentralization of institutions would require that local communities take much greater responsibility for the well-being of their population. Politics would probably assume a more humanistic orientation as people came to see the intimate connection that exists between the processes of personal growth and social change. It could be a society in which political processes were more experimental, error-embracing, and intentional in seeking diversity.

Impact on consumption

Voluntary simplicity consumption criteria are significantly different from traditional patterns. The person living the simple life tends to prefer products that are functional, healthful, nonpolluting, durable, repairable, recyclable or made from renewable raw materials, energy-cheap, authentic, aesthetically pleasing, and made through simple technology. Such criteria will adversely affect many products of conspicuous consumption. On the other hand, the voluntary simplicity lifestyle should create excellent markets for some items:

- first class durable products, such as solid wood furniture, high quality music and television systems, top-grade hand tools, geared bicycles;
- cotton, hemp, and wool clothing – de-emphasizing fashion – which can be mended, handed down, and worn for years;
- do-it-yourself equipment for home construction, home repair and improvements, cooking, gardening, entertaining, and so on;
- inexpensive prefab "flexible" housing;
- easy-to-fix autos and appliances, perhaps using modular construction;
- healthy, natural, unprocessed foods;
- self-help medical, childcare, housekeeping items;

- products for arts and crafts and other aesthetic pursuits;
- simple, safe, nonplastic, nonmetal toys and games for children;
- products or services associated with shared tasks in communal living, cooperatives, recycling, and energy-reduction and food-conversation projects;
- leisure activities geared to country living;
- imaginative ways of refurbishing old city and country homes;
- traveling car repair and parts services;
- machines, equipment, and systems utilizing intermediate technology.

A growing and appreciable portion of market activity will move to the "alternative marketplace": flea markets, garage and yard sales, classified advertising, community bulletin boards. Consumer co-operatives and mail-order operations will increase as voluntary simplicity consumers become less willing to support superfluous merchandising costs. Purchases will be increasingly localized to diminish the costs of transportation and to encourage the utilization of intermediate technology. Specialty stores will likely increase, especially for food, shelter, and clothing.

Impact on work

In a simple-living society, the role of work would be downplayed as a status and power symbol and upgraded as a means of contributing to the collective good. Cooperation rather than competition would be the hallmark of work. Complaints would be directed more toward matters of ethics, social responsibility, and aesthetics rather than issues of pay, office size, and promotion. More part-time jobs, enabling people to earn enough to fulfill their essential needs and yet have much more free time to pursue personal development and perhaps aid others, would be desirable.

Significantly, management would tend to be highly participative, to be organized around tasks, and to be less hierarchical than present. Ultimately, the traditional proprietary attitudes of business might yield to greater openness and inter- and intra-industry cooperation. The aggressive expression of the profit motive (exemplified by "making a killing" rather than "making a living") – although it is not likely to vanish in the near future – would likely be a diminishing force in business.

It seems likely the advocates of voluntary simplicity will, as a consumer group, continue to exert political and economic pressure to change business and industrial practices. As individuals, people may very well try to influence business by buying in accord with rating criteria applied to long lists of specific products and specific manufacturers, retailers, banks, and the like. Such activities, accompanied by word-of-mouth publicity, might be one way in which adherents of voluntary simplicity will try to enforce their sense of social responsibility.

A business founded in the San Francisco Bay area may be one template for new small businesses. Their network includes businesses from food and clothing stores to auto repair. The operating principles of Briarpatch businesses are significant. They include:

- job sharing, in which two or more people are paid for one position;
- job swapping, through which people can occasionally try out other positions;
- multiple jobs or roles, in which a person might be the bookkeeper as well as a board member;
- functions are generally performed without titles; if a title exists, it would probably be facilitator instead of president;
- meditation is increasingly scheduled on the job;
- if there are end-of-year surpluses, they are "recycled" in various ways; but generally there is a desire to help other projects rather than passive investors;

- directors serve as facilitators rather than watchdogs;
- a favorite practice is to set prices according to the rule that the best price is what you would charge your friends.

Long-term significance

Voluntary simplicity specifically addresses the critical issues of our times – the problems of ecosystem overload, alienation, the unmanageable scale and complexity of institutions, and so on. Voluntary simplicity is a creative, comprehensive, and holistic approach to a host of problems customarily considered to be separate. By coping simultaneously with scores of interrelated specifics, voluntary simplicity seems to provide a solution that could not be achieved via the one-by-one route.

It meshes with the eternal needs of individuals to continue to grow. The emphasis on the inner life permits people to grow psychologically. There is reason to think that the kind of growth fostered by voluntary simplicity is especially appropriate to our times and circumstances. In brief, the need of the individual uniquely matches the need of the society.

Of what other emergent life patterns can these things be said?

How to Live Better with Less – If You Can Stand the People
Milo Thornberry

During the 1970s, British science writer Robin Clarke abandoned London to join a rural commune in Wales. What he learned during the experience became the subject of his book, *Building for Self-Sufficiency.*

Clarke and his associates bought a 43-acre farm, and their first job was to convert the small and near-derelict stone cottage into a house that could shelter a community of 16 people. Setting themselves up as BRAD (Biotechnic Research and Development), Clarke and his friends planned to turn the site into a research center to investigate such things as wind power, heat pumps, and methane generation.

"We wanted to devise a life-style that would be valid, not for just this generation living off a depleting stock of natural resources, but for generations far into the future. So we planned to be self-sufficient not only in food, but also in energy, water, and, eventually, perhaps even materials...

"I and my family left 18 months later, and another five people left a few months after that. Nearly all of us left for the same reason: the struggle to do the things we wanted to do against a background of mounting inertia and community dissent proved too great. Just over three years later, the community was officially disbanded, and the farm sold."

But Clarke doubts that anyone involved feels that the experiment could justly be called a failure. "Certainly, I spent some of the most depressing moments of my life at Eithin. But equally, certainly, I experienced some of the highest points I have ever known, and, for at least a year, reveled in a freedom of spirit which I had never dreamt was possible. But, above all, I learned more, I think, in 18 months there than in 15 years of being an editor, journalist, and freelance writer."

Clarke and his friends lived, technically, far below the poverty line, "but we were certainly never deprived." The most important discovery for Clarke was his ability to do all kinds of jobs he previously had no idea he could do.

"Concrete-mixing, drain-laying, carpentry, joinery, roofing, plumbing, wiring, guttering, rendering, farming, and even vehicle maintenance soon became part of the daily life," he says. "And we did them well. So, I suspect, can everyone else. Yet in our society there is a mystique attached to such crafts which leads 95 percent of us to declare ourselves incapable of them."

The divorce which modern society has effected between the heads and the hands is, for Clarke, its greatest evil. "It turns us all, in the end, into less than half a person. And anyone who learns again to use them together will, I guarantee, experience a rejuvenation not normally associated with the mundane tasks of laying drains and learning to make a ridge ladder. It is all something to do with bringing your life back under your own control. And of spending your time at a number of highly different jobs. The human being, surely, was never intended to do the same thing for hours on end for most of his waking life. There is more to living."

Anyone who really wants to save money should join or found a community, Clarke says. The many obstacles that Clarke had feared would occur – such as failure to get planning permission, or the difficulty of finding community members – did not materialize. But the one obstacle he felt confident of overcoming proved their undoing.

"We failed to make it as a community. Not all the time, in that I and many others there almost certainly spent some of the best moments of our lives at Eithin. But, in the end, after the first year, those at first intangible differences between us rose up and smote us most mightily.

"With such a history, it may seem strange to urge anyone to join a community. Yet I believe it is a sensible way to live... if you can do it...

"Most communities, of course, fail in the end through lack of competence, lack of money, or both. That we seemed to have both these problems licked makes our own failures if anything more significant. We didn't have those hard economic facts forever draining away our morale. We were just unable to live with one another as human beings with any enjoyment. It was as simple as that.

"So, if you are planning to do it, what advice could I offer? First, perhaps, never join a community because you want to live in a community, or because you think you do. Do so only if you discover a group of people, or even one or two, with whom you positively think a shared life would be a turn for the better."

What Can One Person Do? Spread the Word!
Carolyn Pogue

Native elders use sweetgrass to teach us. They say that one blade of sweetgrass is easily bent and broken. But a bundle, woven into a braid, is strong.

Sometimes we feel much like a single blade trying to withstand the pressures of modern living. In community, we become like the braid – always distinct, but with the strength of others to support us.

All of us network in some sort of community, whether it is our community of faith, our friends at the coffee shop, our local PTA, our hiking group, our political association, or our work mates. All of us have information and experience in living. Usually, we share this experience and knowledge one to one, and one person at a time. We recommend books, shops, magazines, teachers for our children. But the sharing is often sporadic.

With new technology working for us, we now have access to publishing in varying degrees of sophistication. Why not gather your information and experience and publish it? Why not start a newsletter for your community, or contribute to one that is already published by your community? (Hopefully, the newsletter is published on recycled paper, with canola-based ink.)

A good time to publish is in the Fall, as people begin to think about the holiday season. Your newsletter could easily be distributed at such events as community suppers, Fall fairs, or garage sales. Help people break out of the routine of seeing Christmas as mainstream society sees it. Hopefully, this breakthrough will carry over into people's lives throughout the rest of year.

Your publication may be a collection of lists, or may include articles on ways to simplify life in your neighborhood. Suggestions for topics include:

- names of people willing to trade services. For example, a potter may be willing to trade pottery for Christmas baking or dried flower arrangements;
- a list of clothing consignment shops in your neighborhood;
- a list of secondhand book shops in your neighborhood, and the information (if applicable) that they have gift certificates;
- a list of the names of international organizations working for justice, peace, and the environment (such as Amnesty International, Greenpeace, Bread for the World, UNICEF), and the information that they have gift certificates;
- a list of local organizations, religious groups, or centers working for justice, peace, and the environment

(could you also ask them to send certificates for donations made in another's name?);

- a list of local writers and artists who may be willing to sell their work at a discount to neighbors;
- a list of books that help us choose healthier lifestyles, such as *Unplug the Christmas Machine* (Quill-Wm Morrow, NY, NY, 1991), *The Alternative Wedding Book* (Northstone Publishing Inc., Kelowna, BC, 1995), *Extending the Table Cookbook* (Herald Press, Scottdale, PA, 1991), and this book, *Treasury of Celebrations;*
- samples of coupons or gift certificates to help people give of themselves, such as "This certificate good for one dinner, delivered to your door," or "This certificate is good for one evening of free babysitting";
- names of parents willing to trade babysitting services, and teens willing to babysit in exchange for tutoring or sewing or....

Browse through the remainder of this book, and let it assist you in creating new, local ideas. Once the community begins generating ideas, the sky's the limit. And remember the lesson of the sweetgrass.

Gift-Giving

Earth
Provides Enough
For Everyone's
Need
But Not
For Everyone's
Greed
           – Gandhi

Giving and Receiving Gifts

Reprinted from *To Celebrate: Reshaping Holidays and Rites of Passage*

The practice of gift-giving is as old as Adam and Eve. It may be the original basis for economics. Some authorities believe that in ancient societies gifts were a precursor to bartering, which in turn gave way to buying and selling. Lands and possessions were passed on to children as gifts, beginning a system of family inheritance which kept strict control on land distribution. Gift-giving to deities through sacrifices was an integral part of ancient religions. The purposes of sacrificial gifts were quite varied: to give tribute to the deity as king; to express gratitude; to gain favor; to establish or reestablish ties; to be purged of

sin; or to provide sustenance for the deity's earthly visits.

In many ancient cultures there were special injunctions to make gifts to strangers or sojourners. Some anthropologists suggest that the reason for such behavior was that sojourners, who were thought to have special powers, were mistrusted. The gifts were to ensure the friendship of these transients. In the Hebrew Scriptures, however, injunctions to care for sojourners are not based on fear but on compassion and remembrance: "...you were once sojourners in the land of Egypt" (Leviticus 19:33).

All of the world's major religions

have provision for giving gifts, usually as alms to the poor and needy. However, little is said about this in the Hebrew Scriptures. While Israel made it a practice to give alms to the poor, concern for the poor was expressed in broader terms, and involved providing for their overall needs and protecting them against injustice. In one of the classic texts, the prophet Isaiah proclaimed that religious fasts were acceptable to the Lord only when they included freeing the oppressed, sharing bread with the hungry, bringing the homeless into one's own house, and clothing the naked (Isaiah 58). In the New Testament, Jesus identifies himself with the poor and makes acting on behalf of the poor the standard by which the nations will be judged: "Inasmuch as you have done it to the least of these, you have done it to me" (Matthew 25:31–46).

Connections between gift-giving and ritual celebrations also began quite early. It was customary to exchange gifts on New Year's Day long before exchanging gifts at Christmas became tradition. On New Year's Day, Persians exchanged gifts of eggs – symbols of fertility – while Egyptians gave flasks to each other. Romans exchanged objects bearing the imprint of Janus, the god of two faces for whom the month of January is named. The Celtic-Teutonic Druids made gifts of their holy plant, mistletoe. Ancient peoples also celebrated birthdays and weddings with gifts. The Greek poet Aeschylus wrote about the custom of giving presents to children on their birthdays as early as the sixth century BCE.

The practice of gift-giving at Christmas has several origins. The early Roman feast of Saturnalia was already a well-established time for exchanging gifts when the date for celebrating the birth of Christ was set on the same date. But Christians had their own reasons for gift-giving at Christmas. Patterned on the gifts of the Magi – gold, frankincense, and myrrh brought to honor the birth of the Christ Child – gift-giving was a symbolic reminder of the great gift of God's Son.

As Christianity spread into different cultures and through time, various customs and traditions developed around giving gifts at Christmas. In Germany, the Christ Child was said to bring small presents on Christmas Eve. Among the Dutch, it was St. Nicholas who brought gifts to children on December 6, the eve of his feast. The practice of gift-giving at Christmas was firmly established in the 19th century when the traditions of the Christ Child ("Christkindl") and St. Nicholas ("Sinterklass") became anglicized into one – Santa Claus.

Gifts in the Consumer Society

Reprinted from *To Celebrate: Reshaping Holidays & Rites of Passage*

Gift-giving is no less important today than in earlier times. It is still viewed as an acceptable way to express love and to celebrate relationships. But gift-giving has a history of abuse that continues today. We abuse the practice of giving gifts in several ways: we use gifts to bribe or manipulate; we make gifts because of social pressure; we use gifts to alleviate guilt; we give gifts that are inconsistent with our highest values and ideals. While this abuse is not new, the practice of gift-giving has been affected by our consumer society. As even *The Amy Vanderbilt Complete Book of Etiquette* recognizes, "Today, in our materialistic society, the custom [of gift-giving] has grown to exaggerated absurdity..."

Consider how our consumer-oriented values have shaped our gift-giving practices:

- **Conformity is prized over individuality.** Despite society's rhetoric about individuality, the "if-you-don't-have-one-you-are-inadequate" message of mass culture relentlessly bombards the senses from the air waves and print media. Consumer society's emphasis is to create needs rather than to create products to meet needs we already have. This results in conformity in how needs are perceived and the ways we meet those needs. The more far-reaching result of our conformity, however, may be an absence of dissenting voices in today's mass culture.

- **Whatever is bought and sold is better than whatever isn't.** A broad assumption in the consumer society is that the only way to be happy is to accumulate things. Friendship, contentment, and security are significant only as they involve consumption. The way to express love and affection for another is by buying some "thing." By implication, gifts that are not "bought things" – including things made with one's own hands – are not worth much. The restrictive nature of this assumption rules out a whole host of wonderful ways to give, including the giving of time and skill. Not only does preoccupation with "buying to give" overlook other ways of giving, it also seems to make gift-giving less personal.

- **More and bigger are better. Less and small are chintzy**. In a society which produces consumer goods far beyond the needs of its members, consumption without restraint becomes an ideal. This society's extraordinary levels of consumption have resulted in unparalleled amounts of waste, thus earning the title, "the throwaway society." Unrealistic ideas that Earth has unlimited natural resources, cheap energy, and adequate means of waste disposal have undergirded our consumption and waste. Yet all three of these assumptions are known to be false. The issues raised by this knowledge are more than ecological. Recognition of our planet's limited resources forces us to address the question of a just distribution of goods and resources. New consumer values, ideals, and practices are urgently needed so that all people can share in what the world has to offer.

As gift-giving practices have been symbols of the consumer culture's values and ideals, it is time to give voice to new values and ideals:

- Give in ways that enrich human relationships, a process that requires the investment of self. Proper timing and creativity replace quantity and monetary value as the essentials of good gift giving.
- Give in ways that enable physical, mental, and spiritual growth beyond the expectations and restraints of popular culture.
- Give in ways that are life-supporting and conserving. Be aware of how your giving or nongiving affects people and Earth. Consider who profits from your purchase and who suffers. Think about the ecological cost of creation and disposal.
- Give to those who work for those intangibles most needed by our loved ones and future generations: a world at peace, an inclusive society, and a healthy environment. Let celebrations be occasions to reaffirm your relationship to Earth and all humankind.

As you think about ways your gift-giving can give voice to your ideals, consider:

- **Time and skill.** Gifts of time – especially to younger children or older relatives – are very important and can take many forms. Teach a skill in cooking, writing, carpentry, a foreign language, etc. Gifts of time and skill to justice organizations can be as useful as gifts of money.
- **Homemade gifts.** This nasty phrase in consumer society's vocabulary can be rehabilitated with personal gifts from the workbench, kitchen, and desk. Planning and creativity, more than skill, are the essential requirements.
- **Gifts from self-help craft groups.** Your purchase helps keep alive old crafts. A larger percentage of the purchase price goes to the artisan than if you bought the same thing in the mall, and you are helping

to provide employment for low-income people. Many of these shops have mail-order services.

- **Selective buying.** Exercise your right not to buy from organizations that produce objectionable products or that exploit children, women, men, animals, or Earth. This is a vote for justice and a healthy environment in a consumer society.

- **Organ donation.** Even in death, you can give the gift of sight or life through donating your organs to others. You need to sign a statement indicating your desire, but more importantly, you need to speak to your family now to make sure they understand your wishes. You may also wish to learn exactly what this means by discussing it with your doctor.

Double Your Gift of Love

Reprinted from *To Celebrate: Reshaping Holidays & Rites of Passage*

Retail store advertisers make a great effort to resolve all Christmas (Valentine's Day, birthday, Mother's Day, Father's Day, etc.) shopping problems. To make sure they don't lose the confused, uninspired shopper they go to great lengths to create gifts for the "man or woman who has everything."

You may not know anyone who has everything, but there may be friends or family members on your gift list who are not in need. Do something different for them. Make a gift to a church, synagogue, temple, or charitable group in lieu of an unnecessary gift. We call this a double gift certificate, a gift to the charity and a gift to your friend or family member, a gift that complements a shared concern for a better world.

Send a card announcing your gift with your message of love for the card's recipient and your concern for peace and justice in the world. Better still, make your own card to send.

The Hidden Price Tag
Kathy Hoffman

We make a grave error when we think that the only cost of our celebrations is the price tag on the gift. The actual cost includes the effect on the environment and our natural resources, taxes, and the human and social cost. How many manufacturers and merchants think about the actual cost when they unleash their massive advertising campaigns for Christmas, Mother's Day, Father's Day, weddings, and other celebrations which are ripe for sales? How many celebrators have considered these costs to society when they perpetuate consumption-oriented celebrations?

"Celebration" is big business! More than 50 percent of the annual retail income occurs in November and December.

The effect the millions of dollars in holiday sales have on our Earth's resources and the lives of people is devastating. Irreplaceable resources are exhausted. Think of all the coal and oil tied up in the production and operation of the thousands of non-sensical electric gadgets we buy as "gifts," or the mass-produced plastic and metal decorations your local Chamber of Commerce erects shortly after Thanksgiving; or the miles of Christmas lights we trail over our buildings and trees. Consider the ravaging effect on land and commu-nities of strip mining for these energy resources.

The gift items and paraphernalia we purchase also embody work hours of productive effort along with hours of creative energy spent on trying to convince us that we must buy these things. Our labor resources could be better used in more life-supporting and enriching pursuits such as housing, health, safety, and the eradication of poverty.

Our grandchildren may never see living jaguars, leopards, or crocodiles if we support the market for these skins. If we can't mend the hole in the ozone, they may never enjoy the sunshine without worrying about skin cancer. Drinking from a stream in the countryside is a thing of the past. They may never engage in ocean and fresh water fishing. The Christmas trees we use for a few weeks and then throw away represent lost wood and timberland. The packaging, wrapping, trim, and cards that accompany our gifts also use up wood pulp and energy. Most of the millions of tons of household garbage we throw away annually comes from virgin resources; almost half of municipal waste is paper. (Industrial waste outweighs by millions of tons the waste produced in mining and agriculture.)

What price tag can justify the

value of the human lives that are lost or destroyed due to the increase in accidents, suicides, psychic strains, and highway holiday carnage that surround our "celebrations"? How do you say "Happy Fourth or First of July" to a boy who's been maimed by fireworks? Our insurance rates reflect this holiday carnage even if tragedy doesn't strike us personally.

In addition to the cost of wasted resources, we burden ourselves with increased social costs and taxes. The number of broken homes and troubled children could be reduced if more love were expressed in the home. Family love and closeness can't blossom fully when plastic toys and money are the only gifts exchanged between family members.

The unique pleasures of creating, sharing, and self-involvement are lost when a gift is chosen from a store shelf that contains 100 items just like it. The people we love are special to us, yet so often we express this special love by sharing gifts that are mass-produced rather than unique. We pay for our consumer orientation (in contrast to people orientation) in the form of the increased social costs of supporting juvenile courts and homes. We also pay for the waste generated by our consumption through increased taxes. The rate of our consumption of material goods is increasing faster than the rate of population growth, so that there is an increasing rate of

garbage being generated per person. If taxes aren't raised to meet the increased costs of collecting and disposing of our ever-growing pile of trash, then the costs of removing that trash will have to be at the expense of other municipal services such as schools and parks.

In our celebrations, we exploit not only ourselves, but the resources and quality of life of the rest of the world. Limited land and mineral resources are devoted to export by developing countries while their people struggle at, or below, subsistence levels to feed our insatiable consumption. African resources provide our gifts of diamonds. The rain forests are sacrificed for exotic lumber. South American minerals are formed into cars built with planned obsolescence in mind. These same cars and electrical gadgets then demand the importation of energy resources to keep them operating.

Richard Easterlin, professor of economics at the University of Pennsylvania, surveyed the relationship between happiness and income and came to a paradoxical conclusion. In the U.S., the average happiness level had not risen in 30 years, even though the purchasing power of the average income had risen by 60 percent.

Satisfaction doesn't come from the number of goods we can buy, but from how this number compares to what we think we need. What we think we need depends on our social and cultural impressions and experiences.

Our materialistic orientation has us running on a treadmill, seeking new pleasures and goods to maintain old levels of subjective pleasure. Happiness and human fulfillment are not conceived on Madison Avenue, produced in Detroit, and delivered at your local store.

Although we can't buy happiness, we can give gifts that support life, conserve the Earth, and enhance the human spirit. For example, educational toys give pleasure to a child and also enable the child to learn and develop new skills. Giving to non-profit and social service groups helps not only their functions, but may also allow them to increase their staff, training, and outreach programs so that jobs, skills, and new opportunities are opened up for more people.

Our usual response to a child's "Trick or Treat" is a sugary treat full of empty calories. Wouldn't it be better if Halloween resulted in UNICEF feeding the hungry rather than in your dentist drilling out cavities? One child's coins diverted from a candy bar to UNICEF has a tiny but positive impact on the world.

Imagine the possibilities that our billions of dollars worth of holiday retail sales could have if we spent them in life-supporting celebrations.

Why don't we do it? We've been indoctrinated with the virtues of growth as measured by increased consumption. We have been led to believe that unemployment results when we don't buy what our labor churns out. Greater demand for people-oriented goods and services involve a beneficial shift to human resources. Social service groups need people, but usually don't have the funds to pay their wages. Diverting our dollars to these groups helps them hire permanent staff, as opposed to the temporary holiday help retail stores hire. Also, the "products" of social service and self-help groups improve the quality of life much more than "plastic" gifts off an assembly line.

It's possible to shed the burdens, stresses, and costs we tolerate and impose upon our world by our commercial celebrations. We can affirm life and our love and care for each other and our world with alternative celebrations. We have nothing to lose and a whole world to reclaim. Let us celebrate life!

On Creative Deprivation
Based on the article in *The Alternate Catalogue, 2nd Edition*

Colman McCarthy's article about "Creative Deprivation" in a past issue of *The Washington Post* states that "children have little need for marketplace temptings." That belief still holds true today. Now, the marketplace gurus work even harder at convincing our children that they "need" that toy, that article of clothing, that new computer program. These marketers are skilled, pervasive, and in the long run, destructive to family harmony. There seems little recourse (other than heading for the hills) than to meet them with equally pervasive tactics.

McCarthy wrote:

By definition, to creatively deprive children means to keep their senses and minds free of material goods that overwhelm them, the kind soon to be washing in from the immense commercial ocean of Christmas. How can children not be emotionally drowned when wave after wave of toys rolls over them?

How can a child have a sense of value for any one toy when so many are given at once? How can the potential of one gift be explored when the attraction of so many others is pulling? The whisper of newness becomes a deafening roar. It is hard to imagine how this surfeit of Christmas toys can lead to new levels of playfulness.

It may sometimes feel as if you are standing alone holding your finger in the dike. But there are two factors that can help you. One is a supportive community of like-minded people. The other is to become more involved in offering alternatives.

While a computer game, for example, may stimulate a child for a time, eventually, it can be mind-numbing. On the other hand, a walk in the park with corn kernels in your pocket and your child in tow, can be a rewarding and wondrous event for both of you. (Not to mention that it allows you to get some air and exercise.) Before bedtime, reading about whatever creatures you happened to meet there prolongs and enriches the experience. Drawing or writing about the walk can put the proverbial icing on the cake.

Einstein once said that imagination is of more value than knowledge. It is good to remember these words when raising children. They are born with imagination in abundance. Some commercial gadgets and toys can stimulate, of course, but so can a walk in the park, helping to build and maintain a bird feeder, and so on. A well stocked dress-up box can be the greatest gift to the imagination. (Adults like them, too!)

Creative deprivation also teaches children that there are limits – to re-sources, to what they can ask for, and to what you can and will give. Certainly, debt-ridden and anxious parents are not the gifts that children want. They want and need your at-tention and love. They want you.

Choosing and Using Toys
Allenna Leonard

Even when the toy maker and the toy buyer work together to assure children of toys that are well made and appropriately chosen for their ages and skills, buying a toy is not always easy. When the interests of the toy industry and the toy buyer are at odds, the problems multiply.

Huge conglomerates and retail chains now dominate the industry. The hard evidence is that the industry's "best toy" is the one that sells best and makes the most profit rather than the one that brings hours of safe, creative enjoyment to a child. As a result, par-ents must face unsafe toys, mislead-ing toy ads, toys which grate against the values many of us hold – realities few of us are equipped to deal with when we go into a toy department.

The toy buyer should also know that no matter what the problems, appropriate toys can be found. The toy industry's practices can be im-proved by consumers who will accept no substitutes for what they need.

Numerous small companies build appropriate toys. They must be sought out, often by mail.

The most serious problem fac-ing the toy buyer is that of safety. The toy market is still far from hazard-free, though the establish-ment of a Consumer Product Safety Commission and the issuance of some standards for quality have im-proved the situation in recent years.

The buyer should be able to ex-pect that any toy on the market is safe. But the reality is that toys are safe enough if used only as directed, or if they don't break or operate de-fectively. The toy with glass parts (yes, they still can be found) won't cut unless the glass is broken. The projectile toy with the rubber tip in-jures no one if the rubber tip remains in place and the projectiles aren't fired at living beings. The electrical toy – essentially a small appliance not designed for constant use, and consequently cheaply made – may develop a short and shock a child, or worse. Small toy parts present no hazard to a school-aged child, but a younger sibling may swallow them or get them stuck in the ears or nose. Painted toys can be a problem for children at the age when they put everything into their mouths.

Even when toys are reasonably safe, parents and guardians must exercise responsibility in choosing them and in guiding play.

Because some children are well-coordinated and have good balance while others do not, buyers should be careful to choose movement toys appropriate to the child in question. Roller skates that are fun for one child may be dangerous or frustrating for another. The heavily marketed and glamorous skateboard fad has led to many injuries for both children and adults. If skateboard play is approved, helmets and pads should be mandatory and extreme care should be taken to find a safe skateboarding place free of traffic, rough surfaces, and pedestrians. Other movement toys such as bicycles and tricycles should be carefully investigated for balance, braking, and reflective material, if the child is old enough to use the bicycle after dark.

Parents also need to be aware constantly that injury is most likely to occur when directions for using toys aren't followed properly. The quiet play offered by a craft or science kit can be dangerous if the child is not mature enough to use it. Children cannot be counted on always to use toys in the proper way, so adults must be on their guard when there is a potential problem.

Another hazard buyers should beware of is the emotional ploys advertisers use to sell their products. Advertising research has plumbed our deepest yearnings to find out what triggers the urge to buy. It has used sophisticated psycho-physiological testing equipment to measure such subliminal body reactions as eye movements and sweating palms to see what makes us tick. (Some questions might be raised about the ethics of using methods of psychological investigation in the interests of a commercial third party. A certain amount of probing is appropriate in the hands of trained personnel if the object is to give an individual insights that could lead to better self-knowledge and adjustment, but the same techniques become insidious when they are used to influence an individual for another's gain.)

The toy industry pours millions of dollars into advertising to get parents and children to choose a certain toy out of a possible 150,000 on the market. Hundreds of thousands of dollars may be spent in planning the promotion of a single toy even before air time is purchased! And the adult who makes toy-buying decisions on the basis of emotion rather than reason may be easy prey.

In December, especially, it is difficult not to give in to the nostalgia for a childhood when the pace was slower, extended families lived near each other, and family rituals and familiar things gave a sense of comfort and well-being. We wish to create a similar atmosphere for our own children and are led to believe that "things" will do it – calico decorations, old-style puzzles and games, or new ones which "give a sense of unity to the family that plays them together." We must understand that our yearnings are not for things but for human relationships – the sharing in wreath-, cookie- or gift-making rather than the objects themselves.

Another advertising problem is the difference between what a toy appears to be and what it is. Although the code of the National Association of Broadcasters on children's advertising has eliminated most of the obviously deceptive practices in the preparation of advertising copy, it does not cover whether or not the toy will perform as well as it appears to on television. A study by the engineering department at the University of Georgia showed that only two of the ten toys most widely advertised on television performed as described in the ad, and one of these was a doll. Close-ups, camera

angles, and other techniques may enhance the toy's performance. For instance, cars go much faster when viewed from the bottom of an inclined plane. Or, though the toy is shown in one scene with the child to establish its actual size, other shots may counteract that impression. Also, children do not usually comprehend the statement "assembly required" though they know very well what "you have to put it together" means.

Toys based on television and movie characters may be the biggest cheat in town. Several product lines have been designed based on the attraction of a show's popularity rather than on the toy's playability. Often they amount to nothing more than character dolls one is encouraged to put through the motions of the same story plots again and again. They are generally far more expensive than the products merit – after all, the makers had to pay for the rights to use the television characters as well as the cost of heavy promotion for the toys.

One advertising practice that adults need to watch carefully is the selling of the products directly to children. Advertising toys to children on television creates a value system in which certain needs can be satisfied only by the purchase of things. The ads sell an idea that money can buy happiness, that owning rather than doing is the way to feel good about yourself, and that we are somehow not complete without this or that. And if that weren't enough, the commercials show a heaven on earth where no one gets angry or hurt, where parents are always loving and responsive, and where the lifestyle of plenty has erased every care. A child's own family cannot compare to this and may even seem different and shameful. If a child is part of a poor family, these messages can increase the sense of inadequacy and isolation to the point of hopelessness. Low-income families can feel forced to purchase expensive items to prove that they are as good as anyone else.

These messages presumably are more influential than many others because most of the consumers in the two- to eleven-year-old market have a limited understanding of what advertising is and how it fits into their lives. Much still needs to be learned about how children process the information in advertisements. Adults who are concerned about this advertising practice can choose not to buy any product that is advertised to children rather than to adults. They can also let the manufacturers know why they made their decisions in the hope of influencing future advertising practices.

Advertising directed to adults can also be misleading. For instance, many adults are conditioned to think well of a toy labeled "educational." We all want to see our children learn new things and develop skills they can use later in school or in life. But the toy labeled "educational" and put in a fancy package may be similar, except in practice, to any other construction set, puzzle, or game. Celebrity endorsements and the use of characters from educational television shows may add nothing at all to the play experience of the item. Adults should remember that child development experts still say a set of plain wooden blocks is one of the best toy investments that can be made.

Another problem parents face when buying toys is that many of those which are most widely sold grate against their values. Parents can and should hold out for toys which support their values.

If we want our children to grow up peace-loving and cooperative, we do not need to give in and allow submachine guns, tanks, pistols, or any of the other toys that encourage children to think that disputes and differences are best settled by force, or that the world is divided up into good guys and bad guys: us and them. Gun play and war play can trivialize a child's understanding of the value of life. Does a 13- or 14-year-old who pulls a trigger and shoots someone have any idea of the gravity of the act, or is it just an extension of play?

Children do need to learn how to deal with aggression, but there are more constructive ways to do this than through war toys. Practice in solving problems through talking things out or negotiating compromises is one way to develop skills in coping with aggression. Sports and games also provide ample opportunity for the expression of aggression within set boundaries. If one kicks the ball and runs as fast as one can, this is aggressive and competitive play. But it is conducted against opponents rather than enemies, has standards and rules, and develops physical skill. Playing Cowboys and Indians with toy guns does none of these things; moreover, it is deeply offensive to native peoples.

Toys that support stereotypical views of sex, race, ethnic heritage, or age tend to restrict, rather than open, a child's play opportunities and personal growth. Therefore, care should be taken in examining toys for evidence of these stereotypes.

Research has shown that sex stereotyping is detrimental to both boys and girls because it robs both sexes of full development. Masculine and feminine elements both are included in a well-developed personality – strength and vulnerability go side-by-side; nurture and discipline overlap in the parental role; boys and girls, men and women are much more alike than they are different. Yet, when asked why a certain line of transportation toys included play scenes from one of the few all-male

fourth grades in the country, the manufacturer replied, "We wouldn't sell as many toys if we used a group of girls." And women in toys and games continue to be depicted in relation to dating, baby care, and a few traditional women's jobs rather than in the whole range of life activities which they share with men.

Racial and ethnic stereotyping are a disservice to both minority and nonminority children. Yet Native American character dolls continue to be clothed in beads and feathers, the Spanish-speaking ones in sombreros, and the Chinese in coolie hats. It is important for minority children to feel that they are fairly represented in all aspects of our society. It is also important for nonminority children to see other racial and ethnic groups included to reinforce the concept of a diverse population and to lay the groundwork for feeling comfortable in multi-racial communities.

Age stereotyping is also a problem in toy design and packaging. Grandma and Grandpa dolls were a welcome first step on the doll shelf. It is desirable to show the world as it really is, with people of all ages. Why shouldn't grandparent characters be shown as they are, ranging from people in their early 40s on up? Grandma may not have her hair in a bun and wear long dresses; she may go to work in a business suit. And Grandpa may not hobble around with a cane; he may be on the golf course, or volunteering with Greenpeace. Grandparents may not be white either. They come in the same variety children do. Why don't we see it?

The best toys usually foster open-ended play and have multiple uses. The complicated toy with a single use will not retain a child's interest very long and may leave both the adult and the child feeling bad about the choice. Toys that do it all for the child contribute little to growth. The sad joke about the parent who buys a large, expensive toy for a child and finds out that the child would rather play with the box is too often true. Sometimes an adult and a child have very different ideas about which toys are fun. It's a good idea to ask ourselves whether we think a toy would be fun for the child for whom it is intended, or fun for the child in us. If the second instance is more to the point, maybe two toys are in order. Adults can play, too.

Age appropriateness is another important consideration. If a toy is too far behind or ahead of a child's stage of development, it will not be a good choice. Many toy companies are including some mention of age range on the packages, but they do not do it often enough or consistently enough. Even when the age range is given, it may not be appropriate for a particular child. Children de-velop large and small muscle control, a sense of color and shape, and skill in manipulating objects and concepts at varying rates. Therefore, the buyer needs some sense of the individual child and a knowledge of the general range of toys for that age in order to make wise choices. Local early childhood educators may help make appropriate decisions if the task seems difficult.

Here is one thing we toy buyers should keep foremost in our minds: as consumers, we are in charge. Whatever toys are offered us, it is our responsibility to decide which are appropriate and to refuse to buy those which aren't. Children need toys that foster growth, add to a sense of skill and mastery, expand creativity, develop positive self-images, and encourage interaction between adults and children or among children. Children need a mix of active toys and quiet toys, toys which encourage both nurturing and challenge, that stimulate both muscles and minds. These are the toys we should insist upon; we cannot settle for any substitute for what our children need; and we can find the toys they need if we refuse to take anything else.

Our toy selections, whether they are given as holiday or birthday presents, have a substantial impact on the values we communicate to the children who receive them.

Toys ARE Us! A Parent's Perspective
Rachel Graner Gill

The door before me opened soundlessly. But as I walked down the entrance hall, colors on the wall – geometrical patterns in vivid, angry colors – screamed at my senses. I rounded the corner to the display area and was completely overwhelmed by floor-to-ceiling shelves spilling over with merchandise for children. This was Toyland!

My initial shock at the raucous enormity of the place was soon accompanied by nostalgia as I walked those aisles, remembering with pleasure and pain, times when decisions about toys were an important part of my life, when the pull between our children's programmed wants and our value-oriented perspective on their needs were often in conflict.

Certainly, my husband and I were not always successful in providing creative substitutes when we, with studied deliberation, questioned our children's wants. Specific toys were important cultural symbols in their world, and it was difficult to explain why we rejected those symbols. My brief visit to a modern toy store convinced me that today's parents of young children face an even more difficult task. Giant shelves stocked with violent dolls and grotesque monsters – along with perfect imitations of military and police weapons – included every imaginable accessory for creative destruction.

Those symbols of violence – even scaled-down versions – gave off an oppressive, almost hallucinatory atmosphere. Children became "hyper" as soon as they entered the so-called "super action heroes" section. Their shrill screams of excitement could be heard throughout the store. Adults were affected, too. One mother walked up and down the aisles in a distraught state, lamenting loudly to anyone who would listen, "There's not a single puppet in the store! Can you believe it? Not a single puppet in the entire store!" That woman's anguished cry was real. And as I looked around me, her distress became mine. I realized that the absence of simple, creative playthings in that great toy depository is not accidental. It is a fact that speaks with authority about today's world.

It is a lamentable truth that we feel surrounded by violence; we live in an atmosphere that not only tolerates but encourages violence. In television programming, movies, and the print media – as well as current interpretations of America's role in the world – adults are surrounded by unspoken macho ideals such as "might makes right" and "survival of the fittest," supported with military might. We are encouraged in insidious ways to deal with weakness in other people and with other countries from a position of strength and always with "our best interest" in mind.

It is alarming, but not surprising, how these ideas of power and domination have penetrated our children's world. As participants in those values, toy industries believe that self-interest dictates both their role to provide and their right to sell violent toys. And their profit indicators support their good business decisions. Since 1982, the sale of war toys has risen more than 500 percent! Adults must face the fact that it is not children who supply the toy industry with their profit margins, it is adults who buy for children.

Also, adults may be contributing to the violence factor for today's children by providing another disturbing wrinkle to this complicated mixture of children, toys, and war games. It is possible that children who play violent war games are not simply victims of television advertising and an unscrupulous toy market. They also may be imitating adults with whom they live. This new phenomenon, The National Survival Game, is a complicated adult version of a child's game often referred to as Capture the Flag. Wearing camouflage trousers, jackets, gloves, heavy boots, and often using face-masks, these weekend war-game players carry pistols whose pellets

sting and raise welts, making it necessary to wear goggles. Players confess to getting hooked on the "adrenaline high" and "instinct toning" of a three-hour game, and many of them claim they have never felt so alive.

What does this mean? An admittedly simplistic analysis of these activities suggests that our society encourages adults to play like children and children to play like adults, with both groups using war games as a means for having fun. And on another level, national and international leaders also play at war with deadly games of "I dare you," in which nuclear holocaust – rather than the enemy's flag – may be the result of battle.

It may seem a drastic leap in logic from the danger of war toys for our children and the specter of a nuclear holocaust. Unfortunately, the connection between the two may be more real than we want to believe. Today's adults and children are caught up in games that are far more frightening than those provided by the contents of shelves in a toy store. We have bought into our world leaders' obsessions with military solutions to people's problems. And if we believe, with most child psychologists, that play is a child's work, we make our legacy to future generations when we decide to provide our children with up-to-date symbols of war. The values of our truculent, embattled society will become the norm for our children.

What can we do? To use words that come directly from war terminology, we can protect our children by providing them with a buffer zone – a "game against war" to which every thoughtful adult should be committed. But this means taking risks. We will certainly encounter the displeasure of our children if we interrupt their involvement with the symbols of their world. Even more than adults, children have difficulty trying to distance themselves from their culture. They are highly impressionable and easily conditioned to want what their friends have or what they see on television. Children who are allowed unrestricted exposure to mass-media hard sell – calculatingly and carefully designed by well-planned market research – are unlikely to want anything other than what they are told to want. Adults must assume some responsibility in determining when children's wants conflict with their needs.

Jesus once asked a question that may shed some light on this current dilemma with children. "Which one of you, if your child asks for bread, would give a stone? Or if he asks for a fish, would give him a scorpion?" We know the answer: no loving adult would feed a hungry child on a diet of stones and scorpions. But what is a parent to do if a child asks for a Voltron, a Gobot, or a Rambo doll? We believe that responsible, loving parents will refuse to feed a child's hunger for play on a diet of violence and savagery.

Each Christmas we are faced with questions about gift-giving. What do we give our children? What is appropriate for celebrating the birthday of the Prince of Peace? With that as a point of reference, some disciplined thinking about creative substitutes for violent toys is certainly in order.

Here are some alternate ideas:

1. Do not take your children to "regular" toy stores. If you feel you must, take them to an alternative, educational toy store instead.
2. Share toys with like-minded families.
3. Purchase toys at garage sales.
4. Make your own toys – and have children make them, too. Go to the library for some ideas.
5. Look for quality, low-priced toys at craft fairs and Third World craft shops.
6. Teach your child simple games that don't require the expensive purchase of prepackaged board games.
7. Give an alternative toy to your child's teacher as a gift for the classroom.

Food and Celebrations

Hunger and the Lifestyle Connection
Milo Thornberry and Colleen Shannon

Into the consciousness of a nation already troubled by the repercussions of political intrigue, war, poverty, and urban unrest, the 1970s brought reports of a scourge which was ravaging the world. Hunger hit the headlines with compelling intensity: Famine in Bangladesh! Drought in the Sahel! Even as the century comes to an end, the hunger has not ended.

Most of us learn about the existence of hunger through televised pictures of dying babies and starving people waiting in line for food rations. We listen to the statistics of the food crisis affecting hundreds of millions of the world's poor even as national leaders gather time and time again to discuss the problem.

Others of us do not learn of hunger via television or other media. Others of us live our lives in a food crisis every day. Tucked away on reservations, in migrant worker camps, in former plantation regions, in urban ghettos and sharecropper shacks are the very old and the very young, the men and women whose stomachs are rarely full and whose bodies are never properly nourished.

What is not so generally known is that all of this has been happening in a world which, from a global perspective, has enough food to meet the basic nutritional needs of all its people.

We live on a planet with food resources more than adequate for its population, and yet malnutrition continues as the world's most widespread cause of physical and mental debility, disease, and death.

Why?

• Because some countries allow corporations to use their best farm land to produce crops (coffee, sugar, cocoa, beef, etc.) to export to wealthy nations rather than produce food for their own people.

• Because some companies entice women to relinquish their own natural food resource for their infants – breast milk – in favor of a commercial product which, in unsanitary conditions of poverty, is too expensive, inappropriate, and even lethal.

• Because "aid" from wealthy countries is often designed to develop and protect commercial markets, not to eradicate poverty in the poor countries.

• Because federal programs to alleviate malnutrition in this country have all too often been motivated by corporate and political self-interest rather than genuine attempts to eliminate hunger.

• Because lack of employment opportunities prevents many from gaining the economic resources necessary to purchase the food which is available.

• Because some nations spend so much money for arms that they can't afford to develop their agricultural potential.

• Because a legacy of colonialism has left the control of international trade and intercourse between nations in the hands of the wealthy nations.

• Because the potential contribution of women to development in the developing world has been ignored and their traditional status undermined.

• Because systematic discrimination against some ethnic/racial minorities has been so institutionalized as to effectively cut them off from the means of self-development.

• Because the fruits of the green revolution for the most part aided only wealthy farmers and widened the gap between the rich and poor.

• Because the breakdown of the larger family has resulted in many old persons being left poverty-stricken, alone, and unable to care for themselves.

• Because those who know enough do not seem to care enough to end hunger.

What must be done?

If the causes of this scourge are so many, so complex, and so interrelated, is there anything that can be done? Or are we doomed to see a world in which the "Haves" build ever-higher walls to protect themselves from the ever-growing numbers of the "Have-Nots" and pay ever-increasing amounts of money for arms to keep the "Have-Nots" from storming the walls of plenty? To know what must be done if malnutrition is to be eradicated is not as difficult as knowing how to do it, and neither is as difficult as actually doing it. But knowing what must be done is the starting point. So, what must be done?

1. Each nation has to decide that providing adequate nutrition for all its people is among its highest national priorities. In many developing countries, agricultural priorities are first, food for export; second, food for industrial processing; and only third, food for the population at large. That is a formula for malnutrition. The agricultural priorities must be reversed if all people are to be adequately fed.

The determination to provide adequate nutrition for all its people involves more than a nation's agricultural priorities. Other priorities must include making possible employment for all who can work so that they will have the money to buy food that will be available when the agricultural priorities are changed. If the opportunity for employment for all people is realized in the society, the cancerous core of the cause of malnutrition will have been eliminated.

Employment opportunity, however, will not solve the problem of those who cannot work: the young, the old, the sick, and the disabled. A society that can decide to change its agricultural priorities and provide full employment opportunities is also a society that can provide for the welfare of its helpless in ways beyond the imagination of those who have experienced the impersonal and dehumanizing welfare system in the United States.

2. The international community of nations must decide to accept a more equitable basis for mutual intercourse than presently exists. With justification, the poor nations of the world cry out that "the rules of the game are unfair." It is not too difficult to understand why those countries, with 70 percent of the world's population, reject a system which awards 70 percent of the world's income to the other 30 percent of its inhabitants. That inequity is due less to ignorance, laziness, and lack of resources than it is to the fact that the "rules" of the world economic "game" – as applied to trade, the international monetary system, the operation of large multinational corporations – are "fixed" in favor of the industrialized nations of the world. Those rules are the legacy of Western colonialism.

What the developing nations of the world are calling for is a New International Economic Order (NIEO), in which the poor countries get fair prices for the goods they produce for the industrialized countries and in which poor countries are not forced by wealthy countries to produce goods for them at the expense of providing food for their own people.

There should be no illusion about the difficulties in getting the community of nations to play by a new set of rules. As Geoffrey Barraclough, an analyst of the world economic crisis, has reminded us, if one looks at present indications, the prospects for a new world economic order look slim and those for new world economic disorder look alarmingly large. However, just as it was possible for slavery to be ended in this country, and just as it was possible for Western political colonialism to be ended in most of the developing world, so it is also possible to end economic colonialism.

While there are many other decisions that need to be made if hunger and malnutrition are to be eliminated, there can be no substitute for the decision at the international level providing for more equitable dealing among nations, nor for the decision at national levels to provide adequate nutrition for all their people. The implications of these two decisions are far-reaching. How the decisions will get made may not yet be clear, but that must not detract from the necessity of seeing that they are made.

What can I do?

Specifically, what can I do to ensure that the decisions at national and international levels are made and implemented? Commensurate with the seriousness of the problem and the difficulties in getting the important decisions made is the seriousness with which we approach the problem personally. What is required of us is nothing less than a lifestyle focused on the problem and its solution. We suggest that there are five vocations in this responsible lifestyle.

1. We must be students so that we can see beyond the headlines and political and corporate rhetoric to understand the fundamental issues. Both study and reflection can lead us to a recognition that employment, welfare, and the New International Economic Order are hunger issues.

2. We must be activists in our local community. The integrity of our commitment to the hunger concern is reflected in our ability to recognize the dimensions of hunger at home and in our willingness to be involved with the poor in its elimination. There is no substitute for direct personal involvement. In the 1990s, tens of millions of North Americans are hungry. Forty percent are children.

3. We must be advocates at local and national levels on government and corporate policies and practices. We must stand in those arenas where the poor are not present, whether at a company stockholder meeting or at a Senate hearing; our voices must echo those of the poor whose access to the decision-making process at both government and business levels has traditionally been blocked. Several excellent organizations exist that can assist you in the effort: for example, Bread for the World, the Inter-religious Taskforce on U.S. Food Policy, and the Interfaith Center on Corporate Responsibility.

4. We must be responsible stewards of our financial resources, committing them to church and other voluntary efforts to combat hunger, and monitoring their use in our individual and corporate lives. Through both our charitable contributions and our financial investments, we can make strong statements about our stand for equality and justice. As government and churches develop programs which are more controversial, your informed support may well be critical.

5. We must be pioneers in finding new ways of living which are characterized by using only that which is absolutely required. This means developing a lifestyle that will be a microcosm of the kind of world order which must come to be. It means developing immunity to that disease which is endemic to our society: consumerism and consumption for its own sake. The life of voluntary simplicity is a luxury which we receive in exchange for rejecting our bondage to consumerism. It becomes a sign of our personal liberation as well as a symbol of our solidarity with sisters and brothers for whom simplicity is a "given," not a choice.

Over the years many of us have worked to mobilize people in our churches and organizations into the kind of lifestyle just described. We have sought, through this mobilization, to build a broad-based consensus of concern among our church constituencies. In doing this, we have adopted a style which sought to be inoffensive and low key and an approach which, while straightforward regarding facts, sought to be moderate regarding actions.

That mobilization must continue to be strengthened through individual commitments. Moreover, it must be strengthened through deepened commitments which carry with them a sense of urgency about implementing solutions to hunger. We must end the complacency with which we deal with the "statistics" of hunger by making it our own struggle, and by joining hands with the victims of hunger and working toward their victory.

Food and Celebrations

Reprinted from *To Celebrate: Reshaping Holidays & Rites of Passage*

Food has been an important part of celebrations for people of various cultures and religions from earliest times. Museum exhibits of ceremonial bowls and goblets used by the ancient Greeks, Latin writings describing Roman banquets, religious documents giving instructions for feasts and festivals, traditions of the First Nations for sharing meat from the hunt – these are reminders that festive food has been an integral part of celebrations throughout history.

The Bible includes accounts of many special meals; in fact, food is a recurring theme in scripture. In the story of the prodigal son, the "fatted calf" is killed and prepared for the son's homecoming feast. And when Jesus becomes aware that the time of his arrest and death are near, he makes careful preparations for one last intimate sharing of the Passover meal with his disciples.

Food and celebration seem to go together. Even a casual look at the cookbook section at most bookstores or a glance at space given to describing holiday meals in newspapers and magazines will reveal the keen interest our culture takes in food. Special meals for national, religious, or family celebrations add variety and zest to our daily routine. They afford opportunities to share family anniversaries, to recognize important events, to affirm or to comfort a family member or friend, to increase our understanding and enjoyment of many holidays.

How can we emphasize the creative and joyous aspects of celebrations and avoid both the anxiety of having everything "just right" and the extravagance of preparing and eating foods that are too rich and too expensive?

1. **Share responsibility.** Invite members of the household to take part in planning, shopping, preparing, and serving a special meal. This change from a pattern of assuming that one person, usually the wife and mother, will do it all may not be easy. Sometimes the person usually responsible likes being in charge and feels threatened by having others do her or his job. Conversely, members of the household may not want to take on additional tasks. But if planning is done far enough ahead, if new ideas are considered, if there is some choice about who does what and when, and if a team spirit can be developed, then sharing responsibility becomes more plausible. The investment of time and energy into this

kind of joint planning and job sharing is worthwhile because it can yield exciting dividends.

The first dividend goes to the one who has customarily taken responsibility for the meal. That person will be less tired, less anxious, less resentful and, therefore, more able to enjoy the celebration. One year, "The Best Christmas Gift," a contest sponsored by Alternatives, was awarded to a woman who was a mother, grandmother, minister's wife, and annual hostess of her large family's Christmas dinner. A few weeks before Christmas, her son and daughter-in-law notified her that their gift to her would be a "Kitchen-Free Day" on December 25. They planned, shopped for, prepared, served, and cleaned up breakfast, lunch, and dinner for the whole family. On that day she did not feel torn between duties at the church, visiting with family and friends, and kitchen tasks. She was a guest in her own dining room.

The second dividend goes to the children and adults who help with the meals. Because they are involved from the beginning, they are spared those vague feelings of guilt about one person "slaving over a hot stove"; they share credit for the results – especially their own dishes – and feel more a part of the festivities. Talents

might be discovered and later tapped for regular family meals.

The third dividend goes to the guests. They join wholeheartedly in a celebration atmosphere where nobody seems worn out or uptight. In the rush and strain of daily routines, the gift of a leisurely visit with friends is enjoyable and renewing.

Another way of sharing responsibility for a meal is by asking guests to bring some of the food. This can be a true potluck, with guests bringing whatever they like, or a planned potluck, where each is asked to bring one specific part of the meal, or even a specific item. In addition to sharing the work, guests and hosts also share the expense of the meal.

Gifts of food can be part of special occasions in many ways other than meals at home. A gift of food, especially a favorite recipe, can be taken to the celebrant for a special occasion. If the person is a friend of the family, preparation of the food can be a joint endeavor. Many people traditionally take food to bereaved families, an effort that is practical as well as comforting. Members of the North Decatur Presbyterian Church in Decatur, Georgia, have a tradition of packing goodie-filled Valentine boxes for students away at college.

2. Work ahead. The most crucial step in arranging food for celebration is planning. First, choose a workable, affordable menu. Divide up such tasks as shopping, advance preparations, and cooking on the day of the event. Children enjoy making table decorations if they are not rushed and if they are allowed to use their own creative ideas. They are also tireless helpers for a cookie-making project, but the project supervisor must be sure to allow enough dough for pre-party sampling! Members of the household with demanding work schedules can make cook-ahead dishes such as breads, desserts, or salads, and they can prepare ingredients for dishes to put together later (shell and chop nuts, cut up dried fruits, prepare raw vegetables). Advance preparation frees the kitchen from last-minute congestion, allowing family members and guests to enjoy each other in a more leisurely manner.

3. Keep it festive but simple. Set a festive table with attractive mats or table cloth, a pretty centerpiece of cut flowers or a bowl of fruit and a special card or gift for the guest of honor. Have an eye for color – parsley, cocktail tomatoes, or pimento are pleasing garnishes. Serve the food in bowls and platters different from those used every day. Keep the meal simple by serving fewer dishes. Even for a party meal, a hearty main dish, fresh vegetable, salad, bread, and light dessert are enough. Prepare a sufficient quantity of each dish. Try new recipes, but include some familiar ones, especially if there are children in the group. If those who share the feast leave the table feeling pleased and satisfied, but not "overstuffed," those who prepared the meal deserve to be complimented.

Some meals are fun to eat! Set up your own Salad Bar, Rice and Toppings, Potato Bar or Pocket Bread Sandwich Bar. Young people seem particularly pleased with food they put together themselves.

When the moderators of two main branches of the Presbyterian Church were to lead a joint worship service in Richmond, Virginia, the hospitality committee wanted members of the congregation and visitors to greet the moderators. But it was not feasible to serve a regular meal unless a sizable number of people missed the church service for kitchen duties. The committee devised a plan that worked well. A large quantity of rice was prepared ahead of time in the church kitchen. Members of the congregation were asked to bring any kind of vegetable, meat, fish, or cheese sauce that would combine well with rice. Those unable to prepare a cooked sauce were asked to bring peanuts, raisins, coconut, or other toppings. The pastor of one of the congregations in the city opened his remarks of appreciation for the event by saying, "We Koreans like rice!" That was a plus for the menu that the committee had not even considered. Since rice is a staple in so many parts of the world, it is a good choice for meals prepared for people from other countries.

4. Invite others to share the meal. In planning a dinner for any traditional special occasion, let members of the household suggest persons they would like to invite: foreign students, friends who have no family members nearby, or persons they have met from the church shelter. For a birthday dinner, a child might want to include a scout master, church school teacher, or a new school friend. For a wedding anniversary, a couple might want to invite friends who attended them, or the person who performed the ceremony.

Each Christmas, I enjoy thinking of friends who joined our family celebration in past years and of the special contributions each made to the occasion:

- A young couple from Kenya, students in Louisville, Kentucky, were away from their families at Christmas for the very first time. They good-naturedly played a game of shuffleboard on the front walkway with our four children.

- A mother and two young children wore traditional Japanese dress for our special celebration. They spoke no English and we spoke no Japanese. Fortunately, a cousin visiting from Chicago acted as interpreter.

  When my husband asked the little boy if he would like more turkey, the question was repeated by the cousin to the mother, and by the mother to the son, who said one word in Japanese which must have been "Yes," because the plate was passed along with the cousin's very polite, "Yes, thank you very much."

- A couple from Lesotho, Africa, and their four children were political refugees. The father had to flee for his life in the middle of the night when government soldiers shot into his house and ordered him to come out. It was not until the next morning that the wife discovered that one of the bullets had killed their little grandson. The family managed to escape to Kenya and from there came to the United States for a rest.

  After dinner we sang carols around the pump organ. They sang in Lesotho and we in English, but the tune was the same. Then, with the mother beginning in a very high voice and the others coming in with different parts, they sang their beautiful national anthem. With great depth of feeling, they sang this haunting song of a country from which they were exiles.

- A Japanese mother and three-year-old daughter decided on Christmas Eve to accept our invitation, if the father could come later when he had finished his duties at the hospital. One of our sons was at home for Christmas. He shared our loneliness for the other members of our family – children and grandchildren. When he heard about the guests, he perked up immediately. He went shopping to fill a small stocking and offered enthusiastic help in the kitchen. The visit from that family was our best Christmas present that year.

Children who grow up in families where guests from other countries and cultures are often in the home find it easy to relate to persons from different backgrounds. Money cannot buy the kind of educational experience that growing up with friends from different places provides.

Change is possible

Experiencing the beauty and variety of other cultures in their growing-up years is a privilege not many adults can claim. But most of us are aware of a thread running through every culture: humanity's common need to celebrate. A second commonality is a penchant to organize celebrations around good food and warm friends amid pleasant surroundings. As noted earlier, we have done it this way for centuries. But recent history tells us that millions of the world's people are in a constant struggle simply to survive. With this in mind it seems no longer appropriate to celebrate by imitating opulent, self-indulgent, Roman-style feasts.

It is not necessary to give up celebrating in order to be sensitive, compassionate world citizens. However, celebrations that take into account the world's hungry people and Earth's finite resources demand discipline and commitment to ethical eating, and changing our style of living to consider all who inhabit Earth. If the way we live includes good habits in food buying and preparation on a daily basis, our festive occasions will be easier to plan and execute within the context of responsible living. And we will be rewarded for our efforts by nutritious meals that attest to our involvement with the world's hungry people and by celebrations that are both life-giving and life-enriching.

Almost everyone agrees that certain changes in our diet may be to our benefit. Studies by the Senate Select Committee on Nutrition and the U.S. Department of Agriculture suggest that we should:

- consume fewer calories;
- eat more fruits, vegetables, and whole grains;
- eat less fat, especially saturated fats (butter, red meat, hard cheese) and cholesterol (animal products, egg yolks, ice cream).

Doris Janzen Longacre in the *More-with-Less Cookbook* also urges avoidance of over-processed foods, convenience foods, large amounts of refined sugar, and saturated fats. But change is difficult – or, at least, we think it is – and, oftentimes, we resist. Three statements are frequently made when new approaches to eating are discussed:

1. It is too time-consuming.
2. It's hard to find those ingredients.
3. The members of my family won't eat it.

Family cooperation is sometimes achieved when each member helps in the planning and decision making. Those who accept responsibility for meals (husband, wife, children, etc.) have a better chance of success if there is a firm conviction about the benefits to be reached – better health, lower cost, greater satisfaction, more to share, and happier memories!

Dare to experiment! Make a few changes at first. The daily papers and monthly magazines are full of practical suggestions for new dishes – pastas, stir-fries, frittatas, Oriental and Eastern vegetable dishes, quick breads, unfamiliar fruits (kiwi, papaya, mangoes), lentils, etc. Many communities have good farmers' markets and some have stores featuring health foods. Even traditional grocery stores are becoming more responsive to demands for brown rice, rye flour, spinach noodles, bulgar wheat, pita bread, snow peas, and carob candy.

Celebrations are more joy-filled when, in conjunction with good fellowship and delicious, simple meals, we carry out commitments to conserve resources, share our bounty, and follow good health practices.

Shopping

Good shopping habits trim the food bill, save time, and help change eating patterns. First, get a cookbook that encourages thrift, good health, and awareness of the world. *Extending the Table* and *More-with-Less Cookbook* are basics. Read them until you are saturated with the fact that what you do at the market and in the kitchen matters!

Think about meals as a testimony of faith, not just as an act of survival. Enjoy planning, reading food ads, making a few new menus and thinking ahead so that meal time is a joy and a celebration.

Rearrange storage space so that buying and storing a few items in bulk is possible; for example, whole wheat flour, brown rice and a variety of pastas. Get rid of those things in your refrigerator that you have not used in weeks, and stock bulk yeast, unflavored gelatin, fresh herbs (ginger, dill, mint), fresh fruits and green vegetables in the newfound space. Cut down on canned items which usually are heavily salted and sugared. Stock a few new spices on your pantry shelves. Try oregano, basil, thyme, rosemary, and whole nutmeg. Buy spices loose at one-tenth the price and keep them in small labeled bottles.

Find a store that caters to the "new you." Farmers' markets and health food stores are good sources for these foods. Or, if you live in an area where such markets are not available, ask your grocer to stock these items. Wherever you shop, do two things: make a list, and have an eye for bargains. Prepare for shopping by doing three things: read weekly food ads, mark "specials" that fit agreed-on standards (no junk!), and list items needed for selected menus.

Do incidental shopping by keeping the list in your purse and stopping by the store when you are in that area. Be firm about steering clear of sections of the store that tempt you to binge on sugary doughnuts or to indulge in impulse buying. But be flexible enough to snap up a bargain.

Cooking

Experiment with stir-fry cooking. Children usually love it, especially if they can help. Try new soups – cheese broccoli, corn chowder, fresh spinach, gazpacho, or even cold fruit soups. Make enough for more than one meal.

Discover pasta salads, using raw marinated vegetables and a variety of salad dressings. Serve hot pasta with bits of beef or chicken. Chop fresh vegetables for a salad. Use homemade dressings which are cheaper and free of additives. Cut down on the number of different items on your menu – hot pasta, vegetable salad, and fruit dessert are adequate and nourishing.

Get acquainted with beans and legumes. They are nourishing, protein-rich and less costly than meat… for your wallet and for Earth.

For dessert, try to stick with fresh fruit, simple puddings, or healthful cookies. Find simple, reliable recipes for making a batch of cookies or a sheet cake on Saturday afternoon, and hide it to use during the week. Breads are delicious but high in calories – presenting a problem for some people. Hot breads with bran, nuts, or raisins furnish protein and make an ordinary meal special.

New kinds of cookbooks

When we are looking for responsible kinds of cooking, we now have many alternatives offering Earth-friendly recipes. Look for them at secondhand book stores, rummage sales, or book sales, or borrow them from the library. Many of these books do more than present new recipes. They provide incentive to change by making us aware of the dangers of additives and preservatives, giving us a new appreciation for natural foods and enlisting us in the war against needless starvation in the world. Some of the books are general in nature, covering a range of foods and kinds of preparation. Others are specifically directed toward certain kinds of food, for instance, desserts. All ages can profit from these exciting, challenging books. No one is too old to change or too young to begin right!

Getting Started

Family Transition Is Half the Battle
Carole G. Rogers

The idea of celebrating an alternate Thanksgiving, birthday, or Christmas, of remembering family and friends with love instead of with wasteful, expensive, here-today-gone-tomorrow gifts seems very contemporary – an answer perhaps to the problems of an overcrowded, underfed planet. But it is not really new. In 1513, Fra Giovanna was expressing similar sentiments in a letter to a friend:

I salute you. I am your friend and my love for you goes deep. There is nothing I can give you which you have not got; but there is much, very much, that, while I cannot give it, you can take.

No heaven can come to us unless our hearts find rest in it today. Take Heaven! No peace lies in the future which is not hidden in this present little instance. Take Peace! The gloom of the world is but a shadow. Behind

it, yet within our reach, is Joy. Take Joy!

...And so, at this Christmas time, I greet you. Not quite as the world sends greetings, but with profound esteem and with the prayer that for you, now and forever, the day breaks and the shadows flee away.

For those of us already convinced of the rightness of an alternate Christmas, however, the question often is not Why? but How? None of us finds it easy to resist the lure of the marketplace at Christmas. (And no wonder – every possible attraction, from gaily-wrapped packages and carols to the scent of evergreens and the ho-ho-ho of Santa, has been arrayed against us.) But it is possible. Families who have already made the transition are most encouraging. Here are some of their suggestions as well as some of my own; all are based on practical experience.

Start early

Last year was our first try at an alternate kind of holiday and we started to talk about it in October. It was none too early. Other families, who plan to make all their gifts, start in the summer when there is still time to stitch, carve, preserve, gather herbs, or whatever.

The Advent wreath tradition, which is again enjoying a renaissance, focuses attention on the coming of Christ instead of Santa. The lighting of candles – one during each of the four weeks preceding Christmas – is such a beautiful yet simple ceremony that even young children can participate and understand.

Discuss

Tell the children what you're thinking, why you'd like to change and ask for their opinions. Expect them to understand and be enthusiastic. But be open to their ideas and honor any of their objections.

One woman, a widow with two children, aged 13 and 14, wrote me and said, "The thing that convinced them to go along with me and to try the alternate Christmas was the fact that it was so ecologically right and, too, because we decided that the money we saved would go to help others less fortunate than ourselves."

Some parents call a special meeting or a family council. The Keip family from Pacific Grove, California, went out to dinner together – "a very special treat for us – to talk about and plan for our Christmas celebration."

When you and the children have agreed, tell grandparents, aunts and uncles, cousins, friends – anyone with whom you normally exchange gifts – so they'll know what to expect, too.

Last year we decided that, instead of exchanging lots of expensive presents, we would "adopt" a family in our own country who would not be likely to have any Christmas at all without somebody's help. We sent long letters to our families telling them what we were going to do and explaining that even though we would not be buying gifts as usual, we still loved them. "As we make our attempt at a new kind of Christmas we want you to know that we will be doing it with all of you very much in our minds and hearts..."

Substitute new traditions for old buying habits

One family with three boys spent a weekend cross-country skiing. That worked out so well that at Easter they planned a theater trip instead of giving in to the Easter basket ritual. That was not so much of a success, however. The key, they told me, lies in selecting something everybody will enjoy. No mean feat for most families, but perhaps the choosing can in itself become a festive event.

You can make a tradition of the

alternative gifts themselves. At their planning dinner the Keip family discussed "coupon books" – tickets "for things we will do for each other." After Christmas I learned from Mrs. Keip that the coupons had been a big success on the day itself and continued to be long afterward. "I think this will become an increasingly important family tradition with us in the Christmases ahead," she wrote.

"Our adopted family turned out to be six fatherless children whose mother was gravely ill in the hospital. So we still had to fight the Christmas crowds to buy food and necessary clothing for them. But we tried to turn the chore into a special day and we must have succeeded because we enjoyed it more than any other Christmas shopping we've ever done."

Make the transition gradually

The friend in Connecticut, who took her family cross-country skiing, compromised last year by putting a few things under the tree. "They were all lost or broken within 30 days. We're still talking about the skiing. So I think next year we'll just forego presents entirely."

It's part of the commercial mystique that surrounds Christmas that says it must always be a perfect day. Don't be pressured and don't be rigid. Families who have established their alternative traditions say they had to be flexible, willing to change and adapt. If something doesn't work this year, try something else next year. Eventually you'll evolve an alternate Christmas that is truly life-supporting and also truly yours.

When you first begin you may wonder if the idea will work for you at all. Have you really ruined Christmas forever? No, say the families that have persevered. Jane Mall, from Hinsdale, Illinois, wrote that her family had many doubts last year. "It wasn't until after Christmas that we realized what we had done. It was when we received the thank-you notes. The homemade things were so much appreciated; the idea of an alternate Christmas was new to the recipients and they wanted to know more about it. Then we felt very good about what we'd done and vowed to do the same for other celebrations. It really is worth it! In fact, we can never again go back to the wasteful, selfish way of celebrating Christmas again."

Last year was our first attempt, too, and I had the same doubts. Our children are still very young, our families loving and open-minded even if they do sometimes think we're a little silly. So change seemed possible – even necessary – at this time in our lives. But for us, too, the insights and rewards didn't come until after Christmas. For me there was a feeling of freedom, of having truly enjoyed a day that had always been marred by last-minute trips for that elusive perfect gift. And then there was the enthusiasm of others. One teenage nephew sent us money he'd earned to buy "something" for our adopted family. A cousin sent a donation to a favorite charity in our name.

We still don't know how our future Christmases will turn out, but we'll never go back to our old buying habits to celebrate it.

One Family's Program for Change
Carolyn C. Shadle

My children used to complain to me that they were the only ones in the school lunch room who had sandwiches made of whole wheat bread. I understood their desire to be like their peers, and I didn't want them to feel like "oddballs" or outcasts. Yet, sometimes it surprised me that they are not more different than their friends because I know that my values and my perspective of the world are quite different from that of my neighbors. Then I realized that my values were not those of my children. Perhaps you have noticed a similar gap in your family. Why is that? How can we change it?

I have two sets of values which conflict. On the one hand, I value good nutrition, elimination of heedless consumption, and life in harmony with Earth and its people. On the other hand, I value the freedom of children to choose and to make mistakes. I value their autonomy. I do not believe that we have the right to impose our values. In fact, while my way may be right, I find that I'm not very effective when I endeavor to impose my value system. It usually backfires and they work long and hard at rejecting my values!

If we wish to give our children their right to individuality and yet wish to live out our own values with the hope that they will someday adopt these same values for their own, we have to deal with the question, "How can we most effectively influence the values of our children?"

I have found that my values will be accepted by my children only when the atmosphere in our home is conducive to teaching and learning – only when there is an atmosphere of trust and respect for the children's individuality.

In Paul Tournier's book *The Meaning of Gifts*, he cautions us to avoid projecting our own taste into our gifts. "It is hard," he acknowledges, "to accept the fact that our children's taste may be altogether different from ours, but," he says, "the true meaning of love is understanding the other, attempting to know him and to recognize him... even if he be one's own child... as a person. The child needs to feel that his own particular identity is respected; otherwise, either he will withdraw and become a stranger to his own parents or else he will cease to recognize his personal tastes and will remain a dependent child."

To unilaterally choose gifts which reflect only our values or to unilaterally eliminate gifts because we believe them wasteful and unnecessary is to lack the very values of respect and consideration for others which we are endeavoring to teach.

Trust and respect

Listening, and letting our children know that we hear them, has been the first step in our home in establishing an environment of trust and respect. Listening to them when they complain about lunch or when they plead for the latest toy advertised on television, we need to hear their claims, their needs, their feelings, their frustrations, their wants, and their joys. It is only within an open and respecting relationship that our values can be taught and "caught."

Disclosing ourselves

Next to listening, however, the next most important component in building a respecting relationship is the giving of ourselves. We must speak up, too, and disclose our feelings, wants, needs, joys, frustrations. We must tell them how we feel about using white bread – and why. We must tell them if we feel cheated when we buy cheap plastic toys which break soon after they are opened. We must tell them if we feel concern for a poor worker in Asia or Mexico who has worked long difficult hours so that we can enjoy an inexpensive consumer item. We must tell them if we do not have enough money to buy all the things on their lists because there are other priorities toward which we wish to put our money – such as food, clothing, and charitable contributions.

Learning takes place when we disclose ourselves. *When* we choose to share ourselves is crucial. To lecture about poor Asian women in direct response to their eager request for a gadget or toy means to them that we have not listened, and they certainly do not hear our story about the low-paid Asian worker. (Do you remember how much empathy you acquired for the poor starving children when you were little and your parents lectured to you about their needs while you sat alone in tears staring at your peas after everyone had left the dinner table?) At such a time, we are wasting our breath; we probably induce hostility rather than a feeling of concern and sympathy.

Discussion starters

Our family has made use of "no problem" times, when tempers are even and tummies are full, to address ourselves to value-laden topics, particularly our materialistic lifestyle and our commercialized celebrations.

One of the teaching strategies we have used at the dinner table is called "unfinished sentences." On index cards I write a "sentence stub" which each person at the table must complete. Here are some that we have used:

- The best thing that happened to me today was...
- The nicest thing about Christmas is...
- What I remember most about last Easter is...
- My best friend is...
- The thing that worries me the most is...
- Birthdays mean...

Another strategy we use to provoke discussion is "fantasy." Some of the fantasy situations we've proposed are:

- If you were given a million dollars, what would you do with the money?
- If you could live any place in the world except where you live, where would it be?
- If you could spend a day with anyone except a family member, whom would you choose?

- If you could not spend any money at Christmas, what kind of gifts could you give?
- If you had all the toys and clothes you could possibly want, what then would you want for your birthday?

Another strategy we use involves "ranking" – prioritizing our needs and wants and desires:

- List, in order, the five things you want most to happen at Christmas.
- Which of these would be the worst for you?
  a) to have to go to church on Christmas Eve
  b) to do without new toys on Christmas
  c) to make Christmas gifts instead of buying them
- What is the most important thing about Christmas?
  a) remembering Jesus' birthday
  b) giving and receiving gifts
  c) family and friends getting together
- What would be the most meaningful wedding gift?
  a) a silver place setting
  b) a tuition gift for a marriage enrichment course
  c) a live plant to symbolize the life and growth in a relationship

These strategies are intended to give family members a structured opportunity to share their views and to discuss the topic. If each person's view can be heard and discussed non-judgmentally, then a lot of relationship building happens as family members get to talk about themselves and as we become more intimately acquainted with each other.

By using a variety of value clarification strategies, we have accustomed the children to talking openly about value-laden topics. Then, when it comes to holidays and celebrations, it is not so strange to discuss the values inherent in our styles of celebration.

While there exists a gap between our values and those of our children, there are, in the words of Sidney Simon, two things children need before there is a possibility of their changing their values: the first thing is nourishment, and the second is alternatives.

Nourishment is something we provide when we listen to and relate to our children, as well as when we provide them with nourishing meals. Emotional nourishment comes about as we build a relationship – as we care about one another, listen to one another, and share. The alternatives come as we disclose our values, as we discuss different ways of doing things, as we read good books together, and as we try alternative ways of celebrating.

Alternatives

At Halloween we have tried to adapt the traditional candy giveaway in a variety of ways. Instead of candy, we have baked nutritional goodies and handed out raisins, nuts, apples, and homemade popcorn. We have talked about UNICEF and have tried to focus on Halloween as a time to give to and collect for UNICEF. The Gerhards of Walla Walla, Washington, inspired us; they pass out a copy of this note:

Dear Trick-or-Treater:

We are giving 50 cents to UNICEF for every child who comes trick-or-treating at our home. Because you have come other children around the world will receive a gift of food and medicine to help them have the joys of life which you have. Thank you for coming to our home and helping us to help other children like yourself all around the world.

Another alternative was suggested by a friend in Eden, New York. She was disgusted with the tradition of the birthday child handing out candy to classmates, so she arranged with the teacher to give, instead, a real celebration. She invited a guitarist to visit the classroom and lead the children in singing. Following the singing, each child was given a donut carefully set on a circle of cardboard. In the middle of each was a birthday candle. Following the singing of Happy Birthday and the eating of the "cake," the children were able to appreciate the picture on the cardboard circle. My friend had covered the circles with wrapping paper decorated with butterflies. To carry out the butterfly theme, 25 butterflies were drawn on a large sheet of shelf paper. Each child was invited to write his or her name in one of the butterflies and a birthday wish. The mural was hung for the duration of the day and then taken home by the birthday child as a permanent memento of the class's good wishes.

At Eastertime we have sought alternatives to the needless chocolates in the Easter basket. The solution has been gradually to cut down in number and ultimately to eliminate the candy by replacing it with other items which focus more on the meaning of Easter. One year it was a large button-pin with a picture of bunnies and the phrase, "Love is the answer." Another year it was an inexpensive ARCH book entitled *Kiri and the First Easter*, purchased at the local religious supply store. Another year it was a poster that read "Sharing is Caring."

Our Christmas celebration changes began by adding things that were more meaningful and by eliminating that which was least threatening to do without. As we could talk more about the meaning of Christmas and about the effect of our consumption-oriented celebration, we were able gradually to substitute homemade gifts. One of the early nonthreatening changes we made

was a shift from the use of Christmas wrapping paper to the use of the colored weekend comic pages of the newspaper for wrapping. The change made sense to our children because they had been involved weekly in recycling newspapers as well as old school papers and mail. They had observed the piles of wasted paper and recalled our saying that it takes 17 trees to make a ton of paper.

House decorations were also an area where early changes were made. We ceased buying the expensive plastic commercial items and instead surrounded ourselves with homemade decorations and those which reminded us of the religious meaning of Christmas.

The cutback on gifts was accompanied by discussions about our family budget and priorities, and the addition of an "Alternative Gift Certificate" to all of our relatives and to our own family. (Alternatives for Simple Living issues Alternate Gift Certificates which allow the recipient to receive a book or make a donation to a designated justice or hunger group.) The presence of such a certificate under our own tree gave our children an opportunity to discuss which life-supporting group they wanted to see receive our gift.

The shock of fewer toys and things under the tree was reduced by inviting family and friends for Christmas dinner at our house on Christmas Day.

It made the day very busy, but the hustle and bustle was centered on preparing for company instead of on the hurried tearing open of boxes. An after-Christmas trip also involved us in the joy of reuniting with friends, and it saved our children from counting their presents and comparing their "loot" with that of their neighbor friends. By now they are becoming accustomed to nonmaterial gifts.

Last Christmas we designed and mimeographed this gift certificate for use by others:

To _____
                              (name)

This certificate entitles the above named bearer to receive:

_____

_____

from me, with warm Christmas greetings.

_____
                           (signature)

I heard that the gifts given by way of the certificate ranged from back rubs to promises to cook or clean!

On our last wedding anniversary, our daughter, wanting greatly to give us something, went to the garage, sawed a piece of scrap wood, added two clay sculptured faces, and "engraved" the plaque with gold paint; it read, "The Great Parents Award." We like to think that her creativity was a result of our introducing alternatives throughout the year to the traditional "buy-a-gift" syndrome.

We like to think that what we believe and what we do has an effect on the lives of our children. If we can relate to our children in a trusting and respectful manner and provide them with alternative ways to view the world and relate to it through our celebrations, our children will be open to our values. It is even possible that they will one day apply these same values more vigorously and with more commitment than we now have the courage to do. Perhaps they will ultimately lead us!

Celebrations in Extended, Single Parent, and Blended Families
Milo Thornberry

Once upon a time, "family" meant mother, father, boy, girl, and dog. Today, one parent may be absent, or people may live in an extended family (with grandparents, aunts and uncles, friends) or in a blended family (with "your children," "my children," and "our children"). It can be confusing for children and adults alike.

When you are adjusting to a different family configuration and at the same time, trying to consciously simplify celebrations, it is most important to focus on *celebration*. The event, whether it is a birthday or religious or civic holiday, must never take precedence over the feelings of family members. This means that it may be necessary to celebrate when it is best for everyone, rather than when the calendar dictates.

Many of us have difficulty dealing with extended family members (including former spouses) when their values are different from ours. Stepparents particularly may have a difficult time in staying focused on the joyous aspect of the event. The alternative, however, is to remember that many of us become extra sensitive around holidays, and to ask for physical or emotional help when it is needed.

Celebrations are not always steps to reaffirming and strengthening ties in the extended family. Conflicts about how to spend limited time or whose traditions to follow and new patterns of celebration are commonplace, but not easy to deal with. Blended families may be more complicated. Children's time must be shared between former spouses, and perhaps four sets of grandparents. Tension between former spouses and differing values can make celebrations times of extreme anxiety.

There are no easy answers! It does little good to rail at the high divorce rate, or the fragmentation of the nuclear family. If celebrations are to be occasions for nurture and fun, sensitivity and acknowledgment of these problems are essential. The following suggestions may help in avoiding potential problems:

1. Before you talk with extended family members or ex-spouses, have a clear idea of your own about the significance of the event. Invite the children into a discussion. Hear from them what is important about celebrating with you.

2. Let extended family members and ex-spouses know about your ideas well in advance of the event.

3. Sensitively discuss with your children the different perspectives and

practices they may encounter in their celebrations at Grandma's or at their other parent's home.

4. Eliminate a tone of self-righteousness about your new way of celebrating.

5. Be flexible in the dates of your celebration. Alternatives can also apply to the day of celebrating.

6. Even though your immediate family unit may be in the minority, hold fast to your own plans for alternative celebrations!

7. Resist cultural pressure to outspend the other parent in order to prove your affection. Extravagance cannot compensate for separation. Try talking to your children about this difficult issue.

8. Be courageous as you face changes to your celebrations, but perhaps most important, keep your sense of humor – no matter what. Do your best to make the celebration work; view it as an experiment in growth, and look for the humor and joy in whatever happens.

Women and Celebrations: The Fable of Maybe-Maybe Land
Eugenia Smith-Durland

This story takes place in Maybe-Maybe Land. (It couldn't have happened in Never-Never Land, as you will see.) Maybe-Maybe Land is made up of ordinary folks who try to enjoy life as much as possible because life is good. And because they love each other and enjoy life, they have lots of occasions for celebrating. These celebrations are a very important part of the fabric of life for the Maybe-Maybe Landers. The celebrations are often quite gay and frolicsome, not frivolous, but essential to the balance of life. There is something they all have in common. All seem to call for lots of fine food, dressing up, and above all, lots of gift-giving.

There is just one thing amiss in the lives of these happy people. Although these celebrations are very important to everyone, and all share in the celebration, the women must do all the work! And after the parties are over, they must clean up the mess.

But perhaps the worst problem for the women of Maybe-Maybe Land is their culture and its influence on them. You see, Maybe-Maybe Land culture is afflicted with something known as the "Supermom Syndrome." Supermoms are good wives and mothers, beautiful and well-dressed, even when scrubbing floors or cleaning up after birthday parties. They never become cross or short of bouncing energy. Kitchen floors always shine like mirrors, even while putting on spectacular celebrations single-handedly.

How did the Supermom Syndrome come to Maybe-Maybe Land? Some of it certainly filtered down from the ancestors who worshiped hard work and independent effort. But there is something else. Maybe-Maybe Landers' homes all have little moving-picture sets telling stories about families, *supposedly* just like their own – all with Supermoms. To make things worse, companies pay to make the stories possible, and broadcast their own "mini-stories" to sell products to mothers and children.

Now the women in our story are intelligent, and know the stories they see are not true. But they still are influenced by the Supermom image that is pushed upon them. They often feel frustrated because they cannot keep up with the image that surrounds them. They want their families to be happy and well-cared-for, and they really want every holiday and celebration to be a special occasion. They keep trying, but the harder they work, the more separated they become from their families at those important moments for loving and sharing. Their frustrations make them feel cheated and guilty because they can't enjoy the festivities.

Now the women of Maybe-Maybe Land got fed up with the Supermom Syndrome. (You remember they are all very intelligent – so it stands to reason that they would not put up with the nonsense forever!) And better still, their husbands and children got fed up with the exploitation too. Being bright, creative people, they got together to change the situation.

Some wanted to throw out celebrations altogether, feeling women could handle things if there weren't extra burdens. Their view was not popular. Others wanted to rotate all jobs concerning family living and celebrating. But this sometimes became very complicated.

After much thought and discussion, the Maybe-Maybe Landers realized that it was all right to want celebrations to be special occasions. What had been wrong was their assumption that one had to be a Supermom for it to happen. With family sharing, they could all help mom, and have more fun to boot!

They had come up with an idea for alternative celebrations and there was no stopping them! The possibilities were fantastic! They noticed that "community" and "whole family" celebrations discouraged competitive cooking and decorating. They also discovered that they saved a great deal of money, and were more creative and original as they shared the joy of making gifts and sharing chores and ideas. They also found that their religious celebrations became more meaningful, and they felt much closer to God and their neighbors.

In a nutshell, they discovered, through their alternative celebrations, that in truly authentic and joyful celebrating, the preparations and the occasion itself cannot really be separated! When everyone shared equally in the planning, preparation and work of celebrating – just as they had always shared in the fun – there was no way to distinguish between the preparation and the fun!

Socializing
Bob and Kathleen Keating

Much emphasis is placed on holiday parties, and often they result in unnecessary exhaustion, even sadness. On the other hand, December has become a season of celebration, a time for getting together with special friends. So, ask:

- Is my party one more of many which bring the same people together, or is it for a certain number of friends who otherwise won't see one another?
- Is my party to repay invitations and could it as easily be done another month, or is it to include people I especially want to be with at this time?
- Can I afford the money, time, and energy right now? Will the entertaining be a pleasure for me as well as for my guests?
- Is there an innovative approach I could use, such as taking the party to a seniors' home, or to a hospital where everyone could sing and celebrate?
- Does the invitation list include people who might otherwise be forgotten?
- Will the invitation include children?
- Will I ask people to bring potluck, or to contribute by bringing finger food?
- What is the single most important thing I can do for myself in order to be relaxed and enjoy my own party?

If children are included at your party, you may want to try making a piñata. Make one with the children and fill it with sugar-free candy, nuts, little bags of popcorn, toasted soybeans, fancy crackers, etc. Invite the neighborhood children in on Christmas Eve to break the piñata. The use of the piñata is a Spanish custom, and this should be explained to the children. (A piñata is a decorated shape made of papier mâché. Libraries have instruction books in the crafts section.)

If you decide to entertain, it should be done in your own style, whether that involves careful planning or spontaneity. A way to avoid tension is to be honest about doing things personally. Just because our culture holds up images of elegant decorating and serving, or of having dozens of family members together on Christmas, doesn't mean that's the only way or the best way for you. Try for integrity and you'll enjoy it more.

Alternative Checklist: How Much Is Enough?

Reprinted from *Alternative Celebrations Catalogue, 3rd Edition*

Each day that passes, the evidence mounts up that it is time for our society to start giving back more than we take from our planet and her people. Our taking (buying, having, discarding) appetite has always hurt Earth and those we trampled. We are now reaping what we have sown, and the impact of our gout is both physical and spiritual.

It is almost painful to recall that for thousands of years great and small people of wisdom have declared that the "good life" could not be bought with money and things. Economist E.F. Schumacher, in *Small Is Beautiful*, expanded this idea to include freedom and peace: "Only by a reduction of needs can one promote a genuine reduction in those tensions which are the ultimate causes of strife and war."

"Creative deprivation" for children makes good sense for adults as well. It keeps the senses and mind free of material goods that overwhelm us, in order to have room to experience creative uses of the imagination.

Declaring yourself in the camp of those committed to creative simplicity will happen when you admit that there are limits in life which you have violated. Jettisoning the excess baggage for new ways is a process both liberating and painful and it continues until we die. Fruits come from the daily labor of nurturing the lifestyle which is life-giving. And, as in any garden, there are always weeds and bugs to contend with.

Following is an alternate celebration checklist to stretch your imagination toward specific actions:

Birthdays

- Cut out the junk food.
- Give yourself.
- Make gifts.
- Thank your friend's parents for her/his life.

- Emphasize the uniqueness of the person.

Your wedding

- Create your own wedding celebration.
- Ask friends to help with food for the reception.
- Request gift money be sent to one of your favorite people- and Earth-oriented projects.
- Avoid buying new clothes.
- Make your own invitations.
- Write your own vows.

Other's weddings

- Give homemade, self-help craft shop, or recycled gifts.
- Give yourself (paint their apartment, for example).
- Donate to the couple's favorite cause.
- Give those wedding gifts you never used.
- Offer to take photographs, prepare food, or clean up.

Halloween

- Give fruit or homemade cookies.
- Organize collection for hunger project.
- Plan a block party.
- Give your "treat" money to a hunger project and tell children.

Your funeral

- Donate organs to the living.
- Donate your body to a medical school.
- Have your body cremated.
- Be buried in plain pine box.
- Ask that donations be made to a cause or charity in lieu of flowers.

Other's funerals

- Contribute memorials instead of flowers
- Start a dialogue in your congregation and community about funeral reform.
- Start a memorial society.
- Give the surviving parent, friend, or child a blank book for journaling.
- The age-old tradition of cooking and baking still holds; prepare some food.
- Donate a book to a library, school, synagogue in memory of the deceased.

Your graduation

- Organize an alternate graduation and donate cap and gown, class ring and invitation money to a project.
- Encourage family and friends to give to a project in lieu of a gift.

Other's graduation

- Give the graduate a membership to an environmental group.
- Give a good book or a magazine subscription.
- Make a personal gift.
- Contribute to person's favorite cause.

Hanukkah and Christmas

- Drastically reduce spending.
- Make gifts.
- Give yourself: your time, talent, skill.
- Shop at self-help craft outlets.
- Give a gift certificate for environmental or justice work.
- Organize an alternate Christmas or Hanukkah in your congregation.
- Establish family tradition of giving

"unspent" income to people- and Earth-oriented projects.

- Create new family traditions which are person-oriented.

Valentine's Day

- Do not buy candy and commercial cards.
- Make homemade alternatives.
- Contribute to a prison reform project, or programs to help ex-offenders.
- Encourage your neighborhood school to organize an alternative Valentine program on prison reform.

Birth of your child

- Make your own announcements.
- Encourage contributions to projects which help less fortunate children.

Birth of anothers' child

- Offer to help the new parents – be specific.

- Give the mom herbal bubble bath.
- Give babysitting certificates; parents can call you when they need a break.
- Write a prayer, make a quilt, knit or crochet a gift.
- Give a book.
- Write a letter to the baby, telling how you felt when you first saw him or her.

Thanksgiving

- Plan a meatless dinner.
- Give a donation to hunger and First Nations projects.
- Organize an alternative Thanksgiving campaign.

Passover and Easter

- Plan meatless meals.
- Don't buy candy.
- Don't buy new clothes.
- Contribute to human welfare.
- Plan an alternative children's celebration.

The Shakertown Pledge

In addition to discussing the checklist with your loved ones, you may also wish to discuss the Shakertown Pledge. This pledge was written by a group of religious retreat leaders who felt bad about being members of a privileged minority in a nation guilty of the overconsumption of the world's resources. They recognized that their own lifestyles were part of the problem. They named their pledge the Shakertown Pledge in honor of their original gathering place and because the Shaker community had believed wholeheartedly in lives of "creative simplicity." You, too, may want to sign it, or create a different one that suits your particular family. We suggest you hang it in your kitchen:

Recognizing that Earth and the fullness thereof is a gift from our gracious God, and that we are called to cherish, nurture, and provide loving stewardship for Earth's resources, and recognizing that life itself is a gift, and a call to

*responsibility, joy, and celebration,
I make the following declarations:*

1. *I declare myself to be a world citizen.*
2. *I commit myself to lead a life of creative simplicity and to share my personal wealth with the world's poor.*
3. *I commit myself to join with others in the reshaping of institutions in order to bring about a more just global society in which all people have full access to the needed resources for their physical, emotional, intellectual, and spiritual growth.*
4. *I commit myself to occupational accountability, and so doing I will seek to avoid the creation of products which cause harm to others.*
5. *I affirm the gift of my body and commit myself to its proper nourishment and physical well-being.*
6. *I commit myself to examine continually my relations with others, and to attempt to relate honestly, morally, and lovingly to those around me.*
7. *I commit myself to personal renewal through prayer, meditation, and study.*
8. *I commit myself to responsible participation in a community of faith.*

Conversion: A Letter from Yola
Evelyn Howie

A surprise package with an unlikely postmark was left in our mailbox last December. Since I was rushing to town to select the perfect gift for our friends, I opened it hurriedly, anxious to get on with the shopping.

The package contained four handknit ponchos and four wooden pipes (also hand-made). Yola, who made and sent these to us, is our friend who washed and ironed and made life easier for us while we were in Bolivia. Her salary was 80 cents a day, more money than she'd ever made before! The moment I realized what she'd done, I burst into tears! Here in my quiet kitchen, I was completely overwhelmed with the love and effort these gifts represented, and how could we – with a kitchen full of food, a more-than-adequately-comfortable home, children with more than enough clothes and "things" – how could we continue to spend the time, energy, and money for these meaningless gifts (for which I was shopping) in the name of Christmas?

During the year we've been unable to locate Yola. The only meaningful and honest thing we know to do, the only way we know to reach Yola and Bolivia and all the other people in the world in the same plight, is to send the money we'd ordinarily spend for gifts this year to LAOS, a nonprofit, ecumenical volunteer agency.

Part 2

Gifts

Gift-Planning

Reprinted from *To Celebrate: Reshaping Holidays & Rites of Passage*

Somewhat ahead of time, review the family's (or individual's) expectations for the season or day. If this is not the time for a radical breaking away from gift-giving, try for spending limitations. By planning early, there is the chance to give more careful thought to each gift decision.

Considering one person at a time and giving careful thought to personal interest is not only good practice in caring, but also in deciding what's really appropriate for each individual. It can also prevent the exasperating store-to-store trek, hoping for an inspiration which usually ends up with something impulsive instead of something important.

It's better to think about gifts away from stores, away from catalogues. Think about the person! Only *after* contemplating the type of gift to be given should one selectively shop for that gift.

As for giving to a cause instead of to a person, this must be done with the person in mind. A young person who has always received something tangible may not be ready for a shift to money given for social purposes. But relatives with well-stocked homes and larders are often quite pleased *not* to receive some peculiar item they didn't want anyway. It all depends on the person. The purpose is giving that makes sense to the recipient as well as to the giver.

Another part of the gift-planning is to determine what help children need, encouraging them toward the meaningful rather than the wasteful gift. Give guidance on gift-giving to children who don't have money. All (adults and children) have skills and talents which might create handmade gifts. Most people place special value on those things in which someone has invested time and care, be they pictures, poems, homemade chore coupons, or clever, hand-crafted projects. It is well to ask, "Will the person for whom I'm making this want a homemade gift?" Some people don't find any meaning in them, and that must be considered. Or, if the homemade projects will make one so tired and tied down as to become unhappy, then they shouldn't be attempted. Most of us can't knit three sweaters in the last weeks before Christmas, or sew or carpenter or anything else, if there is time pressure. Planning for the recipient as well as you, the giver, is the key to success.

Different Approaches to Gift-Giving

Reprinted from *The Alternate Celebrations Catalogue*

Christmas fund

About 25 years ago, we decided to stop exchanging gifts in our family and to instead use the money we would have spent to help at some point in the world. In the early years, we used to sit around the table after our dinner on Thanksgiving Day and discuss how we would use our Christmas fund, to which everyone (even the little ones) contributed. In recent years, the family has scattered and the collection of the fund is by mail, solicited by letter. There are 28 in our family group now. Participation is voluntary, and we think it is wise to continue it.

– Carolyn Miller, Columbus, Ohio

Alternative fund

One of the finest Christmas presents you could give your city is to set up an alternative fund like the one in Richmond, Virginia. A small group meets regularly to pool their surplus income resulting from simple living practices. Periodically, the money is sent to local, national, and international projects which have been carefully checked out. For a whole city, the fund works something like a mutual stock fund in reverse. The portfolio of projects is researched for maximum benefit from contributions and low overhead. As money is deposited to the fund, gifts are made to different groups based on urgency and long-range goals.

– Al Watts, Richmond, Virginia

Earth-friendly transport

Give a gift of transportation to help friends carry things and go places with less dependence on the smogmobile:

- shopping carts
- bus tokens
- bicycles
- bike repair books
- backpacks
- baby carriers
- bike touring club membership
- bike baskets
- cloth or net shopping bags.

– Ecology Center, Berkeley, California

New celebration

Last Christmas, our family and some others (who normally spend a small fortune on gifts for one another) decided to put an end to the absurdity of it all. We weren't able to end it altogether, but we did manage to divert $300 to life-supporting celebrations of our own. Four adult couples participated. We met to decide where the money normally spent on gifts would go. In this case, three different areas were touched: the fund for the family whose police-officer father was shot, money to help a boy we knew who was in prison, and money to help someone who was very ill.

Also last Christmas, we got together and gave a party for all of our children. The party was devised around the plan to have the children wrap their own toys to give to other children. We read to them from the Bible about what Jesus said about love and giving, and we saw some beautiful responses on their faces. The children had brought a tremendous number of gifts that they wanted to give away: toys, books, clothing. When all the things were wrapped, we took the children and the gifts to the home of a fatherless family with 16 children. Our children understood that they were not taking these gifts to show that they were good boys and girls, but rather because Christ could show love through them. They were humble; I don't think that they will ever forget the experience.

– Paula Sevier, Birmingham, Alabama

Decorations

What is meaningful is what should be done. The trimmings should take priority over the elegant, the expensive, the extensive. The question to ask is, "What look do we want?" Ask kids how they feel, and proceed from there, sometimes negotiating over a change or over how to put up the decorations.

Certainly, decorating is an area for cautious spending. Not all families like the arts/crafts homemade master-

pieces, but neither is it necessary to spend $10 or $25 more on classy gadgets that catch attention in the store and embarrass the budget later, especially since their use is so limited.

If decorating is a problem, the deciding should be done in consultation with one's own values and tastes. What looks good at the neighbor's, in the store, or in a magazine, may be worth adapting; and then again, it may be a mistake.

For those in doubt, try the pleasant simplicity of decorating with greens. They can adorn shelves, tables, mantels, be tied with thread or wire into swags, or put in vases. Highlights can be a red bow, a shiny ornament, candles (reasonably distant from flammables), fruits, nuts. It's possible to create a very desirable holiday effect and spend next to nothing.

– J. Loerke, Eagle, Wisconsin

Christmas ornaments

Make ornaments for yourself or to give to others. Surely everyone can find scraps of colorful material around their house. Cut two pieces the same (in any number of interesting designs: stars, circles, diamonds), turn inside-out, and stuff with cotton from aspirin bottles, etc. You'll find that they will have interesting family associations as the years go on. (You may like to add some embroidery or painting, too.)

– J. Loerke, Eagle, Wisconsin

Cards

It is clear that holiday cards can be a burden or a pleasure. There is no need to belabor the point that if December is the only communication of the entire year, it may be a very important point of contact – or it may be a meaningless formality, better retired. You may wish to:

- skip a few years and then review your list;
- send cards only to those to whom a letter is also sent;
- send cards Valentine's Day or Thanksgiving, rather than in December;
- make your own cards so they, in themselves, are personalized gifts;
- if you're in the habit of purchasing expensive cards, perhaps make a small donation to a hunger or peace organization instead;
- don't send cards to people you see often; greet them personally;
- invite your children to make your family cards for you;
- if you do purchase cards, purchase from organizations that support life, for example, UNICEF, World Wildlife Fund, AIDS Network, and L'Arche.

Plants: a Gift of Life
Wendy Ward

Their bright blooms and fresh foliage cheer us; we breathe the oxygen they produce. Unlike antique vases or elephant-foot umbrella stands, plants require care and nurturing: they need us as we need them.

Gift plants may be purchased commercially or grown on your window sill. If you go the route of a neighborhood greenery, the following guidelines are useful in selecting a plant and avoiding catastrophe.

Compatibility with its prospective home and family

All plants have basic requirements, especially of light and water. If you're uncertain of its final location, a plant that tolerates low light is a better choice than one needing full sun that it may not get. Exotic or unusual plants often demand special care. Keep the "prima donnas" of the plant world as gifts for experienced indoor gardeners.

Try to include authoritative information on the plant and its needs. If you need help, do a little library research on maintenance, problems, propagation, and pests.

If a plant's recipient has children or pets with a penchant for nibbling, avoid dieffenbachias, English ivy,

Jerusalem cherry, poinsettia, and oleander. These plants are poisonous. Ingesting some or all parts of them produces unpleasant to fatal results. (In place of the traditional poinsettia as a holiday plant, try Christmas cactus or Christmas kalanchoe – both have striking blooms.)

Many children as well as adults appreciate plants as gifts. You may also consider edible plants, such as a pot of parsley.

Potted plants, bulbs, a small avocado or orange seedling you grew yourself, or cuttings from a plant that has been in your family for years or from a special friend far away can add an ounce of extra love to your living gift.

General state of health

Healthy plants are happy-looking plants; they may not have cold wet noses but they do have perky foliage with a good luster. A few bruises and abrasions are natural, but be wary of unnaturally pale foliage or yellowing/browning leaves.

Inspect plants carefully for bugs. Aphids come in a variety of colors and are often found on new growth; scale appears as shell-like growths on stems and branches. Both of these insects leave a sticky residue which denotes their presence. White flies cluster on the undersides of leaves; mealybugs resemble tufts of white cotton. Red spider mites are almost invisible but leave a white dustlike substance (discarded shell casings) along veins on the undersides of leaves.

These practices should be routine when selecting plants. They are practical, yet they also remind us that plants are not merely "decorative objects" but living entities with wants and needs.

The following list is divided into those plants which must have at least a half day of direct sun to survive or look their best (full sun); those plants which will be perfectly happy on less than half a day of direct sun (partial sun/bright light); and those which do nicely in dark corners (shade). Some plants will actually burn if given too much or any direct sun. Plants that are exceptionally difficult to grow are marked (d), those which are exceptionally easy are marked (e).

Full sun
(four hours or more direct sun; south window)

(e) cactus
(e) jade and other succulents
(e) wax begonia
(e) coleus
(e) areca palm
(e) croton
(e) Zebrina pendula – wandering jew
(d) gardenia
(d) citrus

Bright light

(consistent filtered sun;
north window)

(e) grape ivy

(e) maranta – "prayer plant "

(e) nephthytis – "arrowhead plant"

(e) Dracaena marginata –
"dragon tree"

(e) spathiphyllum

(e) creeping fig

(e) piggyback

(d) ferns – "Boston fern" and its va-
rieties, or "table" or "pteris" ferns

(d) Adiantum – "maidenhair fern"

Shade

(interior of a room)

(e) Sansevieria – "snake plant"

(e) philodendron

(e) pothos – "devil's ivy"

(e) parlor palm

(e) Chinese evergreen

(e) aspidistra – "cast iron plant"

Partial sun

(up to four hours direct sun
or consistent indirect sun;
east or west windows)

(e) iresine – "bloodleaf"

(e) peperomia

(e) Dracaena sanderiana

(e) spider plant

(e) Asparagus sprengeri –
"asparagus fern"

(e) Asparagus plumosus

(e) Swedish ivy

(e) gynura – "purple passion" or
"royal velvet"

(e) Hedera helix – "ivy"

(e) Norfolk Island pine

(e) Ficus elastica decora – "rubber
tree"

(e) podocarpus

Grow your gifts this year – it's an inexpensive way of sharing the joy and excitement of your own plants. Cuttings from some of the most colorful house plants root well in water. These include tradescantia, gynura, iresine, coleus, and wax begonia. Such green standbys as philodendron, creeping fig, Swedish ivy, and nephthytis are also easy to root.

Start your gift plants in the spring and summer. Plants have cycles, and one which roots easily in water in June may rot in December. If some cuttings don't root after several attempts, you may not be using the proper propagating method.

Cuttings rooted in water or propagating medium (peat moss, perlite, vermiculite, or sand) should be several inches in length. Cut them just below a leaf or stem node, with a few bottom leaves or stems stripped off so one or two nodes are submerged. Cuttings should be kept out of strong sunlight while rooting.

Sand is best for rooting cactus or succulents. Leaf or stem cuttings from these plants should be left exposed to air for several days before going into the sand.

Newly propagated plants need

a substantial root system on them before being potted in soil. Avoid overpotting. Pots should be just large enough to contain the roots plus a bit of room for growth.

Oranges and grapefruits are a gold mine of potential present plants. Soak the seeds for several days, then plant a half-inch (two centimeters) down in rich sandy soil. Plant a quantity of seeds, as not all of them will make it. Keep young citrus in good sunlight and well-watered, since any wilt is likely to be permanent.

Seeds and pits from dinner table fruits and vegetables are another fun way of growing your gifts. Guacamole fanatics could easily present everyone they know with an aspiring avocado tree. Even an occasional salad will provide a pit for planting, or check local health food restaurants for discarded pits.

Grow an avocado

1. Remove skin and insert toothpicks around the pit's midriff so that it will balance on top of a glass or jar of water.
2. Keep the base half of the pit submerged in water. (The base is the end with the dimple in it.)
3. After the stalk has emerged and grown several inches, pot the pit in a 6- to 8- inch (15- to 20- centimeter) diameter pot, leaving the top third or half of the pit above soil. Several pits potted together will produce a forest effect.
4. When the shoot is about 6 inches (15 cm) high, prune it back to 2 or 3 inches (6 to 8 cm). Traumatic as it may be for you, pruning forces the avocado to branch.

More gift ideas

- packages of seed (such as radish or carrot) with peat pots and soil
- packages of midget vegetable seeds, a bucket or box to plant them in, and a book about growing midget vegetables
- herb seeds or plants and plant books or cookbooks available on herbs and cooking with herbs
- a homemade "gardener's diary" with pictures cut from seed catalogues to match the seeds given, leaving space for growers to keep tabs on their indoor gardening efforts
- narcissus, hyacinth, or crocus bulbs for forcing, with a bowl and pebbles
- current seed catalogue and gift certificate or a homemade gift certificate for a trip/purchase at the recipient's favorite plant store or greenhouse
- a mister made by cleaning a spray bottle with baking soda and decorating it
- a plant owner's "tool kit" made by decorating a coffee can and filling it with a sharp paring knife, small scissors, small soft paint-

brush, magnifying glass, and a supply of organic fertilizer
- an offer for repotting or plant-sitting services
- subscription to a gardening or horticultural magazine

Recyclables

- clear glass jars, brandy glasses, abandoned aquariums, or fish bowls for terrariums
- bowls for forcing bulbs or a single cup for one bulb
- plastic coffee can lids – good for under clay saucers to protect furniture tops from moisture
- jar and can lids for saucers
- plastic and styrofoam meat trays for saucers
- coffee cans or milk cartons as containers for potting soil
- large milk jugs – especially plastic ones – make good watering cans
- styrofoam cups for rooting cuttings

Give a Tree!

Reprinted from *The Alternate Celebrations Catalogue*

A real "gift of life" for many celebrations is a tree planted in someone's name. Think of this alternative for births, birthdays, and adoptions when a tree would grow as a child grows – reaffirming the vital balance between nature and humankind. At Easter, a new tree is a lasting form of new life. Trees can also be planted as a meaningful memorial to a deceased friend or relative.

There are many groups through-out the country which have tree-planting programs of all sorts, either locally or internationally. Contact the Sierra Club, The Heschel Memorial Forest Fund, the Jewish National Fund of Canada, Scoutrees Canada, or similar organizations.

Alternatively, you may wish to save a tree in the rain forest, in the boreal forest, or in an old forest such as Carmanah, British Columbia, by making a donation to a group dedicated to saving them.

Making Gifts

Reprinted from *The Alternate Celebrations Catalogue*

How many of the gifts you've given or received are still used, or even remembered, with pleasure? My own list would include several store-bought items: one of those popular and durable enameled cast-iron skillets, a favorite dress, the complete works of Robert Frost, a fascinating recording of frog calls with a written description of the habitat and habits of each frog. But the majority of those I've enjoyed most are handmade: a large conch shell filled with pansies, a baby doll fashioned from a turkey wishbone and bits of fabric, three handcarved wooden birds balanced delicately in a mobile, a candle made by my five-year-old niece, a jar of calamondin marmalade, a poem, a small bookshelf for my desk.

It's difficult to stop naming them once I start and, thankfully, impossible to stop the warm feelings for those with whom the gift is associated. There is something about a handmade gift that has been designed and created with care, something that strums on the heartstrings long after the gift is given, and both giver and receiver hear it echoing within them.

Many of you may have discovered the joy of making gifts – the act of creation itself, with its satisfactions of self-expression and achievement, and the thrill of seeing someone else's reaction to your work. If you haven't, gather up your excuses and throw them out the window, try making something, and see what happens. You do have the time. Your first effort may not be "nice enough," but chances are it won't matter. Often, it really is the thought that counts. And you can learn how to create something beautiful or useful, just as others throughout the world are doing.

In recent years interest in making various gifts has mushroomed. For various reasons – seeking to regain a measure of control in their lives by reducing their dependence on machines and advanced technology or, ironically, to fill the leisure time these made possible; evading the "buy now" pressures of mass advertisers, creating islands of identity in a sea of anonymity – people have flocked to enroll in arts and crafts courses and to read books and articles on gift-making.

Whatever you want to make, you probably can find a resource through your libraries or community education centers which will help you begin.

A word of caution as you journey through the world of gift-making. Commercialism has crept in before you and is waiting to con you, so beware. Those clever kits you buy at craft shops or through magazine ads are generally more expensive, and probably no more helpful, than the kit or completed item you make from scratch. The crafts course at the local arts center may be more expensive and no more useful than a series of gift-making sessions you and your friends plan, with the help of a few books and articles or a knowledgeable neighbor. And you don't have to buy a book unless you discover it's one you want to use often – libraries, after all, are organized on the principle of sharing resources.

Here are some principles of gift-making that seem essential if you're serious about conserving resources and creating a world where peace and justice prevail:

1. **Use your imagination and make something from "nothing."** In other words, share yourself. Write a poem or a song, give yourself as servant or playmate-for-a-day, weed the garden, clean the house, take your child for a nature walk, pick a single flower and take it as you go to share an hour with a shut-in or an elderly friend. To keep friends who are accustomed to receiving "things" from being disappointed, make a card or write a note or find some other way of communicating why you chose to give yourself, why you feel that you and your time are more valuable gifts than money or things. You may help

liberate them from the trap of materialism. Even if you don't, the way in which you joyfully give yourself to them will create an atmosphere for better understanding between you.

2. **Use materials from nature, but gather them thoughtfully.** It is one thing to pick up a piece of driftwood or a beautiful stone and quite another to gather all the sea grasses in sight. Don't be greedy. If you know a resource is rare, or if it appears to be, leave it to replenish itself or to be enjoyed by others who see it in its natural habitat.

Don't buy natural materials. It encourages the rape of the land and the sea. Someone innocently sees a chance to make a little extra income and starts selling shells or raffia, and suddenly, commercial harvesters have almost depleted a resource. That's the sort of unthinking behavior that has made sea oats a rare plant, done irreparable damage to the coral and tropical fish populations of the world, and nearly killed off certain species of birds whose plumes were once widely sought for pens and hats. In buying natural materials, we may unwittingly create more demand for them than can be satisfied.

3. **Recycle materials you've already had to buy.** Make new

garments from old. Use newspapers for papier mâché crafts; metal or plastic containers for jewelry, fake flowers, or objets d'art; ice cream sticks and burnt matches for clever trivets and decorative boxes. Art teachers and early childhood educators are excellent sources for attractive ways to recycle materials, and some magazines run monthly columns of prizewinning new-from-old creations from their readers.

4. **Don't buy raw materials unless you have to, and when you do, take the time to find the best bargain possible.** Share a portion of the money you save with peace and justice organizations. Take another portion and use it, along with your gift of time, to adopt a family or community organization. Do it with the same attitude that goes into gift making for your relatives and friends – that you will benefit from it as much as the receiver – and see what happens.

5. **Search yard sales and flea markets for used items that can be recycled as is, or turned into a new creation.** Even water-color paints, yarn and fabric scraps can be purchased in yard sales.

6. **Share your philosophy of gift making and giving with your family, friends, and acquaintances.**

Woods Treasures
Mary Norman DeLaughter

My favorite things to use for making gifts at home are little treasures that you can find in the woods, on the desert, in a field, or in your own backyard. There are so many things worth gathering, just waiting to be put together to brighten up a spot in someone's home. I start by gathering bits of bark, flowers, mushrooms, moss, leaves, and rocks. Then I dry them. My process is simple; I just gather them and let them sit. Some treasures may not make it, but most do.

To dry flowers, I put them between the pages of a book.

Bouquets
Woods treasures baskets are small baskets, one or one-and-a-half inches (three to five centimeters) in diameter, filled with a bouquet of small seeds, dried leaves, twigs, berries, vines, and flowers. For a basket I use

the cap from a large acorn, or any other small cap. If I use an acorn cap, I sometimes use a finish on it for a slightly glossy effect. I fill the bottom of the basket with something like floral clay or styrofoam to hold the arrangement. After I've arranged and glued all the tiny pieces to suit me, I glue the basket on a small piece of bark (pieces of bark with bits of moss attached look great).

A similar bouquet in a small vase is a little variation to this. I use any bottle that's handy; food coloring bottles work well. Or, lacking the right size bottle, I just wad papier mâché into a vase shape and make a hole in the top for an opening to hold the arrangement. I cover the bottle with paint, and finish. Here again I use a small piece of bark for a base.

Many times when I find a really great-looking piece of wood, bark, or gnarled root, I'll work with that to make a miniature forest floor. For this I might use lichens or small mushrooms (which will dry by themselves in a matter of days).

Dried flowers

Dried flower plaques are a little more time-consuming, but tremendously satisfying. I buy unfinished wood plaques, stain the outer rim with a wood finish, and paint the middle flat surface with a few coats of black paint. I use dried flowers, stems, grasses, ferns, and leaves. I set and reset them, until I find the arrangement that I like. Then, using a small artist's brush or a toothpick to dab the glue, and tweezers to hold the small things in place, I glue them to the plaque. Then I gently press them down to the plaque with my finger and wipe away the excess glue.

Wreaths

I like using woods treasures to make miniature wreaths out of small acorns, berries, seeds, etc. These tiny versions are great, inexpensive, and easy to do. I cut out a three-inch (seven centimeter) circle of cardboard for a base, and glue an ornament hanger or a paper clip at the top for a hanger. Then I just start gluing on whatever dried things that I have around. On some, I use just acorns; on others, a combination of things. Then I coat it with any varnish and add a tiny red bow at the top. I have done a few wreaths with shells; while they're not as traditional looking, they are rather nice. I've also tried tree-shaped and ball-shaped arrangements.

Stained glass

I've always liked stained glass, but the real way of making it seems expensive and complicated. So I tried something different. From a glass company, I get a number of large, broken pieces of cathedral glass in many colors, for free. And I buy, for very little cost, some sheets of plain glass cut into circles and rectangles. Then I crack the large pieces of colored glass into smaller fragments by putting them into a heavy sack and tapping it with a hammer. I pick out pieces in the right shapes to put together in a flower shape. After the flower is shaped (jig-saw puzzle fashion), I fill in the rest of the plain glass in the same fashion using only one color of glass and glue all the pieces to the plain glass, making sure to press out the air between them (otherwise the glue might not be transparent when it dries). A small wire loop should be glued between the cracks at the top as a hanger.

Then I mix the grout and rub it into all the cracks. (You usually mix grout with a little water; I mix mine with black poster paint or acrylic. This makes the grout black and eliminates having to paint the areas of gray when it's dry.) Using my fingers to fill in the cracks works best. After filling in all the cracks on the surface, I smooth a border of grout around the edge to give it a finished look. Then I put a coat of finish over the whole thing.

Easter eggs

I've made small papier mâché Easter eggs for several years now. I simply ball up some used foil to mold the egg shape, and cover it with papier mâché. After it dries (in a low oven) I paint it a solid color, then decorate it with tiny flowers or other design, using a fine brush. Then I put on a coat of finish. These are especially pretty nestled in a bed of moss or leaves, rather than dime-store "grass."

Gift Ideas

Reprinted from *The Alternate Celebrations Catalogue*

Egg trees

Egg trees delight everyone as a symbol of new life that comes with the spring. (You may wish to use papier mâché eggs instead.)
You will need:
- A branch of a tree that has fallen in the woods. Stand it up with soil or small rocks in a decorated coffee can.
- Collected egg shells, blown out by poking holes in either end.
What you do:

- Dye the egg shells by soaking onion skins (all colors) and then dipping eggs in until desired color appears.
- Paint the egg shells with whatever decoration you wish (enamel or poster paint works well).
- Hang the eggs with wire or string with a button at the bottom to hold string.
- Top each egg with a bow of satin ribbon or colored string.

Stuffed animals or dolls

There are many patterns available for stuffed animals, dolls and pillow toys. These toys can be stuffed with washable, non-allergenic stuffing, which can be found in local stores. (You could also use dryer lint.) Simple embroidery (or fabric paint) can be used for the face to eliminate the danger of a small child detaching the button eyes.

These animals have much more personality than the manufactured toys; they are softer, and show more of a personal effort on the part of the giver.

Cloth picture book

1. Find some sturdy white cotton material, such as duck, denim, or "Indianhead."
2. With pinking shears, cut ten or twelve "pages" a suitable small size, such as 7 x 7 inches (18 x 18 cm).
3. Using bright permanent markers, make simple line drawings of familiar objects, such as ball, boat, house, cup, doll. (Fabric paint, embroidery, or appliqué can also be incorporated.)
4. Print the word beneath the drawing.
5. Print a title, such as "Andrew's Book" on the first page.
6. Assemble pages and machine-sew together down the middle with heavy thread many times.

– Carolyn and Mary Kate Willet,
Larchmont, New York

Baby block

1. Machine-stitch bright squares and rectangles together until you have a patched piece big enough to cover a brick-size foam block.
2. Sew the letters of the baby's name at random in the squares using tape, braid, or a zigzag stitch.
3. Cover the foam block with the patched piece. Stitch securely.

Block is machine washable.

Cork gingerbread people

Making cork gingerbread people for Christmas ornaments is another project for the whole family. The gingerbread people can be made with a lot of variation, perhaps dressed in clothes made from scraps of material. You could have one gingerbread person to represent each family member.

You will need:
- gingerbread cookie cutter to use as a pattern;
- sheet cork (1/8 inch or 0.25 cm thick) available at art supply stores;
- rickrack, or whatever trim you wish;
- felt pieces for the eyes, nose, and mouth;
- ribbon for loop hanger.

Potato printing

No one is left out in your next celebration when everybody makes potato stamps. All you need are a few potatoes cut in half, butter knives, poster paints, and paper towels. Just carve out letters, words, designs, etc., in bas-relief (what you don't want goes, what you do want is left raised). Make several "stamp pads" by covering folded paper towels (recycled) with bright poster paints. Press the potato down on the pad and then onto the desired paper, card, or whatever. Unless the letters and words have been carved backwards, there will be a secret message that will have to be held up to the mirror to be read. If your celebration is centered around a particular person, a special presentation of the stamps (and perhaps one with the person's name on it) would be in order. It's also a good way to teach young children about mirror reflection and printing presses.

Set of glasses made from bottles

Inexpensive bottle cutters are not hard to find. Use the cutter to remove the tops of the bottles for the size of glass you want. We use non-returnable root beer bottles with straight sides, but any shape will do. The sharp edges can be smoothed down with emery paper. We decorate our glasses by wrapping them with carved leather holders.

By putting the bottle top underneath the glass, and applying some silicon glue, you've made a candle holder, wine glass, or planter.

Candle wedding gift

Use a wedding invitation to decorate a candle. Cut around the printed part of the invitation. You should be able to shape it into an oval. Glue the oval to a wide candle. With a match held near the edges of the invitation, let wax seal the edges. For an added touch, put the candle on a stand and surround it with flowers.

– Janet Herringskaw, Akron, Ohio

Railroad spike paperweight

Plan one of your next picnics to take place near an abandoned railroad station. A walk around the station or a short hike along the tracks will soon reveal a few discarded railroad spikes (usually pretty dirty and rusty). Scrub them with steel wool pads or a steel wool brush. Soak them overnight in the strongest (environmentally safe) cleaning solution that you have or that you can concoct from available kitchen supplies. Repeat the process as needed. You'll end up with a fine quality, rustic-looking paperweight. For those so inclined, a library book or Boy Scout handbook will show you how you can electroplate your steel expedition remembrance.

A baby gift

For a family with a new baby, how about making a special calendar with large spaces to record daily happenings or brief remarks.

– Carol A. Watson, Inglewood, California

Chess set

Make the board out of leather glued with contact cement to a piece of plywood. Mark and gouge out the squares, then stain them black or natural with a lacquer finish over the top. The pieces are made by screwing various sizes of square-headed wood bolts into blocks of wood. To further differentiate the pieces, designs can be cut into the heads of the bolts with a hacksaw.

Reviving treasured drawings

For a gift for your parents (or from parents to their children), get a drawing that you did when you were young, one which is treasured by your parents (or done by your now-grown daughter or son). Use carbon to trace the drawing onto linen and then embroider the drawing. They can be completed by using a chain stitch, or satin stitch in the colors that the child chose to use in the original drawing. They make nice pillows or can be framed as a picture. (A collection of them on squares can also be made into a wonderful quilt.)

– Carol C. Keane, Mililani Town, Hawaii

Recipe box

Have the children copy and illustrate their favorite child-tested recipes onto index cards. This makes a nice gift from one child who cooks to another child, or from a parent to a child who is learning to cook. Place the cards in a decorated, personalized box.

– Therese VanHouten, Washington, D.C.

Ideas from Kids

Reprinted from *The Alternate Celebrations Catalogue*

Handmade gifts are always special, but there's something extraordinary about gifts made by children. They may not be as polished as the work of a more experienced hand, but the knowledge that a child spent long hours patiently sanding or painting something just for you adds a different kind of luster to the finished work. The child's sense of accomplishment when the gift is presented makes all the effort worthwhile.

This section on gift-making would not be complete without gifts made by children. They are presented here in the words of the individuals.

Mrs. Tiggywinkle

Mrs. Tiggywinkle is a favorite creature of mine from the Beatrix Potter story.

You get a ball of clay and wedge it up so that there are no air bubbles in it, because if there are, it will explode. You wedge it by banging it on the table in few places. Then you pull little bits of clay out of the top of the ball for prickles. You can make indentations for eyes by pressing with your thumb and draw lines for eyelashes with a pencil or knitting needle. Then pull a nose. Draw a line, or something for a mouth, with any interesting thing you can find. Press your thumb in and down for "feet." Last of all you stick your thumb up the middle inside leaving at least 1/2 inch (1 cm) of clay at the top. You can decorate it with anything (paint, glaze), fire it or put it in the oven, depending on the type of clay you use. – Libby Scribner, 13

Crèche

This Christmas, when I was taking industrial arts at school, I decided to make my family a crèche. I used three sides of an old drawer for the base, then nailed two pieces of plywood for a slanted roof, found some bark and glued the bark to the roof. I cut a star out of Plexiglas to hang over the crèche.

You could make crèche figures to go with the crèche by making simple standing shapes out of clay. Paint faces and clothing on after the clay has baked. – Anne Scribner, 14

Obstacles

I made an obstacle course for my brother's birthday party out in the backyard. I used logs, a sawhorse, trash can lids, anything I could find.
– David Scribner, 12

Gingerbread people

Gingerbread people are fun and easy to make. Make an ordinary gingerbread recipe and make it any shape: a man, a woman or anything else. You can use raisins, chocolate chips, or nuts for eyes, noses, buttons, etc. You can make confectioner's sugar frosting and decorate. Roll up a piece of paper from corner to corner so there is one small end. Put some of the frosting in the container and squeeze it so it comes out the small end. You can make lots of different designs with the frosting such as hair, lace, a mouth, and many other things. Add anything else you want and give as a birthday or Christmas present. Have fun! – Allison Barlow, 12

Rag doll

Make a paper pattern for a rag doll. Pin it on cotton material and cut double. Turn both wrong sides out and sew all around the edges, leaving a hole for stuffing. Right-side it out and stuff with cotton or foam if you want to wash it. Sew up the hole, and sew on eyes, nose, mouth, hair. Make clothes out of scrap materials.

You can make nursery rhyme characters such as Little Miss Muffet or Humpty Dumpty into dolls.
– Collette Surla, 14

T-shirts

Make a personal T-shirt for a present. Draw on a white T-shirt with permanent felt markers. The design will not wash out. – Lisa Hay, 12

Make Your Own Greeting Cards

Reprinted from *The Alternate Celebrations Catalogue*

Using our own experiences, our eyes, our hands, and our thoughts, we can wish joy, love, laughter, God-speed, get-well, peace, with our own handmade greeting cards. We put technology aside for a minute and simply share a feeling. It's exposure of the best kind. Nature provides us with color, shape, rhythm, and line.

Our own backyard jungle might make a water-color birthday card for a grandparent who lives far away; a leaf from a favorite tree could be used for a graduation card rubbing, the sun suggests a string relief for a birth announcement. Folk traditions provide us with a wealth of techniques such as Polish paper cutting, German Scherenschnitte, block-printing, stencil cutting. By searching out our family traditions, by listening to our children, we can also find what to make.

To avoid the last-minute rush to the card store, clear a space (possibly a kitchen shelf) for card-making materials. Store rubber cement, paper, scissors, magic markers, paints, a ruler, sponges, and cardboard there. Experiment with different ways of printing, papercutting, stenciling, painting, until you find a method that's fun for you. Here are some successful ways to make cards, invitations, and announcements.

Collage relief printing

Materials:

- brayer (a small, hand roller)
- ink
- scrap wood
- cardboard
- burlap
- lace
- leaves
- feathers
- any textured material

Method: Choose different textures and shapes to make a design. Feathers make beautiful prints. Glue final design on a piece of wood. Roll a brayer in printing ink. Roll paint on design. Lay paper on design. Rub with the ball of a spoon. Remove print. Re-ink as often as needed.

Styrofoam print

Materials:

- styrofoam meat trays
- water-based printer's ink
- brayer
- cookie tray
- colored paper cut into rectangles
- squares folded to make a card
- dull pencil or dried-up ball-point pen

Method: Cut styrofoam (can be washed in the dishwasher) into desired shape. With dull pencil or dried ball-point pen, draw design on styrofoam, pressing down hard enough to make a clearly indented line. Squeeze ink on cookie sheet. Roll out with brayer to even the ink on the brayer. Using the inked brayer, roll ink onto the styrofoam design. Press the inked design onto a piece of thin pastel construction paper. Lift up. You can glue this print onto a folded piece of construction paper or you can print directly on the card.

Experiment with colors of paper and ink. Make as many prints as you like, re-inking your design each time you print. This is a good method for making bookmarks, notepaper, invitations, and prints to hang on the wall.

Vegetable print

Materials:

- potato
- craft knife
- paper
- sponge
- poster paints

Method: Slice potato in half. Carve a simple design – a holly leaf, a diamond, a circle, a pumpkin. Press potato shape onto sponge that's been soaked in paint (or if you can, dip into the paint in a pan). Print on paper. For greeting cards, you might use construction paper, note paper, rice paper, drawing paper. For wrapping paper decorated with the potato method, use brown paper, newspaper, or ask a printer for offcut scraps. After you've experimented with the potato in repeat patterns, try printing

with half an onion, an apple, a carrot or any odd object – a jar lid, a child's block, a straw, a carved art gum eraser, a meat tenderizer or other roller, your thumb, hand, or foot.

Scherenschnitte: German paper cutting

Materials:

- white paper
- black origami paper
- small, sharp embroidery scissors
- glue
- pencil

Method: Measure white paper with ruler, cut and fold for card. Cut black paper a little smaller than the front of the card. Draw an appropriate design, for instance, a wreath, candles in a candle-holder, a pot of flowers, or a pumpkin, on the white side of the black paper. Carefully cut out design (this takes practice). When completely cut out, apply glue and center the design on the card and press down. This black and white silhouette makes a striking celebration card. Designs are usually more naturalistic than the Polish cuttings, but the technique could be adapted to a fanciful silhouette. Experiment.

Stone rubbing

Materials:

- masking tape
- large pad of newsprint or bond
- black marking crayons or thick children's crayons in dark colors

Method: Make a small, stone rubbing of an angel, bird, or other design for a Christmas card, or make a rubbing of a complete marble or granite carved stone as a gift or souvenir of a trip. Make sure the stone is clean. Tape paper to the top of the stone and make sure it is stretched taut, smoothing with your hands as you tape the sides and the bottom. Using the broad edge of the crayon, rub lightly from the center out. Stroke in the same direction. Your strokes should gain momentum and get darker until you are happy with the result. Try mounting smaller rubbings on colored paper.

Wycinanka Lukowa: Polish paper cutting

Materials:
- gummed paper
- scratch paper
- small embroidery scissors
- pencil
- mounting paper

Method and history: For several hundred years, Polish peasants have made papercuts of birds, leaves, flowers, abstractions of swirls and angles and used them as decorations on their whitewashed houses in the springtime, for greeting cards and notepaper, for decorating Easter egg pictures. Roosters and other birds and trees are favorite designs.

Practice drawing simple outlines of a flower. Cut out a card from white drawing paper. Cut a piece of gummed paper and fold in half lengthwise with gummed side out. It should be nearly the same size as the card. With a pencil draw a flower on the folded paper.

Carefully cut it out and open gently. Center on card and glue it down. This is your basic design. Choose another color and repeat this procedure using the same design, but smaller than the first one. Paste the second layer over the first.

Each additional layer is another color. You can also add a wing to a bird, a leaf to a flower in another color. Try origami paper for its brilliance. The technique could be adapted to hearts for Valentine's Day, or pumpkins for Halloween.

Leaf rubbing

Materials:
- leaf
- crayons
- rice paper

Method: Put leaf under a piece of rice paper that is to be the front of the card. Rub the paper with crayon until the outline of the leaf is clearly visible.

Gift Wrapping Ideas

Reprinted from *The Alternate Celebrations Catalogue*

Wrapping gifts is festive. It makes a gift a gift. Most of our traditional gift wrapping forms must be considered a frill and a waste in this age of approaching scarcity. How can we present our packages attractively without plundering the Earth's resources (and going broke doing it)?

Here are some suggestions:

Wrapping paper

- last year's paper
- newspaper: colorful weekend comics, the sports page, the family living page (a collage of recipes, perhaps), a foreign language newspaper
- shiny illustrated magazines
- grocery bag – plain or decorated
- homemade wrappings (from grocery bags or butcher's paper) using block prints, magic marker or finger paints; draw, color, paint, marbleize, or make a collage
- fabric – a yard of new denim which a teenager can use for a project; scraps of leftover fabric; old sheets, batiked or tie-dyed
- kitchen or bath towel to be useful for itself
- decorate a box with paint or crayons and paste wrapping paper directly onto box
- reuse decorative "shopping" bags

year after year; make your own version of them

Bows and decorations

- last year's ribbons and bows
- cut strips of comic paper with pinking shears and roll them into "bows"
- leftover yarn
- pompoms with scraps of yarn
- pinecones, acorns, milkweed pods, etc.
- fruit or nuts
- a small toy (truck, doll)
- a handmade tree ornament
- a handmade card
- a cookie, iced with the recipient's name

Decorative containers

- a woven basket to be used for bread, plants, etc.
- a decorative and useful flower pot
- a decorative department store box
- fabric bags with drawstring closures
- a canister or cookie jar

Some gifts don't need wrapping

- Canned food with a bow around it is festive and beautiful enough.
- Dolls may greet children, unwrapped, under the tree with a simple note saying "Hello, Merry Christmas!"

More Gift Ideas

Reprinted from *The Alternate Celebrations Catalogue*

More than a tea party

I decided to give a tea party for friends and at the same time do some education on hunger issues. Guests were invited to bring a mug to exchange with another guest and a contribution for Heifer Project International (an interfaith, nonprofit organization dedicated to alleviating hunger by helping low-income families around the world to produce food for themselves and for their communities). Homemade goodies were served to friends who dropped in throughout the afternoon. We enjoyed visiting with each other while learning about and giving to a project that provides breeding stock to low-income farmers around the world. By the end of the party more than $700 had been raised.

– Martha Brooks, Fort Worth, Texas

Cobbler aprons support refugees

Many Hmong people from Southeast Asia have settled in Boulder. One way they support their friends and relatives is by selling beautiful embroidered fabric made by their people still in refugee camps. I designed a cobbler's apron featuring a block of this beautiful fabric which I bought for $5. I made five aprons as gifts for my three daughters, my daughter-in-law, and a friend. I also helped an older friend make an apron for a friend of hers.

– Virginia McConnell, Boulder, Colorado

Jute angels: messengers of hope

Our church offered little jute angels from Bangladesh to give as gifts in appreciation for contributions made to the Lutheran World Hunger Appeal. Lutheran churches are using funds from the appeal to establish a cottage industry for women refugees in Bangladesh. Along with information about the project, we sent a card with the angel. It said:

"I've enclosed an angel for you. Please use it as a 'messenger of hope.' Hang it in your kitchen, in a window, or on your Christmas tree. It can also be an Easter reminder of the angel's message, 'He is risen.' In addition, I've also made a contribution to the Lutheran World Hunger Appeal. Let this angel remind you of the hope we have in life. Tell other people its story."

Last Christmas I sent an angel to my aunt. As a result, for my birthday this year she sent a check in my name to the World Hunger Appeal. So this one little angel has been a gift that has kept on giving – to feed hungry people around the world.

– Eileen Ward, Mililani, Hawaii

Grandparents make talking books

My husband and I sent books to our four-year-old granddaughter along with tape recordings of each of us reading the books to her. On the recordings we rang a little bell each time she was to turn the page. We not only read the words, but talked about the pictures as we would have if she were on our laps. We thought of the idea because she had lived with us and we had grown very close, but then she had moved far away. Our daughter reported that our granddaughter finds the voices so real that she carries on conversations with her "Grannie and Granpap" in absentia.

– Joan Gauker, Norristown, Pennsylvania

Music for parents only

My husband and I are professional musicians. Our parents love it when we play and sing for them on our trips home, especially our original songs. Last Christmas we decided that the best gift we could give them was our music. We recorded a cassette tape full of songs for them. We put some original songs on the tape, and we also picked older songs that we knew they both loved. This year they have told us many times how much they continue to enjoy our gift, and that it was one of the best presents they have ever received. We got a great deal of joy out of giving it to them, and had a lot of fun shar-

ing the recording together. The gift took a lot of time to make, but it was worth every minute.

– Judy Leonard, Conyers, Georgia

Daddy's calendar: A priceless gift of art

Our three children make their father a very special Christmas present each year. Each December, the children and I spend a day making a calendar. I fold large white drawing paper in half; on the top half the children draw pictures and I make the calendar on the lower half. Their father hangs it proudly in his office. The calendars are saved from year to year to show the change in the children's art work. It is a priceless gift which is cherished by their father.

– Deborah Heaton, Enid, Oklahoma

Alternative marketing: Nonprofit gifts that give twice

Every time a handmade jute plant hanger, soapstone jewelry box, velvet Christmas ornament or painted trivet is sold from the Self Help Crafts warehouse in Akron, Pennsylvania, a needy craftsperson in Bangladesh, India, Thailand, or El Salvador benefits. Through Self Help Crafts, North Americans are reaching out to brothers and sisters in developing nations who are victims of poverty, famine, unemployment, injustice, and/or displacement.

Self Help Crafts, a nonprofit program of the Mennonite Central Committee (MCC), creates jobs for skilled craftspeople in developing nations by marketing their crafts in North America. The program began humbly in 1946 when a Mennonite woman, Edna Ruth Byler, traveled to Puerto Rico to visit MCC volunteers and brought back needlework made by needy rural women to sell to her friends and neighbors in Lancaster County, Pennsylvania. Today, more than 3,000 items from 30 developing nations are sold throughout North America. Because almost everyone involved in the program is a volunteer, salaries are few and overhead expenses are low.

Self Help Crafts is one of a growing number of nonprofit Alternative Trading Organizations (ATOS) based throughout the world. Their merchandise works not for the bank accounts of rich multinational corporations, but rather for peace, justice, and global understanding. People who choose to buy items for gift-giving, for their personal, or household use can be sure that a Self Help craft item gives twice: beauty and usefulness to the consumer; dignity, employment, and a fair income to the producer.

[The above description of the Mennonite Central Committee's effort to work for peace and justice by providing a market for skilled craftspeople is different only in history and detail from many other self-help organizations. The philosophy of serving needy brothers and sisters throughout the world is basic to all such groups.]

Self-imposed tax on celebrations: A Jewish response to hunger

The traditional Jewish response to blessing is to share it. It is this basic concept that triggered the beginning of Mazon, a Jewish response to world hunger. Many American Jews are voluntarily putting a surcharge of 3 percent on celebrations such as weddings, bar or bat mitzvahs, birthdays, and anniversaries, and giving the money to Mazon.

Leonard Fein, one of its founders and editor of *Moment*, a Jewish magazine, believes this idea struck a responsive chord among Jews who were looking for ways to share with others but needed a vehicle to do it.

Giving something back to the world in gratitude for blessings – an idea with roots in the Jewish tradition – is a concept that Mazon's founders hope will catch on so that activities around celebrating and feeding the world's hungry are no longer seen as opposing each other.

Mazon supporters also express the hope that churches and non-Jewish social organizations will adopt their idea of celebrating with conscience.

A ministry with scraps

For 25 years, Wilma Watts Buchholtz made clothes for children she did not know. She created them out of remnants and scraps left from her regular sewing and from pieces others gave to her. She then shipped the clothes to missionary friends or gave them to church clothes closets for nearby migrant camps. With creativity and resourcefulness she could make 40 or more children's outfits with materials bought with one $20 bill. One year, in response to the needs of farm workers in her community, she outfitted at least a dozen infants with gowns, diapers, shirts, and handmade quilts, besides making several stacks of children's clothes.

With five great-grandchildren to sew for, Wilma still sewed for her unknown friends. It delighted her to find just the right scrap of material to make a pretty piece of piping for a collar or unusual button on a worn-out blouse that added the perfect touch to a jumper. Each stitch and seam represented her gift of time, talent, and loving concern for others. God has given everyone a gift – some can preach, some can sing, some can visit. Her gift was sewing. Wilma sewed to the glory of God.

– Lois B. Stone

Some of the Best Christmas Gifts
Reprinted from *The Alternate Celebrations Catalogue*

In the weeks before Christmas, our society goes into a shopping frenzy to find just the right gift – or any gift at all – for the people on our Christmas gift lists. Last year Americans spent more than $30 billion on gifts alone. Where is this consumption mania leading us? For years, Alternatives has poked fun at the excesses of commercialized Christmas with a Best and Worst Christmas Gift Contest that had received nationwide press coverage. Winners have received a monetary gift contributed in their names to the non-profit humanitarian organization of their choice. Contact Alternatives for more information about its current campaign. The following are some of the best contest entries over the years.

A whole week of sewing

As a Christmas gift, my mother gave me a week of sewing. Even though I enjoy sewing, my job requirements are such that I have little time to do it. I waited until August when the children needed new school clothes to use my mother's Christmas gift. Then we sewed together: I did the machine work and she did the handwork, pinning, and pressing. While I was at work, she ran errands and did chores so that when I was home we could concentrate on sewing. It was a wonderful gift. It meant so much to me because it was a gift of herself.

– Nancy Angerer, Champaign, Illinois

A house gift in Nicaragua

As their Christmas gifts to my sister and me and our families, my parents made a contribution to Habitat for Humanity. In our names, they gave enough money to enable this organization to build a house in Nicaragua. Since his retirement, my father has been volunteering on these house-building projects in the area where he lives and he knows the value of providing shelter for homeless and needy people. My parents could not have chosen a more wonderful gift to show their love for us and our families.

– Karen L. Weidenheimer, Carson, California

Backrub coupons: A healing gift

My sons, ages 14 and 16, gave me an unusual gift last Christmas. It was a "coupon" for three 5-minute backrubs per month, per boy. In other words, one-half hour of relaxation per month for me.

My life is very hectic, sometimes chaotic. I also have chronic back problems, the result of a childhood accident and genes. Their gift was marvelous for two reasons. First, it relaxes me and soothes my pained back. Second, it provides the two of us with undivided time. If nothing is on either of our minds, the backrub is only a physically healing event. But if there is something important to be discussed, the contact is there. That means the backrub may be over in exactly five minutes, or the conversation can last for an hour or more.

– Virginia E. Stevens, Asheville North Carolina

Michigan mother sees ailing son in Tennessee

My son has cancer. Three days before Christmas my relatives gave me a trip from my home in Michigan to my son's home in Tennessee so that we could spend Christmas together. Because I am disabled and live on a fixed income, I had not been able to see him in three years. It was the happiest, and saddest, Christmas ever.

– Lavonda Teboe, Ypsilanti, Michigan

Family trivia: Make a game of it

The Drey family organized a family trivia game. Each member came to the family Christmas celebration with 20 trivia questions written out on index cards with answers written on the back. The questions were shuffled all together. Then, one by one, family members drew a card and tried to answer the question.

Since I am newly related by marriage, it was a wonderful way for me to get to know the family. Plus, it provided lots of laughs, a few tears, and a general bonding of family members as the past was remembered and enjoyed. This was the best gift I received for Christmas last year!

– Janet Drey, Des Moines, Iowa

Grandma's cross-stitch

My best Christmas present was made by my oldest granddaughter. At age 19, she designed and created an original modern sampler.

Embroidered in the tiniest cross-stitches in Old English black letters is the word "Grandma" on a white background. Over each letter are little figures of my 12 grandchildren (ages 6 to 19) done in the same tiny cross-stitching, each in a pose depicting his or her interest: diving, dancing, playing soccer, gymnastics, drama, gardening, relaxing. The little figures are embroidered in different colors. Even the children's hair is their true coloring.

The four families live great distances from me, so having this lovely picture on my kitchen wall is a wonderful and constant reminder of each of them.

– Anne B. Macosky, Hamden, Connecticut

Surprised by love notes

Christmas was a fun-filled day with loved ones, children, grandchildren, and great-grandchildren in my home. After good-byes were said, they all left for their homes in distant places. What I didn't know is that they had written and hidden little love notes for me that I found over the next weeks. Those notes made me feel loved and needed. This was my best Christmas.

– Mrs. Edward Schreur, Orange City, Iowa

Vintage video

My husband found an old film in my mother's attic. Covered by years of dust and discarded clothing, it proved to be the movies of my parent's wedding in 1932. He took it to a lab where he had it titled and turned into a video tape with background music. This was my Christmas gift, a gift beyond price, and better than the finest store could provide.

– Anne M. Coyle, Fort Washington, Maryland

An open house for Christmas breakfast

For several years two friends have opened their home and hearts to folks who have lost a loved one and who are alone on Christmas morning. They felt that people are usually included in gatherings later in the day, but Christmas morning can be very lonely and a difficult time of day to get through.

They invite acquaintances from past years, and anyone they find who will be alone, to share breakfast in their home. They make them welcome with a breakfast of pancakes and sausage served by a warm fire, making a lonely time of the day comfortable and friendly.

I lost my husband four years ago and have no children to spend time with at Christmas. I will never forget that first invitation. Each year they call with another invitation which I accept with great pleasure. They give much more than breakfast.

– Blanche Buchter, Lancaster, Pennsylvania

Holiday Gifts from the Kitchen

Reprinted from *The Alternate Celebrations Catalogue*

Metric Conversion

1 cup = 250 mL

1 teaspoon (tsp) = 5 mL

1 tablespoon (T) =15 mL

1 pound = 500 grams

Granola

Save your quart jars, fill them with homemade granola, type or print the recipe on an index card, and tie up with a ribbon for a healthful gift.

- 1 to 1 1/2 lbs. rolled oats
- 2 cups wheat germ
- 1 cup brown sugar
- 1 cup unsweetened coconut
- 1 cup nuts
- 1/2 cup sesame seeds
- 1/2 cup sunflower seeds
- 1 cup oil (corn, peanut, sunflower, soy)
- 1 teaspoon sea salt

Mix with hands to get lumps out. Roast for one hour at 325ºF, stirring every ten minutes. Store in refrigerator in airtight container. Add diced apricots, figs, or raisins, according to individual preference.

Herb Vinegars

Save jars and bottles, and put your choice of flavoring in them. Then fill with cider or wine vinegar, cap, and store in a cool, dark place for four weeks. The vinegars are then flavored and ready to use. They don't spoil, either. Use whole sprigs of herbs or spirals of citrus rind for the most attractive effect. Possible combinations: garlic-chive white wine vinegar, thyme and rosemary vinegar, basil and oregano vinegar, orange and cinnamon (stick) vinegar, lemon and mint vinegar. You can also add several peppercorns, grapes, cloves, or dried currants to the combination for added flavor. Make the labels for the jars yourself.

– Pami Bush, La Jolla, California

Liptauer Cheese

(Makes approximately 2 cups.)

- 8 ounces cottage cheese
- 1/2 cup (1 quarter-pound stick) unsalted butter, softened
- 1 tablespoon sweet Hungarian paprika
- freshly ground black pepper
- 1/4 teaspoon salt
- 2 teaspoons caraway seeds
- 1 teaspoon dry mustard
- 1 teaspoon chopped capers
- 1 tablespoon finely chopped onions
- 1/2 cup sour cream (plus 1/4 cup if a dip is desired)
- 3 tablespoons finely chopped chives

With a wooden spoon rub the cottage cheese through a sieve into a mixing bowl. Cream the butter by beating it against the side of a mixing bowl with a wooden spoon. Beat in the cheese, the paprika, a generous grinding of black pepper, the salt, caraway seeds, mustard, capers, onions, and sour cream.

Continue beating vigorously with a wooden spoon or by using an electric mixer at medium speed until the mixture forms a smooth paste.

If the Liptauer cheese is to be used as a spread, shape it into a mound and decorate it with the chives, or shape it into a ball that may be rolled in the chives. Refrigerate it for two hours, or until it is firm.

To make a Liptauer dip, stir the extra sour cream into the paste with wooden spoon or beat it in with an electric mixer. Sprinkle the chives over the dip after it has been poured into a serving bowl.

Lemon French Dressing

- 1 clove garlic, split
- 1 cup salad oil
- 1 teaspoon salt
- 3/4 teaspoon sugar
- 1/8 teaspoon freshly ground black pepper
- 1/3 cup fresh lemon juice

Combine the salad oil, garlic, salt, sugar, and pepper. Let stand at least one hour. Remove the garlic, add the lemon juice and beat with a rotary beater.

Garlic French Dressing

- 1 teaspoon dry mustard
- 1 tablespoon water
- 1 small clove garlic, finely minced
- 1 teaspoon sugar
- 1 teaspoon salt
- 1 cup salad or olive oil
- 1 teaspoon grated onion
- 3 tablespoons cider vinegar
- 2 tablespoons lemon juice

Mix mustard with water and let stand 10 minutes. Combine with garlic, salt, sugar, oil, and onion. Let stand one hour. Add vinegar and lemon juice. Beat with rotary beater.

Here are some delicious spreads which could be used for any holiday celebration when friends get together, or given as a gift. Accompany with whole wheat crackers or assorted raw vegetables.

Homous (Chick Pea Spread)

(Makes 3 cups; uses a blender.)
- 2 cups cooked chick peas (garbanzos) freshly cooked or canned
- 3 cloves garlic, finely chopped
- 1 1/2 teaspoons salt
- 1/2 to 3/4 cup vegetable oil
- 1/4 cup fresh lemon juice
- 2 tablespoons coarsely chopped parsley, flat-leaf type preferable **or** 2 tablespoons chopped mint

If the chick peas are canned, drain them in a sieve and wash them under cold running water until the water runs clear. Spread them on paper towels and pat them dry. Freshly cooked chick peas need only be drained and cooled.

To make the homous in a blender, place the chick peas, garlic, salt, 1/2 cup of oil, and 1/4 cup of lemon juice in the container and blend at high speed for ten seconds. Turn off the blender and scrape down the sides with a rubber spatula. Blend again at high speed, adding as much oil as you need to prevent the blender from clogging. The finished homous should be a very smooth puree. Taste for seasoning and add more salt and lemon juice if you like.

Blue Cheese and Cheddar Spread

(Makes about 2 1/2 cups.)
- 3/4 lb. aged cheddar cheese, coarsely grated
- 3/4 cup beer or ale
- 1/8 lb. blue cheese, crumbled
- 1 tablespoon soft butter
- 1/2 teaspoon dry mustard
- 2 dashes Worcestershire sauce
- 1 dash Tabasco
- 1 teaspoon coarsely chopped chives or onions

Put the beer or ale and the cheddar cheese into a blender and blend for 20 seconds, or until smooth. (If you don't have a blender, beat together until smooth.) Add the remaining ingredients and blend or beat until smooth and well mixed. Spoon into a crock or serving dish and chill. Garnish with chopped chives before serving.

Yogurt Dip

(Makes 4 servings.)
- 6 walnut halves
- 1 tablespoon olive oil
- 1 clove garlic
- 1 cup yogurt
- 1/4 cup very finely diced peeled cucumber
- 1/2 teaspoon lemon juice or vinegar
- whole grain crackers

Place walnuts, oil, and garlic in an electric blender and blend to a paste. This can also be done with a mortar and pestle. Stir into the yogurt with cucumber and lemon juice or vinegar. Chill and serve with crackers as dippers.

Still another present would be to find some inexpensive crocks or pottery jars and fill them with a spread or dip.

Sprouts

Grow your own fresh sprouts and give an ancient gift. Sprout-growing dates back to 2939 BCE in China. A prime source of nutrients, sprouts are seeds or legumes that have germinated and converted their fats and starches into vitamins, sugars, and protein. Sprouted lentils, alfalfa, and soybeans are high in protein, inexpensive, and easy to grow. They can be eaten as a snack, used in a main dish as a natural "stretcher," or served in salads and sandwiches. They are naturally processed in your kitchen and make a cheery winter garden in a jar.

After experimenting with different seeds and flavors, give a sprout jar and some favorite beans or seeds for a winter birthday gift, or a spring Mother's or Father's Day present. A sprout kit might be especially appropriate for someone who cannot grow a garden, an apartment dweller, or a house-bound person.

Equipment:
- wide mouth mason jar
- piece of screening
- aluminum or copper metal ring to hold the screen
- 1/4 cup of mung beans

Basic method: Wash beans. Put beans in the jar with water to cover. Place screen and metal rim on jar. Leave overnight in a dark place. The second day rinse the beans with fresh cool water. Drain well. Seeds should be damp, not soaked. Lay jar on its side in a spot with indirect sunlight, or make a stand out of blocks and invert jar on blocks to drain well. Repeat the rinsing two or three times each day. Sprouts will appear on the second day and are ready to use by the third or fourth day. A small amount of mung beans, lentils, soybeans, or alfalfa gives a high yield of sprouts.

If you're still not convinced about the gift-food from the earth, try the **Golden Temple Sandwich:** Layer avocado and tomato slices, tuna fish (optional), sprouts, and grated cheese on a piece of whole-grain bread. Place in oven on a cookie sheet until the cheese melts. Delicious!

Raisin-Almond Bread

This easy but especially rich bread is delicious at breakfast during the holiday season.

- 1 package yeast
- 4 cups unbleached or whole wheat flour
- 1/2 cup water
- 1/2 cup milk
- 1/2 cup butter
- 1/4 cup white or brown sugar, or molasses
- 1 teaspoon salt
- 1/2 cup ground almonds
- 1/2 cup chopped raisins or candied fruits (I add a bit of rum or whiskey)
- 2 eggs, slightly beaten
- 2 loaf pans

Mix 2 cups flour with the yeast. Stir water, milk, butter, sugar, and salt over low heat until butter melts. Cool five minutes, add flour and remaining ingredients. Knead until smooth and elastic. Divide dough and place in oiled loaf pans, cover, let rise in warm place until dough has doubled. Bake at 375ºF for 35 minutes.

Nut Bread

Bake in greased coffee can; cover with plastic top and decorate or label. If necessary, use a can opener to remove the can bottom before serving.
Combine:

- 1 1/2 cup whole wheat flour
- 1/3 cup powdered milk
- 2 teaspoons baking powder
- 1 teaspoon salt

Add:

- 1 cup milk or water
- 1 cup nuts
- 2 tablespoons oil
- 1/3 cup honey
- 1/2 cup wheat germ

Stir briefly. Fill can or one loaf pan. Push dough into corners and make indentation in top of loaf. Bake at 350ºF for 45 minutes.

Applesauce Nut Bread

Stir together to moisten:

- 2 cups flour
- 3/4 cup sugar
- 1 teaspoon baking powder
- 1 teaspoon salt
- 1/2 teaspoon soda
- 1/2 teaspoon nutmeg
- 1 cup nuts
- 1 beaten egg
- 1 cup applesauce

Fill one, greased loaf pan. Bake at 300ºF for one hour.

Books for Teenagers and Adults

Adapted from *The Alternate Celebrations Catalogue, 3rd Edition*

In an age of rising prices, increasing job insecurity, and uncertainty, it makes sense for more of us to get back to life's basics by producing some necessities at home. It makes sense and saves cents. It also gives tremendous satisfaction and allows us to control our own environment. (You'll know exactly what was sprayed on your plants, for example.) Knowing there's a bountiful garden outside or a stocked pantry also offers peace of mind.

Our grandparents, and maybe even our parents, knew how to take care of themselves, but much of that knowledge is gradually being lost as the supermarket replaces the garden as the food source. Children now think milk and food come from the store. Getting back to basics through efforts to be more self-sufficient means more than just saving money – it means getting in touch with reality.

You can find advice and counsel from older, experienced people, particularly if they have lived through the Great Depression and/or World War II. Marvelous innovations for saving money and staying healthy were invented during those years. During the decades following, though, we arrogantly believed that we "didn't have to do that anymore." We are paying for this arrogance physically, as Earth approaches the breaking point, and spiritually, as we wonder why we don't feel happier (since we have all this stuff).

We can gift ourselves, our loved ones, and our children with information. This could be the gift of a library card, a magazine subscription, a book, or a taped interview with someone knowledgeable.

Generally speaking, books that encourage us and specifically show us "how-to" can be a doorway to increasing personal satisfaction and a relief for Earth. Books on the following subjects may prove especially helpful:

- folk wisdom;
- ancient healing arts and herbology;
- agriculture and organic gardening;
- energy – installing energy-producing or energy-saving systems;
- food gathering in the wild;
- food preservation;
- growing food in your kitchen;
- cookbooks that are long on nutrition and basic Earth-care, and short on empty calories, fat, and Earth-plunder;
- spiritual growth – for example, yoga, meditation, prayer, tai chi (music or talking book tapes abound in these areas, too);
- repairing: machinery, clothing, your garden;
- creation: pottery, wood carving, knitting, sewing, paper-making.

Children's Books Are Butterflies...

Adapted from Wendy Ward's article in *Alternate Celebrations Catalogue, 3rd Edition*

Children's books are butterflies these days: emerging slowly but joyously from a cocoon of traditional values and stereotypes. More and more they are becoming a liberated literary genre in their own right.

The quest continues, however, for the perfect children's book... for books which combine new views and values with quality writing and imaginative illustrations at an affordable price.

Although there has been great progress in the elimination of sexual and racial stereotypes, unfortunately, many books still retain questionable values.

Consider the following images

and their ramifications:

- material goods or economic success as a measure of self-worth or as a life goal;
- emphasis on competition, the importance of winning, and the disaster of losing – rather than on cooperation and community;
- unquestioning obedience to authority with little or no regard for demands of conscience;
- traditional views of achievement and upward mobility;
- acquisition and over-consumption – of food, toys, clothing – in a time when poverty and famine are taking a dreadful toll of human life;
- stereotypes of beauty and ugliness – particularly equating one or the other with "goodness" or "badness" (the typical golden-haired-princess/warty-nosed-witch syndrome of fairy tales).

Of course, all books don't have to be purchased; take some paper, some crayons, and voila! – a book. It may never become a classic, but the caring with which it's done is far more important. Simple picture books can be made by pasting cut-out pictures on heavy poster board and covering it with clear contact paper. If cloth books are difficult to find, experiment with sewing your own using fabric scraps in various colors and textures.

Beyond Disney, toward Shalom with Books
Carolyn Hardin Engelhardt

I've been on a search for young children's lifestyle resources for years. Before I suggest some ways for readers to use their power and influence, let me say that I've been looking everywhere for a long time. What a celebration when occasionally I find good resources!

Our environment shapes us. We become what is around us. Therefore, parents want to share their values with children in natural, casual ways as well as through planned activities and discussions. When values that parents wish to pass on are not readily accessible through the culture – through the media, the books, toys, and music that surround parents – there's an uncomfortable silence. There's a dissonance, a lack of affirmation of one's own values, and an implied affirmation of other values. As a parent working to share particular values with one's children, that's a lonely place to be. It feels as though you're against everything that everyone else is for. It makes you ask whether you're making a "big deal" over something that's not so important. Parenting toward shalom values would be easier if the songs, stories, and toys that surround our children were consistent with what we're trying to teach.

In my lifestyle resources search I look in all kinds of bookstores – from university to small town and big city in various parts of the U.S. and Canada. I read reviews and descriptions, search libraries, and talk to people about what they've found. I'm looking for resources that imply the following values:

- It's okay to be different.
- We are people of many cultures.
- Children and parents of both sexes can do anything.
- Winning and being first are not our goals in play.
- Eating healthful foods is enjoyable.
- We are capable of choosing.
- We don't have to have everything just because others have it.
- Kindness, sharing, and friendliness are a normal way for children to relate.
- Sharing is appropriate.
- We can measure history by periods of peace and human achievement as well as by periods of war.
- We can communicate in some ways even when our languages are not the same.
- Living a responsible lifestyle is okay even if it is different from the lifestyles of others.
- We don't need to follow the dictates of advertising and marketing. We can make decisions for ourselves instead of having others tell us what we want and need.
- Conserving and recycling are a natural part of life.
- It makes sense to buy certain kinds of items that have already been used.
- We can be involved in some social action regardless of age. (For example, even preschool children can dictate a letter to a television station and receive an answer.)
- Repairing items for continued use rather than buying another is a natural part of life.
- Persons of minority cultures live in contemporary settings; they are not just part of past history.

What can be found on these subjects is so minimal that when I do find a book, music or tape, I usually buy it. I want to make such ideas a part of my home surroundings so that my children can pick them up to read or listen to them as casually as they can pick up a picture book of animals.

All around us – in grocery stores, drug stores, music stores, video stores, bookstores, department stores, discount stores – are resources promoting the lifestyles of the latest fad characters, or of the updated versions of "old favorites." "Why do adults buy and use these resources with young children?" one asks. Because they are very available! Adults want to share with the young children they love and they share what is available.

Adults don't share as often the resources described in this article because many of them are not easy to obtain. "You have to order them." "They're out of stock, but will be available in three months." For average busy people who love young children, there are too many roadblocks to obtaining stories of responsible lifestyles. So the T-shirts, mugs, placemats, records, Disney, Barbie dolls, war fads continue to grow – without alternatives. All that would be necessary for other resources to be used is their easy availability.

Adults who are experiencing the inconsistency and frustration of trying to attain consistency between family lifestyle and storybooks on the children's bookshelves are waiting to respond with their purchasing power to appropriate resources. Providing these items for home use can be commercially feasible. Even families that have not consciously made lifestyle choices related to a shalom vision will obtain stories related to these values if they are readily available. Three things are necessary to develop this market:

1. research to find the resources;
2. creativity to develop the resources;
3. marketing that is sufficiently committed to a shalom vision to promote what is wanted as well as (or instead of) what is presented by the usual sales representatives.

Denominational and UNICEF outlets, religious, educational, and environmental bookstores are beginning places for these appropriate lifestyle resources.

Children need to see evidence of a shalom vision in print. Print legitimizes these ideas. Books, music, and video tapes can reinforce what children hear and experience at home.

The same kinds of material are needed to supplement church school studies. When they are available in the church, they reach more children, parents, and teachers.

To describe the search for lifestyle resources for young children is not to say that there aren't lots of good children's books on many subjects. It is to say there is a definite scarcity of resources that include naturally the details of responsible lifestyles. *Our children's literature is too much a reflection of the majority culture.* Just as minorities still do not receive appropriate attention in the literature, minority lifestyles are not affirmed, acknowledged, or included.

We need to change that. We need to distribute broadly what is available. We need to bring the lack of desired resources to the attention of libraries and bookstores. And we can't just wait for them to appear on the market. We need to write the books and make the recordings and games – or encourage our talented friends to do so. (That's how the resources on children with handicapping conditions, for example, have appeared. The people who work with these children – or they, themselves – care, see gaps, and write books.) We can choose to use our influence.

That time of influence has come for me:

1. I have talked to bookstore owners and they have stocked some alternative books.
2. I have purchased books for my family and then taken them to the local children's library to show to the librarian. She has ordered them.
3. I have listed supplementary resources as I've written curriculum resources.
4. I have served on the United Methodist Church's General Board of Discipleship, in its section on Hunger and Value Formation, and heard members talk about the need for assisting people to live responsive lifestyles. I have spoken in committee meetings about my concern for more resources for use in homes. I have suggested topics for those resources. The next time the group met, I brought materials from home and showed them to staff and board members and said, "This is what I mean."

Eventually, a staff committee formed to investigate the possibility of providing lifestyle resources for young children to use at home. I celebrated!

The board engaged a woman to research what was available in lifestyle resources for children. After contacting over 100 publishers, she came to the same conclusion I had. There are so few resources that we certainly cannot flood the market. There are many topics on which new books and songs could be developed, but we don't have to wait for those to become available before we take action.

I urged the Hunger and Value Formation Task Force to select some available items and market them assertively. The staff has selected and is distributing a small selection of books and recordings. Sales brochures describing these resources have been circulated broadly within the United Methodist Church.

You can help. You can support informal learning of responsible lifestyles in homes. You can support parenting that creates responsible lifestyles. You can enlarge the network of persons working toward a shalom vision. You can ask bookstores to carry some of these resources. When you find a wonderful resource, you can promote it by writing a book review for your local newsletter or newspaper. Spread the word! You may use your influence with writers, publishers, and institutional structures and encourage them to promote alternative lifestyles.

How will you use your influence?

Part 3

The Celebrations

January
February
March
April

New Year's and Epiphany

Endings and beginnings

The first day of the calendar year is celebrated as a holiday in almost every country. After the adoption of the Gregorian calendar in the 1500s, January 1 was generally recognized as New Year's Day in the Western world. The Chinese, Egyptian, Islamic, Jewish, and Roman years all begin at different times, but in every culture the first day is marked by special celebrations.

In ancient Rome there were occasions as early as 45 BCE when New Year's Day was celebrated on January 1. Janus – the god of gates and doors, of beginnings and endings and for whom the month of January was named – was honored on that day. He had two faces; one looked ahead and one looked backward. On that day people looked back to the happenings of the past year and thought about what the coming year might bring. Comparative religions historian, Mircea Eliade, has observed that New Year's rites in ancient societies were intended to abolish the past, so that creation could begin anew. In many societies, heavy drinking on New Year's Eve was a personal reenactment of the old year's chaos that would give way to a re-created world in the new year.

In the fourth century, Christians of the Eastern Church began to observe the Feast of the Circumcision, a festival commemorating the circumcision of Jesus on the eighth day after his birth (Luke 2:21). Its observance on January 1 was not established at Rome until the ninth century, over four centuries after December 25 had become the accepted date of Christmas. Its late introduction to the Western calendar has been attributed to the unwillingness of the Roman Church to introduce a festival on a day already characterized as a day of rioting and drunkenness.

The tradition of sweeping out the old year with excessive partying and drinking has persisted. The notion of "turning over a new leaf" for the New Year has also persisted, if often in very superficial terms. It is ironic that the idea of paying off one's debts before the end of the old year, so that the new year could be started debt-free, has been reversed by the use of credit cards and the commercialization of Christmas. Many now greet the new year burdened by their greatest indebtedness of the year.

In the spirit (but not the letter) of the writer of Ecclesiastes, there is a time for frivolity, and a time for seriousness. Times for reflection and personal planning often seem to be casualties of the fast-paced life in our consumer society. An extended holiday vacation or a couple of days off for New Year may offer possibilities for some quiet time. Times for reflection and planning will not only enrich New Year's holidays but can also make a difference in the way we live the rest of the year.

New Year's Eve
watch night services

In 1770, "watch night" services on New Year's Eve were started by St. George's Methodist Church in Philadelphia. Designed to provide an alternative to secular New Year's Eve celebrations, watch night services are still observed in many churches. The evening may begin as a festival, but it always concludes at the midnight hour in contemplation. It usually includes the observance of the Lord's Supper.

Reviewing the old year
with friends

On New Year's Eve, or sometime in the week between Christmas and New Year's Day, I join some of my friends to talk about the old year.

Sometimes we watch one of the network year-end news reviews and then talk about the major events. After reflecting on how we have been affected by the big events of the year, as well as other changes that have taken place in our personal and family lives, we also talk about our hopes for the new year. We joke about our New Year's resolutions, but this annual evening helps me keep things

in perspective. It is also a way to reaffirm old friendships.

– Unknown contributor

New Year's Day

As a rite for New Year's Eve or New Year's Day, write – with suggestions from family members – a very brief outline of outstanding events of the previous year. Make it personal, but be concise.

Decide on a storage place: desk, file cabinet, or safety deposit box. We call our list "We Remember" and include births, deaths, graduations, marriages, employment changes, moves, losing or gaining friends, and so on.

We borrowed this idea from the Pat Boone family back in the '60s, and it has given us a rich family history.

– Era T. Weeks, Dunwoody, Georgia

The Sunday service

Last year, the congregation at Scarboro United Church in Calgary was given two slips of paper when they entered for regular Sunday worship on January 1. During the sermon, Reverend Bill Phipps invited us to write on one our response to: "What baggage would you like to leave behind as you enter the new year?" On the other, we were invited to write one hope for the new year. We were given a few moments of silence to do this.

Bill placed a large pottery bowl (with some sand in the bottom) on the communion table, and then lit a candle. We were invited to walk to the front of the church and burn our "baggage" slip in the bowl. We took our "hopes" home with us.

Many people said that this personal symbolic act was most meaningful because it was performed in our community of faith during worship.

– Carolyn Pogue, Calgary, Alberta

Epiphany

January 6 is known as "Little Christmas," "Three Kings Day," or the beginning of the Season of Epiphany. In some cultures, the gifts (which represent the gifts given by the Magi to Jesus, or the gift of Jesus) are given on this day, rather than on Christmas Eve or Christmas Day. For some, this is a day of special feasting with elaborate traditional foods.

Traditionally, the word epiphany means "a showing forth" or "manifestation." In common usage it sometimes refers to a sudden recognition of something that was there all along, but for which there was only a vague intuition. Often the new recognition can be seen to have a cosmic dimension and can certainly be life-changing. This cosmic aspect of a seemingly insignificant event is well-represented by the Epiphany story of the Magi who followed a star in search of a newborn king whom they finally discovered in a very unlikely Jewish home.

During Advent we often hear the word Emmanuel and the phrase "God with us" as a way to describe the birth of Jesus Christ. Epiphany is a time for discovering what this phrase truly means.

Light for the dark days

Our January and February are particularly long, dark months in Michigan. Our family celebrates Epiphany at dinner time by each lighting a personal candle from the Christ candle we lit on Christmas Day. This not only enriches our lives spiritually, but also adds a good deal of light to some dark evenings.

– Betty Voskuil, Holland, Michigan

Martin Luther King, Jr.'s Birthday

The dream lives on

In 1985, the U.S. Congress declared the birthday of Dr. Martin Luther King, Jr. a national holiday. In Canada, King's birthday is celebrated in many churches on the Sunday closest to January 15.

Born January 15, 1929, and assassinated in Memphis, Tennessee, on April 4, 1968, Dr. King was recognized as leader of the Civil Rights Movement, an Afro-American-led nonviolent protest which brought about the passage of the Civil Rights Act of 1964.

Dr. King was more than a civil rights leader. He called for the United States to live out its ideals of freedom and justice – in the arena of civil and economic rights for its own citizens and in foreign policy.

Because this holiday enjoys widespread popularity, those planning Martin Luther King Day activities are tempted to ensure that popularity by selective celebration: focusing on those things for which King is now publicly acclaimed and ignoring other less popular and less understood ideas for which he was often assailed. While his role in the Civil Rights Movement should be remembered and celebrated, so should his uncompromising stands on those peace and economic justice issues that were not so popular.

Too much effort has been invested in getting this holiday recognized to allow it to degenerate into a day of platitudes about racial harmony. Make these celebrations important occasions for developing interracial solidarity in the continuing struggle for equal rights and economic justice for the world community.

In August, 1995, Reverend Donald Schmidt of Vermont visited Ebenezer Baptist Church, which is down the street from King's tomb in Atlanta, Georgia.

"On the way out of the church I noticed a small stone fountain and plaque, dedicated to the memory of Martin's mother, Alberta Williams King. She was assassinated while playing the organ in this church on June 30, 1974," he later recalled. "The dream lives on, but so does the struggle."

After spending time at King's tomb, Schmidt summed up his impressions in poetry:

Martin!
Did you hear us?
　We were there
singing with you today –
oh it was glorious, Martin!
Over a thousand of us
　marching so proudly down
　　the street,
　gathering at your tomb.

You must have heard us, Martin;
  we sang songs to you
  and thought about you
  and talked about you.

You did hear us,
  didn't you, Martin?

We were right there
  at your grave; you
must have
heard
us.

What?
You didn't hear us?

We will go back home,
  and proclaim the gospel
  with our lives: then
you will hear us.

(copyright Donald Schmidt.
Used with permission.)

Family celebration of Martin Luther King, Jr.'s birthday

King's life can be celebrated many ways in community or within families. The celebrations can also include learning more about Afro-Americans and their struggle in today's world. The learning can be expanded to include: the stories of African people in the Bible; the liberation struggle in South Africa and other parts of the world; and the stories of Afro-American inventors, writers, teachers, and heroes in Canada and the United States.

King's speeches are available in many libraries. You may also want to see what is available on his life on video or in books and cassette audio tapes.

Rosa Parks, a contemporary of Martin Luther King, Jr., refused to obey seating requirements for Afro-Americans on a city bus and started a revolution against segregation. She has written and has been written about. Your reflections and celebrations could include watching a movie or reading about her work. (Look in both the children's and adult's sections of the library or bookstore.)

Because Dr. King followed a philosophy of nonviolence, this is an opportunity to discuss conflict resolution within society or within your family. Churches and libraries are good places to look for nonviolent, conflict-resolution principles. Learning about Mahatma Gandhi is also an option for exploration. His belief in nonviolence and his life are also well documented in books and on film.

Racism is demeaning and harmful to everyone on the planet. Help children understand what racism is, and how its presence in the world scars all of us. You may want to get a copy of the United Nations declaration on the rights of children. Ask them how, or if, these rights apply to *all* the children in the world.

Valentine's Day

Sweethearts and prisoners

Like many holidays, the origins of Valentine's Day are shrouded in mystery and legend. While Valentine's Day is observed on the feast day of two Christian martyrs named Valentine, the origins of today's festival of romance and affection are probably linked to Lupercalia, an ancient Roman festival observed every February 15 honoring Juno, the Roman goddess of women and marriage, and Pan, the god of nature.

In 496 CE, Pope Gelasius changed the date of Lupercalia to February 14 and renamed it Saint Valentine's Day, giving Christian meaning to a pagan festival. According to Christian tradition, there were two Saint Valentines. One, a priest who lived in Rome during the third century, was jailed presumably for aiding persecuted Christians. He is credited with curing his jail keeper's daughter of blindness. Legend holds that on the night before his execution he gave the jail keeper's daughter a note of affection signed, "Your Valentine." Another St. Valentine, Bishop of Temi, was martyred in Rome in 273 CE, supposedly for converting a Roman family to Christianity.

Little is known about the tradition of giving "valentines" before the 15th century when young people in England chose their valentines by writing names on slips of paper and then drawing them, by chance, from a vase. The practice of giving special valentine notes of affection on this day has continued until the present.

For the card, candy, and flower industries, Valentine's Day is one of the more lucrative days of the year. Discovering alternatives to buying these prepackaged expressions of affection for lovers, relatives, and friends is one of the challenges of Valentine's Day!

In recent years, there have been attempts to incorporate the tradition of the two original St. Valentines into what has become a festival of romance by including a focus on prisoners, prisoners of conscience, and the criminal justice system. In some churches, the Sunday nearest February 14 is designated "Criminal Justice Sunday." (In other denominations, "Prisoners' Sunday" is commemorated the third Sunday in November.)

Without taking away from the importance of celebrating human relationships, Valentine's Day can also be a time of learning about and remembering people in prison.

Human rights: An affair of the heart

All over the world people are imprisoned because of their politics, beliefs, religion, ethnic origin, or sexual orientation. Torture is carried out in the name of national security. Executions, official and unofficial, are justified in the name of law and order. People considered dangerous to those in power are detained without trials, while others simply disappear.

When Valentine, on the eve of his execution, wrote a note of thanks to the jailer's daughter who had shown him kindness during his imprisonment and when he signed it "Your Valentine," he probably started the tradition of sending cards to loved ones on this day.

But St. Valentine's gesture had deeper meaning than an expression of personal affection. His life and death upheld the right of individuals to act according to their consciences and deeply-held beliefs, despite powerful national and political concerns. His action symbolizes the strength of human feelings and relationships as a source of resistance to injustice and depersonalization.

On Valentine's Day we can celebrate the importance of relationships by demanding that those in power respect basic human rights:

• Write a letter of thanks to someone whose friendship has helped you to overcome the effects of a depersonalizing situation.

• Form a group to discuss possible human rights violations in your community. Raise questions about what constitutes a "human right." Have a copy of the Bill of Rights handy to help with the discussion.

• Invite someone from an organization such as Amnesty International to explain how your group can encourage international consensus about acceptable standards for arrest, detainment, and punishment.

Prison bars don't stop love and appreciation

In the atmosphere of revenge that is permeating our North American society, it is little wonder that most moderate people feel bewildered about how to break in with a small candle of hope. A Disciples of Christ congregation in Grand Rapids, Michigan, has lit one candle of hope for prison inmates by starting a Valentine's Day tradition.

Each year they assemble 650 Valentine packages that include mixed nuts, candy, a toothbrush, toothpaste, a meditation card, shaving lotion or perfume, and two stamped Valentines for the prisoner's personal use.

This act of human love and thoughtfulness always generates thanks and blessings from the inmates.

Purim

Celebrating survival

First observed in the fifth century BCE, perhaps with roots much earlier in Babylonia, the Festival of Lots (pur means "lot" in Hebrew) or Purim, is a light- and fun-filled festival about Jewish survival. Observed on the 14th day of the lunar month of Adar (in February or March), celebrants read the story of Esther from the Bible, exchange gifts, and sometimes dress up in appropriate costumes.

The story tells how Esther, a Jewish woman who becomes queen to a Persian king, saves her people from destruction. Purim is regarded as a minor festival because the directive for observance is in the book of Esther, not the Torah. Although the day is celebrated, there is an undertone of seriousness. It is the only Jewish holiday that deals specifically with anti-Judaism.

Purim is an occasion for Jews and non-Jews alike to remember the horrific consequences of anti-Judaism in Western history. It is a time for renewed commitment to resist anti-Judaism and any other ideologies that justify the oppression of peoples.

Solidarity

From your children, discover what they understand of anti-Judaism and racism in general. Discuss with them some current examples. Discuss ideologies that are used to justify the oppression of peoples (white supremacy, apartheid, etc.).

Make a contribution to one of the agencies working to counter these ideologies, such as your denomination's office for racial justice, or your local Council for Christians and Jews.

Read the marvelous and courageous story of Esther from a modern translation of the Bible. You will find the whole story in the Book of Esther.

Lent

Preparing for discipleship

Originally a season of fasting and penance for converts preparing for Baptism on Easter Eve, Lent is a period of 40 weekdays, from Ash Wednesday to Easter. It corresponds to Jesus' 40-day fast in the wilderness in preparation for his ministry. (Actually, Lent is a period of 46 days because Sundays were days when fasts could be broken, and were not included in the original 40-day count.)

The Season of Lent includes many special days marking particular events in Jesus' ministry as he approached his death: Ash Wednesday, Passion or Palm Sunday, Maundy Thursday, Good Friday, and Holy Saturday.

When Christianity became the state religion of the Roman Empire in the fourth century, the church was endangered by throngs of new untutored members. To counter the paganism of these new converts, the Lenten fast and practices of self-renunciation became requirements of all Christians. Fasting and self-renunciation were symbolic ways to identify with the suffering of Jesus. Lent became a time of recommitment, a time to ward off the threat of assimilation into the popular culture.

As a time for disciplined re-examination of one's baptismal vows, leading to repentance, and reflection on the cost of discipleship, Lent culminates naturally and directly in the celebration of the Easter resurrection and its implications for participation in Jesus' ministry.

Another kind of fasting

Our most important family alternative celebration occurs during Lent. We used the following idea one year and, at our children's request, have repeated it.

We had become aware of the severely limited budgets of families living on welfare. In order to know how that feels, our family decided to observe Lent by choosing to live on the amount of money a welfare family receives for food. The first year I actually took out the entire amount of money we had to spend on our welfare budget so the children could watch it being spent. Even with the normal amount of food on hand at the beginning of our Lenten experience, during the last week we had some very unusual meals.

We celebrated Easter with a feast, using money carefully saved from our welfare budget. The next day the children and I went to the grocery store, using the money we had saved from our regular food budget, to purchase food and to take it to our local food pantry.

Although this is not like having

to live on a restrictive budget day in and day out, it provides a "hunger" experience and several family discussions on hunger. This also provides the family with the experience of giving up and giving to others.

– Deborah Heaton, Enid, Oklahoma

Homemade cinnamon rolls

Every Sunday morning, except during Lent, our family enjoys homemade cinnamon rolls as a symbol of resurrection. On Easter Sunday morning our favorite cinnamon rolls reappear on our table, this time in the form of the resurrection lamb.

– Betty Voskuil, Holland, Michigan

Stations of the Cross

One year for Good Friday our family did a living Stations of the Cross. We visited places where Jesus suffers today: a welfare office, an unemployment office, a military weapons manufacturer.

The next year we did this on a simpler scale, doing things in which our children could be involved. We visited a hospital and took books for its nursery and we visited in a senior nursing home. We then collected food for the local food pantry.

– Mary and Bill Merrill, Columbus, Ohio

Lenten lifestyle assessment

Lent is a time for expectation, reflection, and self-examination. A group of concerned people from our congregation decided it was important for us to evaluate our lives as Christians and determine if we were living them to the fullest. The result was a family calendar indicating daily Bible readings, along with thoughtful activities for each day during the six weeks in Lent.

As an attempt to gain support for each other, a tree was set up near the pulpit to be used for families to write their experiences on "ornaments" to be placed on the tree. After three weeks of the experiment, a potluck dinner was held for participating families to share their joys and frustrations.

A Lenten lifestyle assessment program gave focus to each week's activities with concrete suggestions for changes in our use of Earth's resources as well as individual gifts and resources. We were challenged to practice and to experiment with voluntary simplicity in television watching, auto, and energy use; in the way we spend our time; in the foods we choose; in recreation and leisure activities; and in the ways we choose to serve others.

Participating families were asked to sign a Lenten Covenant to:
1. engage in daily scripture reading and prayer;
2. focus on specific activities each week, as suggested in the packet;
3. pray for members of the congregation who are participating in the Lenten project;

4. share activities with others via the tree near the pulpit;
5. share the idea of this Lenten Covenant with at least one other person during the Lenten period.

– Mt. Hope Lutheran Church

Walk of the Cross

In Edmonton, Alberta, an ecumenical "Walk of the Cross" is held annually, with dozens of children, women, and men participating. The route takes in "stations" such as the immigration office of the federal government, a school, city hall, social service office of the provincial government, and so on. At each station, someone speaks about such things as how cuts to the health care system are hurting people with mental illnesses, or how education policies meet or do not meet the needs of marginal people. After that, someone provides music on a guitar, and the group sings and offers a prayer. Then we move on to the next station.

This is a wonderful Good Friday event, bringing together people from many different denominations, and providing an opportunity to create a living symbol of solidarity with people who are being "crucified" today.

At the end, one downtown church hosts the group, offering hot cross buns, bannock, juice, coffee, and tea.

– Carolyn Pogue, Calgary, Alberta

Foot-washing

A modern day celebration might include massaging (or washing) each other's feet. It is a delightful experience and involves a level of personal trust that is rarely possible. It has always been done to demonstrate humility and love for the other, stressing the basic equality of all people.

If this celebration is not currently done in your church, you may organize it with a short, quiet worship service which includes the Lord's Supper.

Palm Sunday

Palm Sunday begins Easter Week, celebrating Christ's arrival into Jerusalem. Maundy Thursday commemorates the Passover supper of Christ and the disciples. One old custom had the sovereign of a country wash the feet of paupers, in memory of Christ washing his disciples' feet. Then the king or queen would distribute money, clothing, and food to the poor to be reminded of humility.

I have developed a 21st century tradition that seems fitting for "preparing the way of the Lord." We always spend Palm Sunday afternoon picking up trash on our section of the county road. Usually the snow has melted and fishing season has opened, so the beer bottles alone fill several bags.

– Marion Ellis, Dover, New Hampshire

Stone Soup

The story "Stone Soup," has long been a favorite with many children we know. It is about a wandering minstrel who taught people how to share during a famine. Now through a fairly recently established "tradition," that story has become a wonderful reality in our church.

Each year, during the early part of Lent, we have a time of hunger awareness when church members have at least one meatless meal a week, or cut back on normal eating habits in some other way. The money that is saved by this frugality is set aside for our Hunger Fund. (At some time during this period, the young people also have a 24-hour "starvathon" at the church. During the starvathon they eat nothing and spend their time discussing books and filmstrips about the causes and implications of hunger. They also collect pledges, based on their participation, for the Hunger Fund.)

This all culminates the week before Palm Sunday, on what we call "ComPassion Sunday," with a moving service during which all these gifts are brought forward and put into a large papier mâché loaf of bread. Following this service we always have our famous Stone Soup lunch.

Early that morning, the soup pot is started and as people come to church they bring "fixings" for the soup – vegetables, spices, maybe a soup bone. Children in some of the elementary church school classes cut up the vegetables and everything simmers while we are in church. After the service we all enjoy this delicious soup along with some homemade bread prepared by a group in the church. Those attending contribute what they would have paid for a Sunday dinner at home to the Hunger Fund.

This special occasion concludes with a filmstrip or a retelling of the story and the happy singing of songs in celebration of our sharing. Because of this, the story "Stone Soup" has taken on added significance for our children.

– Khuki Wooleuer, Oneonta, New York

Peace cakes

Palm Sunday has been a time of sharing peace cakes. A homemade bun or sweet bread is given to others with whom communication has ceased. It is a preparation for Good Friday's message of forgiveness and for Easter, in order to reestablish respect and peace. These could be shared in a group, or with another group, between men and women, young and old, or between people of different races, as a commitment to establishing peace among people.

Jesus Christ Superstar

Sometime during Holy Week, our family views the video *Jesus Christ*

Superstar. (It is also available on audio tape.) We have been doing this for years. It is not only a family ritual that brings us together, but it is a wonderful opportunity to discuss theology and learn where our children (and we) are in understanding the story as the years go by.

– Donald Schmidt, Waterbury, Vermont

Lenten wreath

Last year I made a Lenten wreath for our congregation. I cut a piece of 5/8 inch (1.5 cm) plywood into a rough circular shape. The diameter was about 24 inches (60 cm). I screwed a two-inch (five cm) thick triangle in the center, into which I'd drilled six candle-sized holes. I painted this dark brown. I purchased a wreath of thick vines and stapled it around the perimeter of the wooden base, then looped barbed wire through it – a larger than life "crown of thorns." Three small screw eyes were screwed into the wood, and wire attached these to the ceiling in the sanctuary. It was hung in the same way and in the same place as the Advent wreath at Christmas. Six purple candles were placed in it and lit on the first Sunday in Lent. At the end of the service, the minister snuffed out one candle, signifying the coming darkness. He snuffed out another candle every Sunday throughout Lent – the opposite of what takes place during Advent. On Easter Sunday, the unlit wreath was a silent reminder of pain in the world, even though the rest of the church was festively decorated with flowers, candles, and banners.

– Carolyn Pogue, Calgary, Alberta

Symbols at the family table add meaning to Holy Week

Just as the Advent wreath gives children a better understanding of the spiritual meaning of Christmas, setting your table with Easter symbols can illustrate the events of Holy Week. Collect simple household items that depict the events surrounding Christ's death and resurrection. At family worship around the table, use Bible passages to further explain what happened during Holy Week.

Palm Sunday: Place a palm leaf, fern frond, or green paper leaf in the center of a table. The table itself, representing the one where Christ served his disciples the Last Supper, can be your dining table or another space reserved for these symbolic objects. Read from John 12:13. "So they took branches of palm trees..."

Monday: Add a small bowl of water with a folded napkin or towel. Read John 13:5. "...and [Jesus] began to wash the disciples' feet and wipe them with the towel." Talk about the humility and service that Jesus showed by these acts.

Tuesday: Place on the table a picture or molded clay figure of praying hands. Read Luke 22:41. "And he withdrew from them about a stone's throw and knelt down in prayer." Conclude with a family prayer.

Wednesday: Add a picture or ceramic figure of a rooster. Read Luke 22:61. "...Peter, the cock will not crow this day until you three times deny that you know me." Fear of personal reprisal, Peter's reason for denying Christ, is still a reality for Christians. Conclude by praying or singing together.

Thursday: Make a crown of thorns by twisting rough twigs, a rose stem, or weed stalks together. Take turns feeling the crown before it is placed on the table. Emphasize that this symbol of power and royalty was used to mock Jesus. Read Mark 15:17. "...and plaiting a crown of thorns, they put it on him." Sing or repeat the words to "Oh, Sacred Head, Now Wounded."

Friday: Make a small cross of sticks. Read Luke 23:26–33. "And when they came to the place which is called the Skull, there they crucified him." Ask the family to imagine being in the crowd. What would it be like to see Jesus die?

Saturday: Gather around the table filled with Holy Week symbols. After a period of silent meditation, join hands and sing the spiritual "Were You There?"

Easter Sunday: Place a lily or other blooming plant in the center of the other symbols. Read John 11:25. "I am the resurrection and the life..." Center discussion around the lily bulb that is buried in dirt but which grows into a beautiful plant in the spring. Compare Christ's burial and resurrection with the lily. Use this time to separate the Christian from secular observance of Easter. Conclude the Holy Week family worship with joyful Easter music.

To understand our neighbors

In order for us to understand that Jesus was celebrating the Passover with his disciples in what Christians call "the Last Supper," and to understand how this Passover meal is celebrated today, our congregation invited a rabbi to our church during Lent. He led us through the traditional celebration, and then we ate a kosher meal together.

The dinner was well-attended by children, youth, and adults, and the honesty and humor of the rabbi – as well as the fun all of us had – helped us better understand our own religious roots. It also built a bridge between our congregations.

– Scarboro United Church, Calgary, Alberta

Central America Week

The spirit of Archbishop Oscar Romero

Commemorating the life and witness of El Salvadoran Archbishop Oscar Romero, Central America Week is observed in the week around the anniversary of his assassination. While saying Mass on March 24, 1980, the Archbishop was shot and killed. In his final homily that day, he said:

"I implore you, beloved brothers and sisters, to seek a better world from an historical vantage point, to have hope, joined with a spirit of surrender and sacrifice. We must do what we can. All of us can do something..."

Sponsored by many Catholic, Protestant, and secular agencies, Central America Week has become a time to mobilize concern about Central America. Religious communities are urged to set aside the first Sabbath and Sunday service of the week to pray and to commemorate the sufferings and joys common to North and Central Americans of faith. They are further encouraged to plan special events through the week to focus attention on that region's struggles.

For scheduled events and resources contact the Inter-American Task Force on Central America in New York or the Inter-Church Committee for Human Rights in Latin America in Toronto.

At home

You may want to invite some friends to view the video film *Romero*, about the life and death of the archbishop.

Find out who is working to support Central American refugees in your community. Find out if you can help.

International Women's Day

In the United States, August 26 is also celebrated. Known as Women's Equality Day, it marks the anniversary of women's right to vote, won in 1920.

"What time of night it is"

International Women's Day, a day to honor women, is celebrated throughout the world. Set on March 8, the day commemorates a march of women garment and textile workers in New York City in 1857. International Women's Day is a national holiday in the Soviet Union and the People's Republic of China, where women workers are given special recognition.

At the fourth National Women's Rights Convention in New York, in 1853, Sojourner Truth spoke these words:

I know that it feels a kind o' hissin' and ticklin' like to see a colored woman get up and tell you about things, and women's rights. We have all been thrown down so low that nobody thought we'd ever get up again; but see if we don't; we'll have our rights; and you can't stop us from them; see if you can. You may hiss as much as you like, but it is comin'... I am sittin' among you to watch; and every once and a while I will come out and tell you what time of night it is...

Celebrate women!

Throughout history, women have made wonderful contributions for the betterment of humankind. Study the lives of women who have made an impact in various fields: Mother Teresa, Golda Meir, Beverly Sills, and Susan B. Anthony. Celebrate their contributions and learn about women in your community who are working for justice, peace, and the environment.

Host a Women's Day dinner

Invite your friends to a potluck dinner. Ask each of them to bring the name and story of one woman they admire. This could be anyone from Reverend Lois Wilson to Corretta King to your own grandma. (You may invite guests to come dressed as the woman, too.)

"Take Back the Night" march

In many towns and cities in North America, women, men, and children take to the streets with candles and flashlights and march into the darkness. "We will take back the night!" they sing. This march is in defiance of the safety that is still lacking for women on the streets and in homes. If your community doesn't have a march, start one.

Ecumenical Decade of Churches in Solidarity with Women

In 1988, the World Council of Churches declared 1988 to 1998 a Decade of Churches in Solidarity with Women. The aims of the Decade are:

1. Empowering women to challenge oppressive structures in the global community, their country, and their church.

2. Affirming – through shared leadership and decision-making, theology and spirituality – the decisive contributions of women in churches and communities.

3. Giving visibility to women's perspectives and actions in the work and struggle for justice, peace, and the integrity of creation.

4. Enabling the churches to free themselves from racism, sexism, and classism; from teachings and practices that discriminate against women.

5. Encouraging the churches to take actions in solidarity with women.

Find out if your denomination, or your local church is involved in the Decade. Ask if there are special activities or if there will be a special service to mark the Decade.

Celebrating the unnamed ones

In many churches in North America, International Women's Day is combined with Ecumenical Decade Sunday, usually the first Sunday in March. It is a time to celebrate the women in the church today, and to celebrate our mothers and grandmothers. It is a time to remember the many biblical women, including those who supported Jesus' ministry and who were unnamed by biblical writers, whose names are seldom mentioned Sunday mornings.

The men's group at Scarboro United Church in Calgary, Alberta, wrote a collective litany in 1995. It was used during Sunday morning worship.

Litany of Solidarity with Women

Leader: God created humanity; male and female, God created us. God blesses us as equal partners in the human journey.

Men: But women have not enjoyed equality and respect. God's intentions have been thwarted, and women cast into inferior roles.

Leader: World history is awash in the suffering of women; too often religion has been a cloak of legitimacy for maintaining the status quo.

Men: Even today women suffer degradation at many levels in our society.

Leader: So we are grateful for the example of Jesus who accepted fully the humanity and gifts of women.

Men: As women throughout the world seek their equal place in society, we offer our support and solidarity.

Leader: May we all be held accountable for abuse of power, disrespect, and ongoing conditioning which results in indignity and the dishonoring of women as equal partners in the human community.

Men: In this Ecumenical Decade of Churches in Solidarity with women, in our own communities and throughout the world, may we open ourselves to acknowledging past failures, and move forward together with new understanding and action.

Leader: May God be with us in our common journey,

Men: And may women feel our solidarity, and support in the celebration of our common, God-given humanity.

All: Amen!

– Scarboro United Church, Calgary, Alberta.
Used with permission.

During the offering time, in addition to the ushers taking forward the money gifts, women of many ages carried forward a turkey platter, a tea pot, a broom, a small child, a sewn garment, a hymnbook, and a Bible as symbols of women's work in the church throughout time. These gifts were carried high and proudly. They were received (except for the small child!) and placed on the communion table along with the offering plates.

Knowledge is the first step to change

Borrow books from your library, community center, or from friends, and check your library for videos about women in the world today. You may choose to focus on learning about women and poverty, women and pornography, women and violence, or women and war. Invite a group of people to view and/or discuss one of these issues. Ask each one to bring one small gift for a woman. Deliver the gifts to a women's shelter, or to a women's prison.

St. Patrick's Day

The wearing of the green

St. Patrick's Day is an Irish religious holiday. Celebrated on March 17, this holy day commemorates the contributions of that country's fifth-century patron saint. Like many other Irish religious figures, St. Patrick was believed to have had a special rapport with nature, and this helped him to convince the Irish that he was in touch with God.

Forsaking the religious significance of this day, commercial interests in North America trade more and more on the ethnic stereotype of the "hard-drinking" Irish to make St. Patrick's Day an occasion for reveling. Irish societies are working to counteract this stereotype by conducting alternative St. Patrick's Day celebrations.

In addition to "wearing the green" and cooking special Irish recipes, this is a good day to overcome stereotypes by recalling the contributions that Irish people have made here. It is also a day to mourn the civil strife that plagues Northern Ireland and the divisive role that religion has played there.

At home on St. Patrick's Day

Around the dinner table, talk about a "Who's Who Among Irish North Americans," beginning with Patrick Henry and remembering John F. Kennedy and Robert Kennedy.

It is also a good time to connect with people of Irish descent and learn their stories.

Spring

Life after winter

In different parts of the world, the signs of spring differ dramatically, but astronomers can tell exactly from Earth's motion around the sun when one season ends and the next one begins. The vernal equinox marks the beginning of spring in the Northern Hemisphere between March 20 and 21. On this day, the sun appears directly above the equator, so that along the equator there are 12 hours of daylight and 12 hours of darkness.

Ancient people knew that at the vernal equinox winter was giving way to spring. Many rites of fertility and rebirth were observed at the time of the vernal equinox as in the festival of Eostre in Britain (see **Easter**). Even though the manifestations of spring are different in different places, the first day of spring is a good time to celebrate the ending of winter and the renewal of life in nature. It is much better than mixing the coming of spring with the celebration of Jesus' resurrection.

In 1979, another important dimension to the celebration of spring was added when children rang bells at the United Nations at the exact hour of the vernal equinox inaugurating Earth Day. It is a day for celebrating nature and learning about the interdependence of all life. Implicit in that celebrating and learning is the recognition of the threat waste and pollution pose for the fragile ecological balance which makes life possible on the planet.

At home on the first day of spring

Read, and then discuss, the following words of Wendell Berry from his book, *The Unsettling of America: Culture and Agriculture:*

> *...The earth is what we all have in common, it is what we are made of and what we live from, and we cannot damage it without damaging those with whom we share*

it. There is an uncanny resemblance between our behavior toward each other and our behavior toward the earth. By some connection we do not recognize, the willingness to exploit one becomes the willingness to exploit the other... It is impossible to care for each other more or differently than we care for the earth.

Celebrate spring by celebrating life

You may also want to read aloud the following poem by American poet Neal Gladstone.

This is the water, celebrate the
   water
May you always drink your fill.
We can save the treasure
if we stand together and
   celebrate the water.
Don't think we don't need you;
   we need you.
Don't think we don't hear you;
   we hear you.
Those who care just lift your
   voices and join us as we sing.
Save our planet, keep our planet
   green.
This is the air, celebrate the air,
May you always breathe your fill.
This is the music, celebrate the
   music
May you always sing your fill.
These are the people, celebrate
   the people
May you always love your fill.

This is your life, celebrate your
   life
May you always live your fill.
We can save the treasure
if we live together
and celebrate life.

Celebrate Earth

In the past few years, there have been special days set aside to celebrate some special part of life. Earth Day, Food Day, and Sun Day are three examples. Each of these days has made a unique contribution to our image of celebrations, for they increase our sensitivity to the possibilities and dangers of the world around us, and encourage us to action. They have a certain commonality which should be recognized by people working to change their lifestyles. First of all, they break away from tradition by celebrating new ideas. Second, there is no effort to institutionalize these days and "create" a massive self-perpetuating event complete with gifts and cards.

Because these celebrations have been more or less improvised to suit the needs of the current society, one could probably assume that there will be other celebrations of this kind in the future. So, if one of these celebrations comes along, how could you get involved?

The focus has usually been national, but just because you have seen a word or two in a national publication does not mean that anyone in your area is organizing the day. It might be up to you to get something started. Try to find the origins of the event. If it is of a general area, track down a club that might be involved (a Sierra Club might be a place to start for an environmental day). Ask the members to help you with organizing. If they do not know about it, they need your help. Try to take the event and relate it to a very local and common issue – the closer to home you can draw the issue, the better response you will get. A national organization will provide you with tools, and can get you started.

Would you like to organize your own day? A local celebration will often be more satisfying than a national one, because everyone feels personally involved. If it is a Sun, Earth, or Food celebration, you may draw on the experiences of past organizers by writing to them. If it is a special and unique celebration you want your community to have, then you need to have assistance in getting it organized for maximum results. However, start out small, with people who you know will get things done, rather than trying for something big with people who may be unfamiliar to you. Good luck!

A rite for spring: Begin to recycle

Anyone can – and should – participate in recycling. Practically every community has an organization that accepts recyclable material: a junk dealer, a municipal or private drop-off center, a charitable organization that operates a paper drive. Find out what materials can be recycled in your area. Then keep those materials separated from your trash and recycle them as they accumulate.

To make a serious impact on our country's solid waste problem, we need community-wide recycling programs. Private citizens can play key roles in initiating and supporting recycling programs. Without them, solid waste professionals typically underestimate the potential of citizen participation and lean toward high-technology options for dealing with the problem. So investigate what is happening in your own community.

If there is a recycling program, support it by participating in its efforts, by promoting it to friends and neighbors, and by supporting it at the governmental level. If no recycling program is planned or in operation, take the initiative by writing to the newspaper, talking with public officials, or forming a citizens' group to press for recycling.

Community recycling programs not only reduce the trash disposal volume to more manageable levels, but also contribute to more effective use of scarce resources on our spaceship Earth.

– Earl Arnold, Eco-Justice Task Force, Ithaca, New York

Let Earth breathe!

Encourage your Scouts, women's group, Guides, men's group, or your friends and family to take an afternoon for garbage pick-up in your area. Consider that the garbage lying around after winter is lying on the face of our Mother, Earth. Give her a chance to feel the sunshine and breathe the air! Do it with love. Make a party out of it by singing as you go. Have a potluck picnic – indoor or out – to finish your celebration.

All-night vigil

Hold an all-night vigil. It might be Easter Eve or the night of the spring equinox. Read favorite poems, literature, scripture having to do with Earth, people, life, love, change. Incorporate First Nations wisdom in the readings, and wisdom from religions other than your own. Share skills on the guitar, recorder, flute. Tell of the last time you were up all night. Sit silently in a circle. Sing appropriate songs.

Dig a pit and build a fire. Every hour, have two people go out and watch the fire and stoke it so it doesn't go out while the rest sleep. Bake a meal in the fire by placing food in a suitable pot and burying it in the coals. This is a traditional way of cooking for many African and Hawaiian peoples. Keeping the night fire allows the two watchers to talk and watch the changing sky in a very personal way. Have an astronomy book accessible.

Each team of people wakes the next team to watch. It builds communication, group solidarity, and offers an experience full of wonder. Every hour offers something special and different to the two fire-watchers.

Passover

Freedom from slavery

Passover, or pesach in Hebrew, is the Jewish festival commemorating the Exodus. Passover refers to the night before the Hebrew slaves were to leave Egypt, when an angel of the Lord would kill the first-born of the Egyptians. The Hebrews had been warned that only houses marked with lamb's blood on the door posts would be spared. The angel would "pass over" these houses.

The directive for observing the Passover is in the 12th chapter of Exodus. An eight-day festival, Passover begins on the eve of the 14th day of the lunar month of Nisan – usually between mid-March and mid-April – with a Seder, or feast, in the home. This ceremony, celebrated with family members around a special Seder meal, is a retelling of the Exodus story and has been done in the same way for hundreds of years.

A child asks four questions and the elders answer, recounting why Passover is such a significant occasion. (See Exodus 12:25–27.) Although the Seder is the central part of the Passover festival, there are many observances, activities and special foods for the other days.

The Passover has long had significance for Christians. On the night he was arrested, Jesus celebrated the Passover with his disciples, using that sacred feast to institute the Eucharist – sometimes called the Lord's Supper or Holy Communion (Matthew 26:17–30). Beyond that unique connection to Passover, many Christians observe the Passover Seder as a way of affirming their own Jewish (spiritual) heritage. Given the long and tragic history of Christian persecution of Jews, such affirmation is most appropriate.

What links are in place in your community?

Find out if there is a branch of the Council of Christians and Jews in your community. Learn about it, and attend open gatherings and events.

Ramadan

Month-long fast for Muslims

Ramadan, commemorating the revelation of the Koran to Mohammed, is the most sacred celebration in the Muslim world. The observance begins on the eve of the ninth month of the lunar year. Since the lunar year is 11 or 12 days shorter than the solar year, the incidence of Ramadan moves through all the seasons of the year in cycles of approximately 33 years.

Celebrated for 30 days, the observance affects a large portion of the developing world. According to Islamic law, fasting from sunup to sundown is required of every able-bodied Muslim. The fasting is meant to help keep the observance in mind, encourage spiritual discipline, create an identification with the poor, and remind people of their ultimate dependence on God.

Popular celebrations of Ramadan sometimes involve lavish feasts after the sun goes down, but this custom does not represent the holiday's true spirit, to bring about inner strength through austerity.

Learning about our neighbors

Because Islam is a religious tradition little understood by most Westerners, perhaps during this fast, non-Muslims can use this time to learn more. During dinner one evening, identify popular stereo-types of Muslims. Then do some reading. Search out not only non-fiction, but also poetry and fiction written by Muslims. Make the ac-quaintance of some Muslims in your community. Then, at another family meal one evening, try to go beyond the stereotypes to real people.

You may wish to invite Muslim people to a community gathering as guest speakers. Find out if your religious community has an interfaith council and learn about interfaith gatherings in your community.

Easter

Celebrating resurrection

Easter, the most important festival of the Christian church, celebrates the resurrection of Jesus from the dead. The Feast of Easter was well established by the second century, but controversy developed between the Eastern and Western churches over the proper day for its observance. In 325 CE, the Council of Nicaea settled the dispute by deciding that Easter would be celebrated on the Sunday following the first full moon after the vernal equinox, making it fall on variable dates each year between March 21 and April 25.

We celebrate Easter on Sunday because it is the day of the week when Jesus rose. The Council's decision to time the celebration with the vernal equinox, however, suggests that the day replaced one or more pagan rebirth festivals observed at the time of the vernal equinox.

The derivation of the word "Easter" is not clear. The Venerable Bede, an early English historian (672–735 CE), connected Easter to Eostre, an Anglo-Saxon spring goddess whose festival was celebrated at the vernal equinox and whose symbols were the hare and the egg. It seems likely that the hare and egg traditions of the goddess Eostre became the Easter bunny and Easter eggs.

Still other pagan practices came to be associated with the feast of Easter. For example, sunrise services, while having some basis in the early dawn visit of the women to Jesus' tomb (Luke 24:1), were also part of traditional vernal equinox rites which welcomed the sun and its power to bring new life.

One wonders if the popular preoccupation with Easter as a time to celebrate hope for life after death also has its roots in ancient rites of spring. The New Testament clearly links hope for a general resurrection to Jesus' resurrection (1 Corinthians 15); however, the spring and rebirth symbols often used in churches at Easter may actually distort the meaning of resurrection. These symbols (e.g., butterflies) suggest natural cycles of life, death, and rebirth. Resurrection in the New Testament sense is not natural. Rather, it is a radical action contravening nature for God's own purposes.

Through the resurrection, Jesus' ministry of healing, teaching, preaching and standing in solidarity with the marginalized became the universal ministry for those who would follow. As Jesus said to the fearful, unbelieving disciples on that first Easter, "Peace be with you. As the Father has sent me, so I send you" (John 20:21).

The commercialization of Easter makes it difficult to keep the real purpose of the resurrection celebration in perspective. In addition to the annual Easter clothes, card, flower and candy blitz, attempts by business interests to make Easter a "second Christmas" have spawned an Easter-oriented toy industry and a massive live-animal business selling millions of rabbits, baby chicks, and ducks each year.

There is another significant level of concern with our Easter celebrations. Although many attempts have been made to link the Easter bunny and Easter egg traditions to the resurrection, those traditions actually divert attention away from celebrating the resurrection. "What happened on the third day?" asked the church school teacher to a group of preschoolers one Easter morning. "The Easter bunny brought eggs," was the immediate and unequivocal reply. As children grow and learn that the Easter bunny is a myth passed on to them as truth, they have less reason to believe what is taught them as truth about the resurrection.

Better than chocolate eggs

Consider placing a book in your child's Easter basket – one that expresses the love and sacrifice represented by the observance of Easter.

Signs of faith

At Easter we help our children understand the significance of the season by adorning our home with signs of faith: a dove sculpture or crucifix hung on our wall only during this season, or a banner with an Easter message hung temporarily on our refrigerator or front door.

Since Easter is our family's most festive occasion, we celebrate with an all-day open house. Two homemade grapevine baskets (no chocolate Easter eggs, no Easter bunny) are filled with dogwoods, violets, daffodils – whatever is blooming – as a symbol of new life. Gifts for the children specifically celebrate life. Last year they got umbrellas to play in the life-giving spring rains. We end Easter day with the Paschal vespers at dusk.

– Ed, Andrea, Nathanael and Rebekah Wills,
Memphis, Tennessee

Easter in the Philippines

In the fresh air of the Philippine countryside, families met in the early morning to read together from the Easter text. After a short period of meditation, each family offered symbols of new life: plants, seeds, eggs, hand-painted butterflies, and a pair of booties! These symbols were put on dry twigs to make an Easter tree. Older children planted quick-sprouting mango seeds in an earthen pot and were told to watch carefully for an amazing demonstration of new life.

– Ana Maria Clamor, Quezon City, Philippines

Easter Seder: We remember

Easter is the most sacred holy day in the Christian church. It marks an extraordinary event – the resurrection of Christ – and is supposed to remind us of the meaning of that event. Commercial interests, pushing Easter bunnies, new clothes, cards, baskets, candy, and toys, sometimes make it hard to stay focused on the real purpose of celebrating Easter. The Easter Seder helps us remember.

The idea for the Easter Seder comes from the Jewish Passover Seder. Jewish people observe the Passover, which commemorates the Israelites' liberation from slavery in Egypt, about the same time of year that Christians celebrate Easter. At the heart of the Jewish festival is the retelling of the story behind the Passover meal which is called the Seder, or "order": "When your children say to you, 'What do you mean by this service?' then you shall say..." (Exodus 12:26).

In response to a set of questions from the children, the different generations at the table recount the story and the meaning of the observance. The rite has proven to be an important way to keep the significance of this celebration before the children and the whole family. We remember that the Last Supper was Jesus' Passover meal with the disciples.

The following questions and answers, using the form of the Jewish Seder, attempt to retell the story of the death and resurrection of Jesus, helping us understand what that event 2,000 years ago has to do with the way we live now. The Easter Seder is designed for use by families or other groups on Easter Sunday. If you decide to use the Seder in a worship service or with a group at church, also consider using it at home when you have your traditional Easter meal. This Seder, like the Jewish one, assumes the presence and participation of more than one generation. The younger generations ask the questions and the older generations answer and explain.

Feel free to adapt the following Seder to your liking. Create one that you will use year after year so that the Seder becomes an Easter tradition in your family.

The Youngest Child: *Why is this day different from all other days?*

An Elder: On this day, almost 2,000 years ago, God raised up Jesus from the dead. Jesus had been crucified. His friends took his body down from the cross and placed it in a tomb. Early in the morning, three days after he was buried, some women went to his tomb. When they got there, they found the stone that sealed the tomb had been removed and the body of Jesus was gone.

A Child: *What happened to his body?*

An Elder: The women thought his body had been stolen. But an angel appeared and told them not to be afraid. The angel brought the good news that Jesus was alive. He had been raised from the dead, just as he had promised, and he would see his followers later. The women ran to tell the other disciples what they had seen and heard. Some of the men didn't believe the women's story until Jesus actually appeared to them. Then, they knew he was alive.

A Child: *Who killed him?*

An Elder: Roman authorities executed Jesus. The Romans had occupied Judea for almost a hundred years, but the Jews never stopped trying to regain their freedom. Since Jesus, who was Jewish, was popular, the Romans were afraid if he became king he would be successful in driving them out of the country. Some of the religious leaders who had received special favors from the Romans were also afraid of Jesus. Together with the Roman officials, they cooperated in a plan to bring Jesus to trial and to have him executed.

A Child: *Why were they afraid of Jesus?*

An Elder: For three years, Jesus and his disciples traveled all over Judea, preaching, teaching, and healing people. Great crowds followed wherever they went. Jesus taught that God loves all people and that to love God and to love your neighbor are the two most important commandments. He enlarged the meaning of neighbor to include the poor, the outcasts, and even one's enemies. He spent most of his time with society's rejected, giving them hope.

But many people did not like Jesus' teachings, and he was often in trouble. His teachings about accumulating wealth, injustice to the poor and needy, and religious hypocrisy were hard words for those who were neither poor nor outcast nor had any concern for the destitute. In his manner of living and in his teaching, Jesus sided with the poor, exposing religious leaders in their selfishness and bringing fear that they would lose their privileged positions.

A Child: *Were all of the religious leaders opposed to Jesus?*

An Elder: No. Some were amazed at his healing, his teaching, and his courage in confronting authorities. Some believed that he was sent from God.

A Child: *Did God really raise Jesus from the dead?*

An Elder: The New Testament tells us that the risen Jesus appeared to his followers on the seashore, on the road, and in a house where they had gathered to pray. One of the stories tells about a disciple who doubted that Jesus was really alive. But after Jesus appeared to him and invited him to touch his wounds, he believed. These stories also make it clear that the risen Jesus appeared to be different.

Whatever the differences, his followers recognized him when he appeared to them. Their sense of his presence was so real that they began doing the things he had done during his lifetime, although they knew that could mean suffering, persecution, and even death.

A Child: *Why do we celebrate Easter?*

An Elder: Jesus came into the world to bring God's good news of love and forgiveness for all people, including us. Because Jesus included the poor, the outcasts, and even enemies of the people in the circle of God's love, he was persecuted and finally killed.

God raised Jesus from the dead as a sign of approval for the work he had done on Earth. His preaching, teaching, healing, and his identification with the poor was the work God intended. For two days after the crucifixion, Jesus' followers were desolate. They were afraid and hid. It seemed that all Jesus had done was nothing more than a beautiful, fleeting dream. But that was not the end! God raised up Jesus as if to say, "The words he spoke in my name are true! The deeds he did are my deeds! And they are now the work of all who follow him." When Jesus appeared to his followers after the resurrection he told them, "As the Father has sent me, so I send you."

And so we are called!

Children: *The Lord is risen!*

Elder: The Lord is risen, indeed!

All: Hallelujah! Amen!

May
June
July
August

May Day

May Day has roots in prehistoric times as a spring festival, marking the revival of nature after winter. Maypole dances and flowers still mark the celebration.

Meeting in Paris in 1889, a congress of world socialist parties voted to support the United States labor movement's demands for an eight-hour work day and chose May 1, 1890, as a day to demonstrate in favor of the eight-hour day. That action set a precedent, and May 1 became the traditional time for labor demonstrations in Europe.

In the former Soviet Union, May Day is a national holiday marked by giant banners, patriotic speeches, and military parades.

[See also **Labor Day**.]

At home on May Day

If spring comes late to your area and March 20 and 21 goes by without any visible signs of new life, celebrate its coming today. If possible, spend some time outside. Consider how different your life is because the labor movement won the struggle for an eight-hour work day.

Pentecost

Courage is born

Pentecost (from Greek pentehoste meaning 50th) celebrates the post-resurrection descent of the Holy Spirit on Jesus' followers (Acts 2:1-6). This occurred on the Jewish Pentecost which is observed on the seventh Sunday after Easter, or 50 days after Passover (see **Shavuot**). On that day, a group of frightened disciples hiding in Jerusalem were empowered to become fearless witnesses, even in the face of opposition by the civil authorities. For that reason, Pentecost is said to be "the birthday of the church."

Although setting the Christian observance of Pentecost on the existing Jewish feast day was probably intentional, the two days have only the name and date in common. Also known as Whitsunday, Pentecost was celebrated as early as the third century, with celebrations sometimes including the whole 50 days. Because it was a feast of joy, any kind of penance was forbidden.

The Lent/Easter season concludes with Pentecost, celebrating a universal ministry empowered by God. According to the story of Pentecost, many nationalities were represented in the crowd that listened to the disciples preach the good news of Jesus that day, but they all heard the message in their own language. Pentecost is a good time to hear the message in your "own language" and to consider what participation in God's Shalom means for you.

At home on Pentecost

Recall heroes of faith who were empowered to participate in Jesus' ministry despite great personal cost. Well-known public figures include: Dietrich Bonhoeffer, Dom Helder Camera, Dorothy Day, Martin Luther King, Jr., Mother Teresa, and Desmond Tutu. What lesser-known people would you include?

Shavuot

First Fruits and the Torah

Shavuot, meaning "weeks" in Hebrew, is observed seven weeks (50 days) after Passover. Other names describe its character: Harvest Festival, Festival of the First Fruits, and Festival of the Giving of the Torah. Originally an agricultural festival, Shavuot was one of three occasions when people were required to go to the Temple in Jerusalem with offerings from their farms. After the destruction of the second Temple in the first century, the people could no longer bring their offerings to the Temple, so the festival was designated as the anniversary of the reception of the Torah at Mount Sinai.

While the agricultural theme has not been removed entirely, the central focus is on the Torah. At the synagogue service the Ten Commandments are recited and the Book of Ruth is read.

Our common heritage

Because Genesis, Exodus, Leviticus, Numbers, and Deuteronomy (Torah) are all familiar books to Muslims, Jews, and Christians, take some time after dinner one evening to contemplate that fact. What do those common roots mean today? Retell the story of Ruth to a child you love. In your women's or men's group, spend an evening focusing on the Book of Ruth.

Mother's Day and Father's Day

Mother's Day, observed on the second Sunday in May, has its origins in the different concerns of two women, Julia Ward Howe and Anna Jarvis. Julia Ward Howe – writer, lecturer, social reformer, and author of *The Battle Hymn of the Republic* – made the first known suggestion for Mother's Day in 1872. She wanted to observe Mother's Day on June 2 and dedicate the day to peace. For several years she sponsored an annual Mother's Day meeting in Boston as a way of connecting her ideals of motherhood and peacemaking.

Anna Jarvis had a different reason for honoring mothers. Never a mother herself, she spent most of her adult life caring for her mother in Grafton, West Virginia. Her concern was for mothers who needed care and whose adult children were neglecting them. Out of this concern, in 1905, Anna Jarvis started a campaign for an annual religious celebration honoring mothers.

Although others started Mother's Day celebrations in their areas, Anna Jarvis is responsible for making it a nationwide observance. In 1914, Congress passed a resolution providing that the second Sunday in May be designated as Mother's Day.

Anna Jarvis envisioned Mother's Day as a time of recommitment to honoring and caring for mothers, especially mothers who were no longer able to care for themselves. But she was dismayed to see the way the holiday was celebrated. She lived to see Mother's Day become the victim of commercialism, when honoring mothers was reduced to giving flowers, cards, and gifts. She died in 1948, disappointed and disillusioned that her work had been so trivialized.

A special day to honor mothers has ancient and worldwide precedents, but a special day to honor fathers seems to be unique to the Western world. Many different people contributed to the creation of Father's Day, all of whom were likely influenced by Mother's Day. The first Father's Day service was probably conducted at a church in Fairmont, West Virginia, at the request of Mrs. Charles Clayton. But the person most responsible for getting the day started was Mrs. John Bruce Dodd of Spokane, Washington. The idea came to her during a Mother's Day sermon in 1909. She remembered her father who had raised six children after his young wife's death. Only one year later, on the third Sunday of June 1910, Spokane became the first city to honor fathers with a special day. Although widely observed since that time, it was only in 1972 that a Congressional resolution put it on the same basis as Mother's Day in the United States.

The founders of Mother's Day and Father's Day would probably not be pleased with the lot of many of today's elderly people. Part of what they were responding to in the early part of this century was more than a simple desire to honor their parents. They feared that the emerging pattern of small nuclear families would contribute to a growing neglect of elderly parents and bring about a growing social disorder and the economic and cultural marginalization of the elderly. Theirs was a prophetic vision. They identified a problem with which this society has yet to come to terms in any serious way.

Mother's Day and Father's Day remind us to honor our parents in special ways. Beyond that, however, calling attention to the plight of the elderly in this society and pressing for serious attention to their problems may be the best way to honor them. Hopefully, the blatantly commercial creation of "Grandparents' Day" will die a commercial death, and the genuine concerns for the elderly which moved the founders of Mother's and Father's Days will find expression on those days.

Although the founders had elderly parents in mind, there is no reason why younger mothers and fathers (including single parents), and the special problems they face, should be excluded from these observances.

Although it didn't catch on as part of traditional observances, Julia Ward Howe's idea for making Mother's Day (or Father's Day) a day dedicated to peace makes sense. Those who bring life into the world and nurture it to adulthood have a special stake in seeing that those lives are not senselessly destroyed in war. Although commercial Mother's Day cards with peace messages may not be available anytime soon, there is no reason why you can't create your own, and encourage others to do the same. You may want to combine honor for parents and the desire for peace in your celebration.

At home on Mother's Day

Recognize and acknowledge that those who care for small children occupy a very influential place in society. Whether at home, in elementary schools, or in day care centers, the kind of care given to small children determines the direction of our society.

Use Mother's Day as an occasion to speak on behalf of better day care arrangements for the growing numbers of mothers who work, and for better prenatal care for poor mothers. Consider the struggles of mothers trying to support families on inadequate welfare allotments and of elderly women whose social security benefits do not meet their costs for living.

Make a special donation of food or clothing or money to welfare mothers in your community by contacting social services.

Mothers mourn in El Salvador

Throughout many countries in the world, Mother's Day is an occasion for mothers to spend time with their children, celebrating motherhood and family. But in my country of El Salvador, motherhood has taken on another meaning. After years of war, more than 60,000 deaths and another 6,000 disappearances of our loved ones, we Salvadoran mothers pass Mother's Day as we do any other day, mourning for our missing children and husbands. While mothers everywhere spend sacred moments with their children, we only have our sorrow to embrace. For us, the greatest homage on Mother's Day would be the liberation of our incarcerated children and the declaration of the whereabouts of our disappeared ones.

– America Sosa, COMADRES,
Washington, D.C.

Mother's Day: A celebration of love, a festival of peace

Mother's Day was initiated in the 1870s as a call to women to work for peace in the world. In that first Mother's Day proclamation, Julia Ward Howe wrote:

Arise then, women of this day!
Arise all women who have hearts.
We women of one country will
be too tender for those of another

country to allow our sons to be
trained to injure theirs. From the
bosom of the devastated earth a
voice goes up with our own. It
says, "Disarm, Disarm!"

As men have often forsaken the
plow at the summons of war let
women now leave all that may
be left of home for a great and
earnest day of counsel with each
other as to the means whereby the
great human family can live in
peace, each bearing after his own
time the sacred impress, not of
Caesar, but of God.

I ask that a general congress
be held to promote the alliance
of the different nationalities, the
amicable settlement of international
questions, the great and
general interests of peace.

On this day we honor our mothers for their constant love. Motivated by that love, let us also make an earnest search for peace.

– Center for Disarmament Education,
Baton Rouge, Louisiana

Older adults: A nonrenewable resource

A television commercial features an older man on his first day at work at a local fast-food hamburger restaurant. The scene moves quickly from his young co-workers' skepticism at his arrival to their frank amazement when they see how effectively he does his work. When he returns home in the evening, he says confidently to his questioning wife, "I don't know how they ever got along without me."

The first time I saw this commercial, I thought the message was good: not only is this man able to do good work, but the quality of his work is recognized by the younger generation. I have since had second thoughts. What does this commercial suggest about a society where selling hamburgers at minimum wage is an appropriate use of a senior citizen's skills and experience?

It is my hope that this commercial will be viewed as a parable about the contribution older people can make to all facets of life in this society. The skills and experience of these people are like nonrenewable resources. When they are gone, they are gone forever. How long can our society afford to waste this critical resource?

– Rev. James G. Kirk

Parents' Days

Our celebration of Mother's and Father's Days has one thing in common with the intentions of their founders – we say we are honoring our parents.

But Anna Jarvis's efforts to call attention to adult children's neglect of their parents haven't had much effect. On Mother's and Father's Days, unfortunately, we honor the

dollar more often than we do our parents.

As adults, and also as children, we often neglect our parents. We take them for granted and fail to show appreciation for their nurturing, or we consider them nuisances rather than people like us with a need to give and receive love. As a result, we are ready targets for advertisers who appeal to our guilt feelings to fill their pocketbooks. "Remember Mom" and "For Dad on His Day" send millions rushing out to buy gifts that will prove affection or pay Mom and Dad back for all their sacrifices.

The sales thrust extends to grandparents, aunts, and uncles, sometimes even sisters and brothers. Anyone who remotely qualifies as a mother or father figure, especially anyone who has been ignored during the months preceding the holiday, is likely to receive some type of acknowledgment. Restaurants, clothing merchants, florists, and candy stores do a bonanza business.

We could suggest doing away with Parents' Days and making every day a people's day, on which we honored them and thought of ways to help them and bring them joy. In fact, making every day a People's Day is what we do suggest. But it's also fun to have special days for Mom and Dad. The trick is celebrating them appropriately, given the influences on us to buy and be done with it.

The original celebrations focused on the parents of adult children – their need to be cared for in old age or illness, and the child's desire to show appreciation for the parent's own years of caring. Our focus could encompass all the needs of our parents or the needs of all the aging and ill in our society.

What do your parents need that you can give them on their day? Or what do they need that you can promise on their day and do another? Pick something that will satisfy them, not something that will make you feel less guilty. A surprise phone call, a surprise breakfast in bed or a weekly game of chess may mean more than a commercial gift. The point is this: don't get entrapped by the occasion, but make the celebration one which shows your sensitivity to their needs.

Sometimes Parents' Days can be complicated by too many parents. When there are two grandfathers and a father involved, a family can get wrought up over sharing time with each person. If you need to divide your attention, talk about it with the people involved and plan ahead. Maybe you can celebrate Mother's and Father's Days, two Grandfather's Days and a Grandmother's Day.

Or maybe you can share your celebration with aging friends outside your family. Holidays, especially those which are highly commercialized,

have a very negative effect on those who don't feel a part of them – like many of our senior citizens in homes for the aged, nursing homes, and hospitals. Use Mother's or Father's Day to focus attention on them, to visit them or to begin a self-education program on their needs. You might enlist your family or a community group in the project as well.

See if your community has resources available for its senior citizens, and if it doesn't, see what your group can do to get something started. Make sure your local government is taking advantage of available programs and resources. Check into local employment practices and see if there is discrimination against those who are "too old" to get jobs while they have the mental and physical stamina to work.

You can also use the day to share your talents and skills with older people. You might help an older friend plant a garden or, if the work is too taxing for your friend, offer the time and tools to start it yourself. Your mutual harvest of goodwill will be plentiful.

If you've always wanted to learn quilting, woodworking, or how to fix a broken toaster, ask an older friend. They have decades of experience! (Consider that if your friend is 80, her memories extend back into the 1880s, since she will have heard stories from her parents and grandparents!)

If you'd rather focus on showing appreciation for your parents, don't rely on a greeting card to convey the message. Try a family or group discussion about what you appreciate in each other. If you live far away, make an audio or video tape and mail it. Or if talking is difficult, write a letter. Try to share what you feel today – tomorrow one of you may be gone. You might also ask children from an orphanage or foster home to join you and your parents for a holiday outing. Through programs such as Big Sisters or Big Brothers, you may pledge to start a regular program for sharing with parentless children the experiences your parents have given you.

A lot of mothers really are uncomfortable about Mother's Day because it's "mandatory." As an alternative, we suggest sending a gift or letter to your mother on your own birthday. She thinks about you that day; in fact, it probably means more to her than it does to you. The people we know who tried it said their mothers were touched and pleased. One woman saved her money all year and on her own 35th birthday sent her mother money – the mother needed money more than she needed anything else – except, of course, the love involved.

The Gray Panthers, a national action group of all different ages, works with a score of contemporary problems facing old persons – representing age realistically, housing, fighting mandatory retirement, transportation, health, schools for all ages, legislation, employment. Each affiliate in the Gray Panthers network is independent and determines its own needs and priorities. A gift to parents could be helping to set up a local chapter.

For Mother's Day, why not give a contribution to local women's centers, libraries, or to some organization in which your mother has shown interest or to which she has given her time?

– Aviva Cantor Zuckoff, New York, New York

Journaling and storytelling

Organize a workshop on keeping a journal. Suggest it to parents as a way of recording their thoughts and feelings as they grow older.

Ask parents to write about their childhood. Give them a notebook, a pen, and lots of encouragement. (Or provide them with a tape recorder and plenty of tape.) Stress how valuable a record of their memories is for them, for their families, and friends. This could evolve into a group workshop, "Celebrating Childhood." Many grandchildren would be happy to receive a story about their grandparent's growing-up years.

Mother's awareness program

Mother's Day need not be limited to celebration of mother, but can be a time to celebrate women. Many mothers bear a heavy load of family responsibility because they work outside the home and still continue to keep the lion's share of the family duties. Mother's Day is a good time to start a "working mother's awareness" program. If your family is one of these, think about how the family runs. Is there work-sharing by all family members, or does mother still do the organizing? Just because she can do jobs with ease when other members of the family cannot doesn't mean she wants to. Families tend to give up on helping because "it's so much easier for her." That is an excuse. Why not sit down with the family on Mother's Day and discuss sharing tasks and readjusting the work load more fairly?

Or start a project on women's rights. There are still discriminatory laws and traditions against women in jobs, getting credit, or owning property. Mother's Day might be a good day to start a women's rights study/action program – either in your own family or in a community group.

– Ellen Dittmer, Jackson, Mississippi

Memorial Day

A day to reflect on world peace

Memorial Day is a day to honor lives lost in all military conflicts. Originally, it was a day to commemorate those who lost their lives in the Civil War. According to one tradition, the day began when some Southern women chose May 30 to decorate the graves of both Confederate and Union soldiers killed in the Battle of Shiloh. More than remembering war dead, the day was to help bring reconciliation to a bitter, scarred, and sharply-divided nation.

Popular celebrations of Memorial Day tend to emphasize the importance of military strength and military preparedness. The day might be more appropriately observed as a time to resolve old hostilities and to work for peace, so that there will not be more war casualties.

Remembrance Day

Canadians honor the memory of their war dead on November 11. It is a legal holiday. Remembrance Day (known in Newfoundland as Armistice Day) commemorates the armistice that ended World War I at 11:00 a.m., on the 11th day of the 11th month in 1918.

In this century, Canadians have officially served in the South African War, World War I, World War II, and the Korean War. Since the inception of the United Nations, Canadians have been involved in peace-keeping missions throughout the world. On Remembrance Day, Canadians also remember women and men serving on those missions.

The Royal Canadian Legion sells poppies as symbols of the fallen and of hope, in recognition of John McCrae's famous poem, *In Flanders Fields*. (McCrae was a physician and poet from Ontario who served in World War I.) Throughout Canada, Girl Guides and Scouts, cadets, and military personnel participate in parades and memorial services.

Patriotic questioning

While it is our purpose to honor our war dead, do we instead glorify war?

What problems are solved because soldiers die? Is our world a better place because we are willing to give our young on the altars of national security?

What about those who are now filling graves for tomorrow's "peaceful" cemeteries? Are bereaved families comforted by the honor they receive?

What about war? Does it bring peace and life, or death, destruction, and empty ceremonies?

Children of War

This Memorial Day or Remembrance Day, let us celebrate life. Let us honor the survivors of war in our time – the children of war.

In 1986, the Children of War Tour brought young people who had grown up in war-torn areas of the world to the United States. Joined by North American teenagers, they toured cities across the country, telling their stories.

"Children have an ability to forgive and forget. We are less sure that we are absolutely right. Adults, who are sure they are absolutely right, they make war over their absolute rightness. Now, look at us, look at us. We represent the places in the world where men are killing each other and yet we are living together."
– Arn Chorn, Cambodia

"We believe that wars are not the solutions in our countries. We must learn to live together because we are the future. We've been learning from old people, and old people are teaching us to kill."

— Hector Recino, El Salvador

Said a 15-year-old boy to his Minneapolis hosts, "We don't call this a basement where you play ping-pong. We call it a bomb shelter."

— Marwan Najjar, West Beirut, Lebanon

Confirming the importance of the young people's mission, Nobel Prize winner Archbishop Desmond Tutu accompanied the children on their visit and told them: "When you go back home and walk down the street and people ask, 'Who is that?' You tell them, 'I am a sign of hope.'"

(The above quotes are taken from *Brave Bearers of Hope, the Children of War Tour* by Judith Thompson, Coordinator of the Children of War Program at the Religious Task Force, Mobilization for Survival, Brooklyn, New York. Used by permission.)

Celebrating Summer

Long days and vacations

In the Northern Hemisphere, summer arrives on June 20 or 21, when the summer solstice occurs. On that day the sun is high in the sky and there are more daylight hours than on any other day.

Traditionally, summer is the time to take vacations. Since ancient times people have recognized the importance of a change in routine to help restore minds, bodies, and spirits. While festivals and celebrations helped to provide them with brief changes in routine, vacations as we know them today were generally available only to the wealthy.

The 19th century labor movement is responsible for the widespread practice of vacations with pay, the only way most working people can afford to take time off from their jobs. With children free from school for a couple of months, vacations came to be associated with summertime.

While the idea of taking a vacation is still a privilege accorded to relatively few people in the world, the tourist business is now recognized as one of the world's largest industries. Although widely viewed as an ideal form of development for poor areas both at home and abroad, there are many questions about whether tourism aids or inhibits development.

Regardless of the time of year they are taken, vacations should be occasions for rest and renewal. But unless vacationers exercise care, they can be self-destructive and exploitative of others. Like other celebrations, vacations can be times to restore the human spirit without sacrificing concerns for other people and the environment.

Have a solstice party

Invite friends to celebrate the longest day of the year with a potluck dinner. Spend as much time as you can outdoors. Ahead of time, invite guests to research and share a known, little-known, or should-be-known fact about the sun or solstice. Invite them to write a letter or poem on the theme of summer, the longest day, or the sun. Seal it in an envelope and mail it back to each guest so that they receive it on December 21 or 22, the shortest day of the year.

What you shouldn't leave home without: Ethics and tourism in the developing world

Travel changed my life. My traditional Mississippi Delta background provided me with a set of stereotypes about life, people, and the world; and though I questioned those values at an early age, I learned to accept their teachings and adjusted my behavior accordingly. But my first trip away from home challenged all that. As a college student I spent a summer working for the United Methodists at a camp in Hawaii.

Everything was different – food, foliage, friends. And for the first time I met people prejudiced against me because I was white.

But I was enthralled by what I saw and felt, and this first experience of tourism became one of the most profound learning experiences of my life. The way I saw myself in the world was radically changed, so I decided to see more of the world in order to have a better understanding of my place in its great diversity. Throughout the rest of my formal schooling, I chose summer jobs with people whose culture was different from my own. After graduation, I became a travel agent – a job that enables me to help others have the broadening, life-changing experiences I have enjoyed since that first trip to Hawaii.

Tourism is now the largest industry in the world. To disassociate ourselves from it is almost impossible. But the more I learn about this international business, the more concerned I become about its ethics and the more I question the effect of this giant industry on our world. The ethics of tourism are highly undeveloped. Church offices and boards, with their huge travel budgets, are among the supporters of this industry, sometimes without questioning the industry into which they invest so much money. The truth is, tourism is no longer a frivolous, middle-class issue; it encompasses human rights and justice causes throughout the world. As supporters of the industry, individuals and institutions must take ethical questions into account.

What are these questions? Last year I attended a conference sponsored by the Center for Responsible Tourism in San Anselmo, California. There I heard reports from people who constantly deal with difficult issues forced upon their countries by the demands of tourism. In Tahiti, tourists consume precious water resources, making water levels sink dangerously low. Hawaiians live on beaches because of insufficient housing on islands sporting luxurious hotels. Puerto Rico's fishermen and land owners are displaced so that hotels and resorts can be built. And in the Philippines, along with other Asian countries, tourism for prostitution is big business.

Stories about tourism's abuses seem endless. Why do these things happen? An important reason is that poor nations are encouraged by world banking institutions to promote tourism as a way out of poverty. Now, however, many countries realize that profits from tourism go out of their countries, back to outside investors. As host countries, they are left with their lands defaced, their people put into degrading roles, and their way of life changed forever.

The Ecumenical Coalition on Third World Tourism was formed in response to these burdening concerns. This group has developed an important concept for responsible tourism: a code of ethics for tourists, helping guests to be respectful and gracious in their visits to other countries.

While tourism presents many problems, the industry also provides an opportunity for people from different cultures to meet – crossing political, social, and religious barriers. However, in order for this human encounter to take place, those of us who travel must be willing to treat people with dignity. While at seminary, I wrote a paper comparing the influx of northerners in the South after the Civil War to U.S. intervention in Central America. I made that comparison to help people understand the powerlessness and frustration felt by citizens in other countries when touring Americans fail to treat them with respect.

This past year I had the opportunity to help a youth group in San Anselmo, California, make their travel plans for a work project in Jamaica. The group was very careful to make sure all Jamaicans who helped with arrangements for the group were adequately compensated. In addition, a group of Jamaican young people were invited to work alongside the young people from California. Together they created a much-needed playground for the village. Tourists in this instance treated hosts with complete dignity, and the experience for everybody was very fulfilling.

A number of organizations are

helping travel consumers meet recreational and educational needs in ways that are not dehumanizing to people in host countries. Among them: Contours in Thailand, and the Center for Responsible Tourism in California.

– Terre Balof, Atlanta, Georgia

A code of ethics for tourists

1. Travel in a spirit of humility and with a genuine desire to meet and talk with local people.
2. Be aware of the feelings of the local people to prevent what might be offensive behavior. Photographers, particularly, must be respectful of subjects.
3. Cultivate the habit of listening and observing, rather than merely hearing or seeing.
4. Realize that other people may have concepts of time and thought patterns which are very different from yours – not inferior, only different.
5. Instead of seeing only the "beach paradise," discover the richness of another culture and way of life.
6. Get acquainted with local customs and respect them.
7. Rather than knowing all the answers, cultivate the habit of listening.
8. Remember that you are only one among many visitors. Do not expect special privileges.
9. If you want a "home away from home," why bother traveling?
10. As you shop and bargain, remember the poorest merchant will give up profit rather than dignity.
11. Make no promises to new, local friends that you cannot implement.
12. Spend time reflecting on your daily experiences in order to deepen your understanding. What enriches you may be robbing others.

– The Christian Conference of Asia

Take a just holiday

Check out your local library and bookstore shelves for books about eco-tours and learning tours. Ask youth hostels, elderhostels, and universities if they can direct you to low-impact vacation ideas. They may have information about working holidays such as the Los Niños vacation described above, or know of courses you can study in other countries in subjects such as archaeology, biology, justice issues, language, or art.

Consider a walking vacation. That's right, your own two little feet. Or maybe cycling or canoeing. Think of the ozone you'll save!

You may also want to look into a house-swapping holiday where you exchange your home and vehicle with people in another country. Certainly less expensive than staying in a hotel, and drier than camping, house-swapping has the advantage of placing you in an established community, rather than in a tourist area where most of the people you meet are other tourists.

One organization which invites people to visit other countries and stay with families is SERVAS International. This organization's purpose is to build world peace on a one-to-one basis. It is nonprofit, interracial, and interfaith. It has consultative status as a non-governmental organization in the United Nations.

Finally, you may take a "vacation" by staying home and hosting a student or other traveler from afar. Take a look at your world through their eyes. You may be surprised at how they see you and your community. Best of all, you have the opportunity to make a new friend. High schools, universities and colleges, as well as community service groups and religious groups often have needs for host families.

National Birthdays

Canada Day

Canada Day, the principal national holiday, celebrates the creation of the Dominion of Canada on July 1, 1867. This civic holiday has also been known as Dominion Day, Confederation Day, and simply, July the First.

From the Atlantic to the Pacific to the Arctic Oceans, Canadians in 10 provinces and 2 territories celebrate with parades, picnics, giant birthday cakes, and fireworks. It has also become an important day for welcoming new Canadians from around the world in public ceremonies where people are sworn in as new citizens.

Celebrate the holiday by entering an Earth-oriented, people-powered float in your local parade. Take time to reflect on citizens of the country who do not feel celebratory on this day. If you are on your way to a picnic, stop first and make a donation to the food bank.

Independence Day

On July 4, 1776, the Continental Congress adopted the Declaration of Independence. The anniversary of that event, Independence Day, is regarded as the birthday of the United States.

Afro-American orator and editor Frederick Douglass once spoke for slaves and other minorities who did not experience the freedom and justice proclaimed in the Declaration:

"What to the American slave is

your Fourth of July? I answer, a day that reveals to him more than all other days of the year the gross injustice to which he is the constant victim. To him your celebration is a sham; your boasted liberty an unholy license..."

Let Douglass's statement be a reminder that while the creation of the United States is unique, it is also a very human and imperfect creation. To disregard the latter is to negate that uniqueness. An alternative celebration may be informed by two considerations. First, unlimited loyalty is "due only to God, not the nation." Second, legitimate patriotism requires that the nation be continually called to live out its vision of "liberty and justice for all."

What if?

In his article for *The Silver City Record* in Kansas City, Terry Woodbury laments the use of noisy, dangerous firecrackers to celebrate freedom. To him, it is nonsensical. After pausing for a moment's reflection, it's only surprising that hundreds of other writers aren't saying the same thing.

What if, Woodbury writes, our public celebrations were organized by librarians, history teachers, museum directors, and "...our refugee neighbors who know first hand freedom's high price? What if, for one day, radio stations played only songs of protest, of freedom, or of cour-

age, of believing in something enough to die for it – just like we hear Christmas carols all day December 25? What if churches and schools dramatized the lives of individuals whose faith and courage have shaped our national character?"

What if the only explosions we heard were explosions of dance, drama, music, and storytelling?

Celebrate by welcoming strangers

The United States is a nation of foreigners. "Give me your tired, your poor, your huddled masses yearning to breathe free," reads the inscription on the Statue of Liberty. Safe harbor for those seeking asylum is a national ideal worth recalling on the Fourth of July.

Are there too many people taking advantage of this offer? Some think so. According to some, "we are losing control of our borders." This is not a new opinion. King George tried unsuccessfully to restrict immigration to the colonies. His action prompted one of the grievances leveled against British rule in the Declaration of Independence.

Actually, we have never had control of our borders. If the First Nations had controlled their borders, most of us would not be here. Perhaps we are afraid that newcomers will treat us like our ancestors treated Native Americans.

Knowing what to do about foreigners in need of refuge is not easy. The social and economic implications of immigration are complex, both for citizens already here, and for those who come from abroad. But this country's ideal for justice for all should be protected as a national goal.

With regard to those who are already here, many citizens' and religious groups recognize their responsibility and persevere in a climate which sometimes questions the presence of refugees and new immigrants, especially if they are poor.

Celebrate this Independence Day by recalling why waves of immigrants have come to North America year after year for more than 500 years. Compare the reasons people are coming today. Discover all you can about this complex problem. But don't stop there. Find practical ways to welcome and assist those who are already here. There are many opportunities to teach English as a second language, for example, or to assist children who need a "buddy" in school for one-on-one volunteer tutoring.

Hiroshima Day

Remembering the past for the sake of peace

Hiroshima Day commemorates the first use of nuclear weapons on August 6, 1945. Peace Day, as it is sometimes called, recalls the insight of Mahatma Gandhi, who said that nuclear weapons would make peace a necessity.

The bomb that fell on Hiroshima killed more than 100,000 people instantly. Three days later, another 50,000 died when a second bomb was dropped on Nagasaki. Tens of thousands died more slowly from radiation poisoning. Survivors, their children, and grandchildren continue to be affected.

Although the events behind this observance are difficult to recall, the possibility that nuclear weapons might be used again is making this day an important time for people all over the world to say "never again!"

Sadako and the Thousand Paper Cranes

A little girl who loved to run like the wind died when she was 13 years old. She died because the bomb that dropped on Hiroshima caused her to contract radiation-induced leukemia. Her name was Sadako Sasaki.

During her illness, Sadako heard of a legend that says that cranes live for 1,000 years, and that if a person could fold 1,000 origami paper cranes, a wish would be granted. In her sick bed, Sadako began folding colorful paper cranes of hope. When she had completed 644, she died. Her friends completed the task for her, and Sadako was buried with 1,000 cranes.

Today, a monument stands in Hiroshima Peace Park. It is a statue of Sadako, the brave young girl who did not stop hoping. At the base of the statue, there is an inscription:

> This is our cry,
> This is our prayer,
> Peace in the world.

Middlebury, Indiana, to Hiroshima, Japan

Students, teachers, administrators, aides, and media center personnel made it happen – from Middlebury, Indiana to Hiroshima, Japan! Highlight of the year for Jefferson, Middlebury, and York Elementary School media centers was the story, project, and journey of the paper cranes.

It all began with a story hour featuring *Sadako and the Thousand Paper Cranes*. Students and teachers at the three Middlebury elementary schools were challenged by this moving story of Sadako's faith and courage and her friends' dedication to peace. Each school adopted an origami project, the art of Japanese paper folding, honoring Sadako by reenacting her story, sharing their

concerns about nuclear war, and their hopes for world friendship and peace.

At each school, students worked hard to reach their goal of folding 1,000 gold and silver paper cranes which were displayed for several weeks as mobiles in the media centers. Most students folded at least one crane; some folded many more to achieve the objective. Principals, teachers, and parents also lent their skill and support.

Plans were made to send the completed cranes by a nine-year-old girl and her six-year-old brother who would be spending the summer with their aunt, a former community teacher now living in Tokyo. Included in each school's carefully-packed box was a photo of the mobile as displayed in the media center with the following laminated message:

> To: Children's Peace Monument
>   Peace Park Hiroshima, Japan
> To honor Sadako Sasaki and to
> share our hopes for peace in
> the world.

The experience of taking the cranes to Hiroshima's Peace Park was described in a letter by their teacher friend to the children of Middlebury: "Your 3,000 paper cranes are at home now under the statue of Sadako Sasaki in Hiroshima's Peace Park. We went straight to the Peace Park and unpacked the beautiful, shiny cranes. We tied each thousand together, attaching the message from each school. A reporter from Hiroshima's Chugoku newspaper asked questions and took lots of pictures. Thousands and thousands of paper cranes were laid carefully around the monument. What a beautiful sight – rainbow colors, patterned origami, silver and gold – all together, made in hopes of peace."

From this activity came rewarding experiences in teaching, learning and teamwork. In many classrooms, Japanese culture and folklore were featured, with projects in haiku poetry and in other origami projects. Besides learning to work together, many students experienced a memorable and positive way to deal with the bombing of Hiroshima. On the 40th anniversary of the bombing, 3,000 cranes from the three Middlebury elementary schools made their dramatic plea for peace.

– Elizabeth Johnson, Media Coordinator,
Middlebury, Indiana

Remembering and hoping

On Hiroshima Day, join others in peaceful remembrances. Many antinuclear and peace groups hold a special event on this day. Search out children's books which tell Sadako's story. Read the story to someone you love. If your community or school library does not have a copy, consider buying one for them as a gift to your whole community.

September
October
November
December

Labor Day

This day to recognize organized labor is a legal holiday observed throughout Canada and the United States on the first Monday in September. The first parades and rallies to celebrate the contribution of organized labor in Ontario were held in 1872.

Peter J. McGuire, president and founder of the United Brotherhood of Carpenters and Joiners, instituted Labor Day to recognize the contributions of laborers and to acknowledge the role unions have played in protecting workers from exploitation. Labor Day has been celebrated in the U.S. since 1882.

In Europe, Labor Day has been celebrated since 1889, and is celebrated on May first. North Americans have traditionally celebrated in September.

Labor Day weekend has become a time for final outings and vacations before students return to school. Leisure activities are particularly appropriate since paid holidays and vacations are possible, in large part, because of the labor movement. Labor Day provides a chance to learn more about the productive history of the labor movement as well as its recent history of decline. This is a day to be grateful for those who labor. It is also a day to be more aware of those who want to work but remain jobless.

(See also **May Day**.)

Autumn begins

Although Labor Day marks the end of summer social activities, autumn officially begins on September 22 or 23, when the autumnal equinox occurs. On this day, like the vernal equinox which marks the beginning of spring, the sun appears directly above the equator.

Learn about the changing seasons. Teach children – with a walk in a park, in the back yard, or out in the country – about what happens in nature. In areas with distinct seasons, autumn is the time when nature prepares for winter: flowers die, trees lose their leaves, animals develop warmer coats.

Rosh Hashanah

Jewish New Year

Rosh Hashanah, celebrated on the first day of the lunar month of Tishri, falls sometime in September or October. In contrast to the frivolity associated with many New Year's Day celebrations, Rosh Hashanah, or Jewish New Year, is a solemn holiday. On that sacred day, according to Jewish tradition, the world is created anew and set right by God's power. Ancient ritual for worship dictates that the shofar, a ram's horn, be blown to call the faithful to purify themselves. Those who are not totally right with God and their fellow humans have ten days, the Days of Awe, before Yom Kippur to make reparations through fasting, prayer, penitence, and righting wrongs.

Yom Kippur

Day of Atonement

Yom Kippur, Judaism's highest holy day, is held in such high regard that it is known as "a Sabbath of Sabbaths." According to tradition, on this day, Moses descended from Mount Sinai with the Ten Commandments after God forgave the Israelites for worshiping the golden calf.

Yom Kippur is a day of strict fasting for everyone except children and sick people. No business is transacted and normal routines are suspended. The entire day is devoted to self-examination and repentance.

Atonement themes found in scripture are read on that day: Leviticus 16, Numbers 29:7–11, Isaiah 57:14–58:14, and finally, the Book of Jonah. When Yom Kippur was observed in the Temple in Jerusalem, the emphasis was on seeking forgiveness from God through the mediation of the High Priest. Since the destruction of the Temple, the emphasis is on praying directly to God for forgiveness.

Yom Kippur ends with the longest and loudest cry of the ancient shofar (ram's horn), sounding a note of hope for the new year. Almost another year goes by before the shofar is heard in the synagogue again.

Both the personal and communal goal of the ten days of purification is to begin the new year in harmony with God. A Jewish legend says, "It is out of kindness toward his creatures that the Lord remembers them year after year on Rosh Hashanah, that their sins may not grow too numerous... [Otherwise] their sins would grow to such an extent as to doom the world, God forbid. So this revered day assures the world of survival."

At home for Yom Kippur

In addition to recognizing that this is Judaism's most important holy day, it is also a good day to recall the common roots of modern Judaism and Christianity. Read and discuss Isaiah 57 and 58, scriptures that are immensely important for both traditions.

Sukkot

Festival of Booths

The Festival of Booths is celebrated for eight days beginning with the 15th day of the lunar month of Tishri, 15 days after Rosh Hashanah and five days after Yom Kippur. Originally a harvest festival, this day is increasingly being observed by synagogues as a time to share food with those who need it. The custom at Sukkot is to build and live in a hut made of branches and boughs in order to recall times of Jewish homelessness and uncertainty (Leviticus 23:42–43). Sukkot also marks the end of the solemn period of the high holy days.

At home for Sukkot

Recall times of homelessness and uncertainty in your family history. Remember those who are homeless on this day – those in refugee camps or on city streets. If you are not already doing so, consider joining the effort of those working with homeless people and other refugees.

Thanksgiving

Harvest festivals have been a part of human history since the beginning of agriculture. With harvesting completed and food stored away for the winter months, those early tillers of the soil celebrated the results of their labor. They also recognized their dependence on elements and forces beyond their efforts that made harvest possible.

Ancient cultures held harvest festivals in honor of the Earth Mother; the Greeks honored Demeter, and the Romans Ceres. Jews celebrated harvest in several periods throughout the year. In medieval times, many Europeans observed the Feast of St. Martin of Tours on November 11, and harvest home celebrations began with the reign of James I in England. Today, Thanksgiving Day is observed on the second Monday of October in Canada, while in the United States it is on the fourth Thursday of November.

Obviously, the first thanksgiving rituals and celebrations were varied. The rituals of Inuit living on the Arctic coast differ from the Pueblo people in New Mexico. In Canada, one of the first observances of non-native people was in 1578, when Martin Frobisher celebrated in the eastern Arctic. In the U.S.A., the first non-native celebration was by English settlers in what is now Virginia in December 1619. Their charter required that their arrival date be observed yearly as a day of thanksgiving to God.

Most American people associate the "first" Thanksgiving with the Pilgrims at Plymouth. Escaping religious persecution in Europe, these colonists attempted to reach the Virginia colony. Their 67-day voyage ended instead at Cape Cod's Provincetown Harbor on November 11, 1620. At a recently vacated Indian settlement, they discovered corn set aside for spring planting. Already on a starvation diet, they were more concerned about their immediate need for food than for anyone's future crop, so they took 10 bushels of the Indian's seed corn in order to survive the winter.

In the summer of 1621, less than a year after their arrival and after a winter when half of the colonists died, hope was renewed by a good corn crop. Squanto, a Patuxet Indian, helped the colonists during that first winter and spring, showing them how to prepare the fields and plant corn. He acted as go-between for the newcomers and tribes of First Nations peoples, and helped arrange the pact that allowed them all to live in peace.

The first corn harvest brought rejoicing, and Governor William Bradford decreed that a three-day feast be held. Chief Massasoit was invited to share the celebration. Chief Massasoit and 90 people joined in, probably to celebrate their traditional harvest feast. They brought five deer to add to the Pilgrims' collection of wild geese, ducks, lobsters, eels, clams, oysters, fish, berries, biscuits, breads, corn cooked in a variety of ways, and puddings of cornmeal and molasses. Sweet strong wine from wild grapes supplemented the feast.

Women cooked, children played, men showed off their marksmanship with firearms and bows and arrows. The feast lasted for days, with little attention to religious services. Some believe that the Pilgrims chose to keep their harvest festival secular because they disapproved of mingling religious and secular celebrations. It seems to have been a one-time occasion, with no thought to future celebrations.

Serious questions have been raised about the nature and purpose of Thanksgiving Day observances in the subsequent 100 years. William B. Newell, a Penobscot Indian and former chairman of the anthropology department at the University of Connecticut, says that the "first" official Thanksgiving Day was proclaimed by the Governor of Massachusetts Bay Colony in 1637 to celebrate the massacre of 700 Indian men, women, and children at their annual Green Corn Dance (their Thanksgiving). For the next 100 years, says Newell, "every Thanksgiving day ordained by a governor was to honor a bloody victory thanking God for the battle won."

In November, 1787, President Washington issued a proclamation for a day of thanks. In the same year, the Protestant Episcopal Church announced the first Thursday in November would be a regular yearly day for giving thanks, "unless another day be appointed by the civil authorities." But for many years afterward there was no regular national Thanksgiving Day in the United States.

In 1863, during the darkest days of the Civil War, President Lincoln proclaimed Thanksgiving a national observance. That he did so was largely due to a campaign by Sarah Josepha Hale, the editor of *Godey's Lady's Book*, the most widely circulated women's magazine in the late 19th century. For nearly 40 years, Hale publicly promoted the idea of

a national Thanksgiving. Even in the midst of civil war, she urged that the celebration not be austere. Fasting, she warned in her magazine, only pointed to the terrible "condition of the country and the deeds of men," while feasting exalted God and the culinary prowess of women.

Each year, for the next 75 years, the president proclaimed that Thanksgiving Day should be celebrated on the last Thursday of November. In 1939, President Roosevelt set it one week earlier; he wanted to help business by lengthening the Christmas shopping season. Finally, however, Congress ruled that after 1942, Thanksgiving would be observed on the fourth Thursday of November and would be a legal federal holiday.

In Canada, too, the day jumped around at first. In 1879 it was celebrated November 6. It was celebrated November 11 in conjunction with Armistice Day, too. It was not until 1957 that Parliament declared the second Monday in October as the national holiday for observance. Premier Drury of Ontario lamented that what should have been a day of consideration for farmers, was instead being dictated and celebrated for the convenience of urban people. Drury said the date was too early in the year. Thanksgiving is sometimes "celebrated" by farmers who are still bringing in their harvest.

According to *The Canadian Encyclopedia*, Canadian Thanksgiving celebrations draw on three traditions:
1. Harvest celebrations in European peasant societies (where the symbol of the cornucopia originated).
2. Formal observances, such as the one celebrated by Martin Frobisher.
3. The Pilgrims' celebration of their first harvest in Massachusetts in 1621 (where the tradition of the turkey, squash and pumpkins originated). The Pilgrim's tradition was taken north by immigrants in the 1750s.

Observations

If celebrations give voice to the ideals by which we are trying to live, how should we observe Thanksgiving? It may be easier to think first of how we ought not observe it.

Thanksgiving should not be a day for thanking God for affluence while others go hungry. The notion that it is God who gives affluence to some and poverty to many not only ignores the role humans have played in arranging patterns of affluence and poverty but flies in the face of the God of love and justice. Nor should it be a time to claim God's special blessing on any nation. As a minority religious group, the Pilgrims knew only too well the problems that occur when the interests of God and nation are identified by a dominant religious group.

Thanksgiving should also not be an occasion to romanticize the cooperation between "the Indians" and the settlers, unless to recall in sorrow the subsequent centuries' genocide of Native Americans. Finally, Thanksgiving should not be a day of rest before the two largest shopping days of the year, when giving thanks is swept out the back door so Christmas commercialism can come in the front.

As a day that gives voice to our highest ideals, Thanksgiving can be a time to remember with gratitude and humility that we alone are not responsible for whatever bounty is in our lives. It can be a time to confess that part of our bounty has come at the expense of others, including Native Americans, slaves, farm workers, and hosts of others we do not even know. It can also be a time to share what we have with others, and include in our celebrations those who would otherwise be alone.

Finally, Thanksgiving can be a time to commit ourselves to creating a world where hungry children are fed, the homeless are provided with shelter, and those who suffer discrimination because of race, sex, religion, or age are respected.

Five grains of corn

In early New England, at Thanksgiving time it was customary to place five grains of corn at every plate. This served as a reminder of those stern days in the first winter when the Pilgrims' food was so depleted that only five grains of corn were rationed to each individual at a time. The Pilgrims wanted their children to remember the sacrifices, the sufferings, the hardships which made possible the settlement of a free people in a free land. They did not want their descendants to forget that on the day on which their ration was reduced to five grains of corn only seven healthy colonists remained to nurse the sick, and nearly half their number already lay in that windswept graveyard on the hill.

– Plymouth Congregational U.C.C., Des Moines, Iowa

Thanksgiving in the woods

Thanksgiving has always been a special time for my family in Suwanee, Florida. Twenty-five years ago, along with various relatives, we began celebrating Thanksgiving in the woods because our homes were too small to include everyone. My father, brother, and other men in the family enjoyed hunting after the crops were harvested. Since they were camping in the woods, this seemed to be the place to meet for our celebration.

Some years there was so much pain in our lives that attempting to celebrate Thanksgiving seemed a farce. I particularly remember the year my husband and I separated. From miles away my mother was trying to comfort me with scripture and song, all to no avail. But Thanksgiving was a glorious day with a vibrant blue sky and warm weather so, as usual, we ate outside. All the people who loved me most were there to affirm that life goes on, even in the midst of the deepest pain.

Then came the year we celebrated without my father, who had helped to start the tradition. As we gathered for the meal, our sense of loss at his death was tremendous and giving thanks was difficult. However, we gave thanks for the memories that are left to us, for the father who never failed to give thanks, and for the many ways that God meets our needs and cares for us. We celebrated in the way we have grown to love – in the woods with the sound of rushing water nearby, the smell of outdoor fires, dogs barking, birds singing, and people laughing and talking – remembering the Creator who made us all.

– Kay Deen Mann, Decatur, Georgia

Thanksgiving: Responsibilities of abundance

If celebrations are symbolic vehicles for nurturing the human spirit, for reaffirming that which is lasting in life, then they need to reflect in contemporary form the original spirit and values of the founding event. For Thanksgiving to look like that it would have to "celebrate Native Americans and the elimination of world hunger." This would naturally require considerable homework: what caused the Native American to become an oppressed people in their homeland, and what are the root causes of hunger which are planted in the soil of our society?

It would cause us to redefine the responsibilities of abundance. So long as Thanksgiving continues to be distorted from its original values we can expect Native Americans and the world's hungry to view it with cynicism.

Hunger

The extent of hunger in North America and abroad has been kept from public view because the hungry tend to be silent, unobtrusive, and hidden away in ghettos or remote rural areas. Only recently has the magnitude of world hunger caught the attention of more than a few. The UN Food and Agriculture Organization tells us millions in the world are hungry. Millions of children, millions of women, millions of men. Many of our own citizens lack the necessary income to provide a nutritionally adequate diet. Many children go to school hungry. Food banks and community pantries are now an established part of the North American landscape. And the future hardly looks bright.

Periodically, hunger can be blamed on drought, skyrocketing grain and petroleum prices, or a shrinking world grain supply. However, overall, world harvests have improved, and grain prices are lower. Yet millions still starve or live stunted, malnourished lives.

The National Council of Churches has named unjust economic systems as an underlying cause of hunger in the world. This includes the neocolonialism fostered by our transnational companies which, when unregulated by government or the host country, tend to cost the development process more than they benefit. A second underlying cause is insufficient food production in developing countries, caused by an influx of capital-intensive systems of agriculture and the trend to develop one product for export rather than balanced food production for domestic use. A third factor is rapid population growth, and a fourth is the consumption patterns of the rich, which make heavy demands on the world's output.

The development of goals which produce personal, social, economic, and political justice – agricultural policies which provide farmers production incentives and which protect them from the often disastrous results of over-production; more ecologically-sound agricultural practices and a goal of domestic self-sufficiency for food production; and the simplification of the North American lifestyle – could help.

The urgency of the world hunger problem is stirring many to action. If the rich of the world are going to provide any more than "Band-Aids" for this serious illness, there must be a more concerted effort from institutions to bring about action. Thanksgiving, with its bounty of food for the privileged, is the ideal time to start consciousness-raising efforts and actions on behalf of the hungry and undernourished.

Feasting has its place in our lives. Few of us are called to unrelenting austerity, and God's bounty is certainly worth celebrating. We don't want to recommend that joyous banqueting be removed from our lives, but that we look at it in a different way. At Thanksgiving, we tend to make a ritual of feeding ourselves and our friends to the point of gluttony, and we only remember the world's hungry in an abstract way. New traditions at this time could serve not only to remind us of our heritage and abundance, but also provide direct action to help those who do not have the advantages we have.

First United Methodist Church in Rule, Texas, lived out a parable. Several weeks before Thanksgiving, their pastor gave each person a certain amount of money – five dollars to one, two dollars to another, etc. She asked them to serve as stewards and see what they could do with that money for the church. The report on Thanksgiving Day was of many projects to help people, to raise money for the church, and to enhance church life; and the congregation learned a new dimension to stewardship.

Individually and as families

1. Extend your family by inviting one or more people who would be alone to share your dinner. Consider especially those who seem unlovely and unloved.

2. Eat simply, or even fast, on Thanksgiving Day. You could use the time you would have spent preparing and eating a large meal in prayers of thanksgiving and intercession. Send what you would normally have spent for dinner to a local hunger pantry or project.

As a congregation

1. Hold a church family dinner. Invite church families to bring their Thanksgiving dinner to share with those who are alone or needy. In one community, several churches got together and held a free, all-day feast (10:00 a.m.–10:00 p.m.), for those in need. Church members agreed to provide food, fellowship, and various kinds of activities (hymn sings, inspirational talks, films, prayer vigils) throughout the day. Radio publicity and posters brought in many who otherwise would have had little to be thankful for.

2. Several congregations hold "Fastathons" over Thanksgiving. Members ask friends to sponsor them at 10 cents to 25 cents per

hour, and join others who are fasting in the church fellowship hall from suppertime Wednesday through suppertime Thursday. (Some bring sleeping bags, others go home to sleep.)

During this fast, films are shown, magazines and books are available, and simulation games are played to teach hunger facts. Worship services, prayer vigils, and Bible studies focus on God's concern for the world's poor. Money raised is donated to projects designed to help people help themselves. Each "Fastathon" concludes with a community supper of rice and tea, and Communion.

– Patti Sprinkle, St. Petersburg, Florida

Action ideas

The following actions are useful in getting people's attention and beginning the education process. Lifestyle change begins with commitment, study, and experimentation, and it takes a good year to bring into effect. Structural change is hard for an individual to bring about so we urge you to join your local hunger coalition to get the most from your efforts.

About eight weeks before Thanksgiving, I preached a sermon on worldwide hunger and suggested that the families of the church establish a "poor meal" as a weekly family ritual. One night a week the family would eat a very inexpensive meal without dessert and put the money saved in a container. The families were to choose a container that would be placed on the table. (We used such things as coffee cans and oatmeal boxes.) During the eight weeks, I suggested scriptural texts and questions on hunger for the families to consider on the night they ate their "poor meal."

Then, on our Thanksgiving Eve worship service, the people came forward as family units and placed their containers on the altar. This was a very moving experience for us as a congregation. Something that had become a real part of our daily lives served as a focus for the worship event.

– Kerry L. Stoltzfus, Erin Presbyterian Church, Knoxville, Tennessee

Consider using the Thanksgiving season as a time to start a voluntary simplicity study-action project which would end with an alternative Christmas campaign. (Or maybe not end at all!)

Cooperation

We had a number of people who were new to the community and without ties to family and friends here. So several men in the church volunteered to cook turkey for Thanksgiving for these people. One woman made a list of things to bring and filled in names of persons willing to bake a pie or bring a vegetable. Many of us were skeptical about how well it would come off, but about two weeks before the holiday approximately 35 people had signed up. We ended up with 60. One of the former ministers of the church came back with his family, so this became a way that they could share in the giving of thanks. While many single people showed up, a surprising number of families did too. Mothers escaped the labor of slaving all day in the kitchen for one big orgy, followed by endless dishwashing while the men watched football.

Before and after the meal, there were puzzles, games, and discussion starters. Someone was going to bring a television, but fortunately it was broken, so all of us escaped the trappings of the "boob-tube." After the dinner, the price of the meal was announced and people were asked to donate about a dollar if they could.

It was a real success. Another event was planned for New Year's Day and people are thinking about it for this year again. While the idea is simple, it provided a real opportunity for people without a place to celebrate Thanksgiving and an alternative for those traditionally trapped by "family."

– Rev. Jerry Haas, Pacific Beach United Methodist Church, San Diego, California

Soup kitchen

In terms of specific Thanksgiving events, we have done basically the same thing each year. The night before, we have a liturgy in the soup kitchen after which we prepare the food for the following day.

On Thanksgiving itself, we serve a regular dinner: turkey, potatoes, dressing, green vegetables, juice and desserts to about 300 people – not quite a small family gathering! We get an excellent response from all kinds of people. That evening at the hospitality/pre-trial house, there is again a large dinner (for about 50) for the people who live with us, as well as for members of the community.

I know that some people have begun a tradition of fasting on Thanksgiving, especially because of the situation of world hunger. I believe it is an admirable response, but because of the work we do, and the kind of people we deal with, we feel that we should feast on that one day, and that the poor deserve the best kinds of food.

Individuals in the community have taken part in feasts of different kinds, vigiling, and so on for people who wish to share their food with the poor. One thing of importance that I would like to emphasize is that while Thanksgiving is a day when we do think of food, it is important that we spend some time on this day attempting to regain a whole theology of food, about the kinds of food we eat, and why we eat them. Thanksgiving should just be a beginning for that kind of reflection.

– Rachelle Linner, Community for Creative Non-Violence, Washington, D.C.

Native foods

As an alternative way to celebrate Thanksgiving, I forward a suggestion from a Native American member of the Panel of American Women. Hold a congregational dinner featuring native dishes. Give recognition for the contributions that Indians made to the beginning of the Thanksgiving tradition. Such a program, of course, would be faithful to the truth in historical facts.

– Shirley Morantz, Executive Secretary Panel of American Women, Kansas City, Missouri

Native Americans – suggestions for action

- Become as well acquainted as possible with the conditions of First Nations peoples.
- Get acquainted with the tribes in your area – and in your state, province or territory. Are there reservations nearby? Are there people off the reservation living in your community? What are their particular needs? Gifts? Concerns? Their place in society? Are there cases of injustice that need to be dealt with?
- If you are a church or synagogue member, how does your congregation relate to native peoples? Is there any local involvement in native affairs? Does your religious community have any national program? Is there a social action committee dealing with native concerns?
- Have you corresponded with your government officials about First Nations issues?
- What is your local newspaper doing? Does it continue stereotypes about native peoples? Does it feature native writers? Is the native community presented positively or negatively?
- Does your television station carry programs that dehumanize or stereotype native peoples? What can you do to change this?
- What do the children learn in the local schools about native peoples, about history from the perspective of First Nations? Are they still studying "How the West Was Won," or have they heard "How the West Was Lost"?
- Make a study of the textbooks used in your local schools. How are spiritual practices presented? Do the texts make it sound as if native people only "lived," or do students have a chance to learn about native peoples living today?
- Examine the resources in your local libraries. Help the librarian become aware of the problem. Suggest books written by native peoples and ask the librarian to subscribe to native periodicals.
- Consider the possibility of forming a study and support committee to involve local and regional people in the native struggle. In many places there are local and

regional issues on which to focus; in other places national issues may be the focus.

- If you are a member of a church, it may have been involved in running residential schools for native children. Find out if your denomination has issued an apology for damage done to families, individuals, and the culture. If it has not, urge it to do so as a first step in recognizing past injustices. The apology needs to be followed by reconciliation and healing.

– Sources: Fellowship of Reconciliation, Nyack, New York, and The Human Rights and Aboriginal Justice Program Office, United Church of Canada

As with most urgent issues of contemporary interest, book and film resources on world hunger and native Americans are nearly boundless. Contact a church, your local library, a university offering Aboriginal programs, or an Indian Friendship Center for help.

World Food Day

On October 16, in the midst of the traditional harvest season, more than 150 nations observe World Food Day. Established by the United Nations in 1980, its purpose is to mobilize concern about the systemic dimensions of food production, food distribution, and world hunger.

In Canada, World Food Day falls around Thanksgiving. Many people combine this sobering commemoration with their traditional or alternative observance of Thanksgiving.

Resolution on world hunger

The Session of Hamilton Union Church adopted and promoted the following resolution within their congregation:

Because of our deep concern for the many, many starving people in the world and the many more who are malnourished while a majority of us in the United States and other affluent countries eat more than we should, your Session urges the members of the congregation to do some or all of the following:

- Have at least one meatless day a week, thereby saving several pounds of grain.
- Have at least one meatless day a week and periodically send the amount of money you would have spent on meat to Church World Service.
- Of your total meat consumption, replace some of the beef, veal, and pork with poultry. Poultry meat takes less grain to produce.
- Eat smaller portions of meat.
- Eat meat once a day if you are

in the habit of having it more often.

- When you eat in a restaurant, ask the server to bring only the amount you think you can eat since whatever food you leave will be thrown out.
- Send as large a contribution as you can to Church World Service as an expression of gratitude that you have enough to eat.
- Write to your congressman, senators, and the president urging that the government do all within its power, compatible with price stability in the U.S., to make food available to the hungry.
- Secure and read a copy of *Diet for a Small Planet* by Frances Moore Lappé.
   – The Session of Hamilton Union Church

Welcome to the Hunger Restaurant!

We did something about hunger! We developed the idea of the Hunger Restaurant. It's a fairly simple project, and any group can do it. What is a Hunger Restaurant?

First, set up a room in the church as a restaurant. Card tables with checkered tablecloths and candles in bottles do a nice job of setting the atmosphere. Regular menus are used. Host, waiters, and waitresses are secured. You even need a couple of cooks. But don't worry, the cooks need not be experts.

The next step is to invite people to your Hunger Restaurant. Your advertising should inform people that it will be an educational experience. It will help hungry people, and a meal will be served. When the people arrive, they are greeted and taken to a table.

A waitress brings in a glass of water and a menu which includes many fine selections at various prices. A little later, orders are taken.

Now the educational experience begins. On two walls, slides are shown, depicting hunger around the world. They are flashed rapidly, so as to create a special effect. On tape, a distant drum beats, which helps us to understand and remember that one person dies from hunger for each beat of the drum. The place mats show pictures of starvation and give hunger information. A person who has experienced hunger, or visited hungry people, shares a short presentation. Hunger information is passed out.

Now we are ready to serve the food. Regardless of what people have ordered, they receive one cup of cooked rice. When it is served, the guests are told that millions of people will receive less food than this for the whole day. As they eat the rice, the hunger pictures continue to flash on the walls. Brief interviews (or news items) about hunger interrupt the taped background music.

After dinner, the bill is prepared

according to the price of the food ordered. When the bill is presented, the guest is told that this is the total amount due, had they received what they ordered. The guest is then invited to pay that amount, or give a portion of it to help feed the hungry world.

The whole experience takes less than two hours. Education has taken place. Money has been collected for hungry people, and a meal has been served. The sponsoring group has done something that helps. Everyone is satisfied, even though they are still hungry.

– Temple United Methodist Church,
Muskegon Heights, Michigan

Offering of Letters

According to a study of the National Academy of Sciences, "If there is the political will in this country and abroad... it should be possible to overcome the worst aspects of widespread hunger and malnutrition within one generation."

We can help to create that political will by expressing our concern to elected leaders, thus moving our government toward policies that enable hungry people to work their way out of hunger and poverty.

We can struggle for reforms which make it possible for the poor to become more self-reliant in providing their own food. Such reforms should be seen in the context of a clear and consistent food policy. At present, the United States has a variety of approaches, developed by various agencies, which lack overall vision and sometimes work at cross purposes. By developing a comprehensive food policy, our government could more effectively deal with such issues as food and development assistance, domestic hunger, grain reserves, and the global economics of food.

Helping shape such a comprehensive food policy is too much to ask of any of us. It is not possible for one person to keep abreast of all fields related to hunger, and rarely can one person, acting alone, change a government policy. The answer lies in joining with others who have a similar concern, drawing upon careful analysis of government policies. With others, we can express our views when key decisions are being made.

To network with others concerned about hunger, contact the head office of your local denomination or organizations such as OXFAM and Bread for the World.

The Offering of Letters is a way for Christians to express their faith in an act of love on behalf of our hungry brothers and sisters in the world.

The Offering of Letters is an invitation to people of faith throughout the country to place in the Sunday collection basket, as an offering of our citizenship alongside our regular offering of money, letters to public officials – the president, congresspersons, senators – on a carefully selected public policy issue or piece of legislation which affects the lives of hungry people.

The Thanksgiving Season provides an ideal time for the Offering of Letters in the churches, though many churches, for one reason or another, opt to have their Offering of Letters at other times of the year. Any Sunday is appropriate.

People may write their letters at home or at church on the Sunday of the offering, depending on local preferences. A special offering basket may be provided or worshipers may bring the letters forward in a procession. In one parish, a procession outside to the mailbox was incorporated into the service.

United Nations Day

On October 24, 1945, the United Nations Charter was approved by a majority of its member nations. The mandate of the United Nations is:
- to maintain international peace; to develop friendly relations among nations
- to cooperate internationally in solving international economic, social, cultural, and humanitarian problems and in promoting respect for human rights and fundamental freedoms.

In 1947, the UN General Assembly passed a resolution designating October 24 as United Nations Day. The importance and hope for peace attached to the UN was so great that the National Council of Churches moved the date of World Order Sunday, a time for churches to reaffirm their responsibility for world peace and justice, to conform to United Nations Day – even before the UN General Assembly had made that day official.

Telling the children

United Nations Day presents an important opportunity to remember how interrelated the world has become, and how critical the need for international cooperation if humankind is to survive. Honor the day by teaching your children about its work, which includes peacekeeping, agricultural research, children's emergency work, the advancement of women, as well as health education, meteorological, maritime, and environmental programs.

Halloween

Halloween refers to the evening before All Hallows' or All Saints' Day and is celebrated on October 31. The origins of the day come from the Druids' New Year celebration. Along with some other groups, the Druids believed that on the last day of the year the dead came back to mingle with the living. In the eighth century, Pope Gregory III moved All Hallows' to November 1, probably in an attempt to provide an alternative to the popular pagan festival. All Saints' Day was in honor of all the saints who had died, whether or not the church had yet officially canonized them. During the Middle Ages, All Hallows' Eve became known as a special time for witches and sorcerers.

Halloween costumes started in medieval times when churches displayed relics of saints. Those parishes too poor to have relics let parishioners dress up to imitate saints.

The tradition of Halloween as Mischief Night, when pranks of all sorts were played on the unsuspecting, likely originated with the old belief that on All Hallows' Eve ghosts roamed the countryside playing tricks. Pranks could thus be blamed on the ghosts.

Many Halloween traditions come from Ireland and Scotland. Bobbing for apples is one of them. The jack o'lantern supposedly comes from an Irish legend about an old sot, Jack, who made a deal with the devil for his soul. The angered devil supposedly threw a live coal at Jack, and it landed in a half-eaten turnip in Jack's hand. The resulting coal in the turnip became a jack o'lantern.

The blend of legend, religion, and mischief has combined to make Halloween a unique celebration. Commercialism has had its effect on the festivities, as children beg for costumes like their favorite television characters and for treats which are hopelessly lacking in nourishment. Because parents fear for the safety of their children, children are discouraged from accepting any treats that are not commercially packaged.

While Halloween is very popular with children, several factors compel us to reexamine current practices in celebrating Halloween. First, more candy is consumed by children on Halloween and the day after than in any other 48-hour period of the year. Second, we have witnessed the return of Mischief Night, with malicious and destructive pranks being played, especially in urban areas. Third, trick-or-treaters find harmful things such as razors and poison in their collected goodies.

Having said that, creativity and planning, combined with moderation and safety, can make Halloween fun.

Halloween Lock-In

For their traditional Halloween Lock-In, our Youth Group discussed Halloween and its connection to the festival of All Saints. Then each person received an unlighted candle before proceeding quietly to the chancel area of the dimly lit church building. Seated on the floor around the marble steps by the altar, we remembered people, now deceased, who had touched our lives in special ways. We recounted ways we continue to be connected to these people in "the communion of saints."

The large Paschal candle by the baptismal font had been lighted, symbolizing Christ's resurrection. With that symbol of resurrection assurance filling our thoughts, we shared the name of the person for whom our candle was lighted and what that person's life meant to us. Then, lighting our candles from the Paschal candle, we placed them in front of the altar.

The light of our candles flooded the church, just as the people they represented continue to illuminate our lives. During a time of quiet prayer we thanked God for the lives of these people, praying that we would be faithful to the light they had shared with us.

– Pastor Richard L. Schaper, Lutheran Church of the Redeemer, Atlanta, Georgia

Community Pumpkin Patch

For Halloween we have a community Pumpkin Patch. Our local social service agency has a volunteer-operated community garden. Garden plots for individual use are free, but all takers must help plant and harvest one crop in the community garden to provide fresh produce for the food pantry. These community gardens are located on city land used as a leaf dump, and we have found that pumpkins grow well in uncultivated leaf mounds.

Just before Halloween our harvested pumpkins, supplemented by others we purchase, are placed in the Pumpkin Patch where customers trade cans of food for pumpkins – two food items for a small pumpkin, four for a medium pumpkin, etc. These canned goods are given to the local food pantry.

We make money for the food pantry by selling homemade pumpkin baked goods and apple cider. Two local residents set up their apple press and make fresh cider, stimulating sales by giving out free samples.

In addition, volunteer artists paint a cute or scary face on pumpkins for 25 cents. For entertainment the zoo brings animals to pet, and the recreation center provides clowns for face painting.

The Pumpkin Patch has become quite a tradition in our community. It raises several hundred dollars for our food pantry and contributes many canned goods. This project requires little work and lasts one

Saturday from 9:00 a.m. to 1:00 p.m.
– Mary and Bill Merrill, Columbus, Ohio

All Hallows' Eve

We celebrate All Hallows' Eve with a hot dog roast and bonfire. Everyone is encouraged to dress as a saint, but no Draculas are turned away. We play games such as "Pin the Crown on the Saint," and sing "I Sing a Song of the Saints of God" (Episcopal hymnal). We end with the service for All Hallows' Eve around the bonfire.

– Ed, Andrea, Nathanael and Rebekah Wills, Memphis, Tennessee

Fall festival

We hosted a family party encouraging everyone (not just children!) to come dressed as Bible characters or saints. As folks gathered, we sang fun, campfire-type songs. Then we all told who we were and were given the prize of a bookmark.

Afterward, the adults played table games (and they must have really enjoyed it, staying as late as they did!) while the kids had their choice of face painting, guessing the number of pieces of candy in a jar, bobbing for apples, bean bag toss, ping-pong, ball toss, or drawing faces on balloons. We had trouble getting people to leave, so perhaps we'll have another celebration next year!

– Susan Landis, Cheshire, Connecticut

Family Halloween celebration

Dress the whole family in costume and visit a pediatric ward. Get permission for your visit in advance, making sure your planned gifts to the children there are appropriate. Balloons, coloring books, or comics may make better gifts than candy or gum. Or, if the hospital has no objections, bake cookies together and take them. Visit a few rooms briefly. The joy you bring to the patients and their parents is a real gift.

– Joel E. Shirk, Cheshire, Connecticut

Finding acceptable alternatives

Although our four children at home – aged 7 to 11 – were reluctant to give up costumed trick-or-treating, my wife and I had decided that the quantity of candy ingested and the risks to the children warranted stopping the tradition. As an alternative, we proposed a Halloween party at our house. After the children compiled their guest list, I called the invitees and their parents. Guests were to come dressed as historical heroes. Costumes were to be simple and made with whatever was available at home. Each person was to learn some factual data about the hero(ine) chosen, part of which would be required for admission to the party. They were instructed to keep their identity secret from the other participants until it would be revealed in a special game of charades. During the game they gave prearranged clues to their identities and acted out their characters.

Among the heroes and heroines were Joan of Arc, Sitting Bull, Martin Luther King, Jr., and Abraham Lincoln.

In addition to the hero-related activities, we did some of the more traditional things: bobbing for apples, eating homemade cookies prepared by their parents, and going through a haunted house designed by our kids in the loft of the barn.

In the spirit of ghosts and goblins, we took the kids out back of the barn in a small pasture where we sat down and talked about the spirits of the people who might have lived at this place many years ago: Indians, slaves, slave owners, tenant farmers, and others. While we tried to make it a little scary, it was more an opportunity to remember those who had been there before us.

This party required a lot of planning as well as time, but the kids did not feel cheated out of Halloween. The next year, we enlarged the party to include the fifth and sixth grade class from our church.

– Milo Thornberry, Alaska

Community-building

Perhaps Halloween offers itself as a good time for us to make our neighborhood more of a community. Groups of parents, who relate only infrequently during the year, could sit down with their children and plan a Halloween block party. Costumes can be made of old clothes, sheets, and paper bags. The party could take place in several homes, interrupted by visits to neighbors' houses to collect money for hunger projects. In addition to the widely promoted UNICEF campaign, you might initiate your own neighborhood project for another of the many international hunger groups, or for a local one in your community.

Hunger project

Because we are turned on by Food Day, natural foods, and taking care of our bodies, we are turned off by the Great Candy Giveaway in October. Consider baking nutritional goodies or giving fruit. Having become disturbed by the greed, and anger (when the "take" is not good enough) that trick-or-treating has produced at our front door, we tried an alternate approach which may interest you. We bought no candy or fruit.

Instead, when children came to the door, we told them of our concern for children who had nothing to eat and explained we were giving the money we would have spent on fruit to a hunger project. And our children collected several dollars in the neighborhood for the project. I might add they rejected candy by choice up to the last house – to the astonishment of our neighbors.

With a little planning, Halloween can be a great family funtime. At the same time, it can be an opportunity to redistribute a tiny portion of our overabundance and to plant a seed of caring in the hearts of our children.

A note instead

This year we decided that in our own small way we would like to turn childhood greed for candy into something that helped to meet the needs of others, and that would also help youngsters to begin thinking about those needs.

We printed copies of this statement and put them in each child's goodie bag:

Dear Trick-or treater:

We are giving [a donation] to UNICEF for every child who comes trick-or-treating at our home. Because you have come, other children around the world will receive a gift of food and medicine to help them have the joys of life which you have. Thank you for coming to our home and helping us help other children like yourself all around the world.

This was a small beginning for us this year, but we hope it may get some parents to do some re-thinking when their children ask them to explain what our "treat" is all about.

– Dan and Jonnie Gerhard,
Walla Walla, Washington

Party activity

Invite children to make "jack o'lanterns" out of apples (just cut out eyes, nose, mouth, etc.). Display them for each other, them eat them up. It's a fun snack. You may also want to insert raisins or nuts in the eyes, nose, and mouth holes. Adult help, of course, is needed for the little kids!

Remembrance Day (See **Memorial Day**)

Hanukkah

Feast of Dedication

This annual Feast of Dedication (*Hanukkah* means "dedication" in Hebrew; it is sometimes spelled *Chanukah*) is celebrated for eight days, beginning on the 25th day of the lunar month of Kislev, falling normally in December. Hanukkah commemorates the victory of the small military force under the leadership of the Maccabees. Against great odds, they defeated the Syrian army which occupied their land. Syria had tried to force a corrupt form of Hellinization on the Jews through a series of repressive decrees, which included turning the Temple in Jerusalem into a house of worship for the Greek god Zeus. When the Maccabees succeeded in driving the Syrians out of Jerusalem and recovered the Temple, an eight-day festival to rededicate the Temple to the service of God was proclaimed.

In 165 BCE, when the Jews were preparing for the Temple rededication, it was discovered that there was only enough sanctified oil to burn in the menorah for one day. However, enough for eight days was required.

The story that is celebrated, in addition to the military victory, is that the small amount of oil lasted for the full eight days. The following year, these eight days were ordained as a time to give thanks and praise for the miracle of the flask of oil. The lights are a sign of God's presence.

Today, Jews throughout the world celebrate by lighting the menorah (which is oil or candle-burning) in their homes and synagogues over an eight-day period. During the lighting, special prayers are recited. On one of the days, families and friends gather to visit, play special games, eat festive foods, and exchange gifts. In some communities, huge outdoor menorahs are lit in public celebration.

Light in the subarctic darkness

The December nights are long in Yellowknife, Northwest Territories. Longer than in southern climes! While her Christian neighbors lit their houses with festive Christmas lights, artist Esther Tennenhouse brightened the darkness within her own tradition. She created a yard-sized menorah from ice and hard-packed snow. Candles burned brightly within the ice to create a wondrous sight.

The local newspaper photographed this menorah. Someone in southern Canada read the paper, and sent a copy to a friend in the United States. The photograph was published there, too. Someone else sent a copy to a friend in Israel, where it was published again. The light from one northern menorah traveled halfway around the world that year!

Advent

The "good news"

"Santa Claus is coming to town!" This is the Advent – the coming – that our children are aware of, for six weeks, morning, noon, and night. Our small children know more about Santa Claus than they know of Jesus Christ. The "good news" of Santa Claus is proclaimed from fireplaces, store windows, and the mass-media. In the name of Santa Claus, celebrations are held, cities are decorated, songs are composed, the gross national product is raised, and children are motivated and disciplined.

The Santa Claus myth had its source in the St. Nicholas celebrations. St. Nicholas was the Bishop of Myra in Asia Minor; he died about 350 CE. Indeed, Santa Claus got his name from the Saint.

The Gospel of Christ

"Report to John what you hear and see: the blind recover their sight, cripples walk, lepers are cured, the deaf hear, dead are raised to life and the poor have the Good News preached to them" (Matthew 11:4-5).

John the Baptist, the Herald of Christ, proclaimed the Advent theme of repentance (Mark 1:4).

"If anyone wants to come with me, they must forget [themselves], carry [their] cross, and follow me" (Mark 8:34).

John the Baptist said, "Let the [one] with two coats give to [one] who has none. The one who has food should do the same" (Luke 3:11).

Blessed are the poor in spirit...
Blessed are the meek...
Blessed are the sorrowful...
Blessed are they who hunger
    and thirst for justice...
Love your neighbor...
Love your enemies...
Befriend the hungry,
    the naked,
    the sick,
    the homeless,
    the prisoners,
    the strangers.
"I have come that they may have life... more abundantly" (John 10:10).

Through the years in North America, the Santa Claus myth has been almost completely reduced to an advertising gimmick. The myth has so deteriorated that it is no longer a "cute" tradition; it is harmful to children. It is easier to teach the Gospel of Santa Claus than it is to teach the Gospel of Christ.

Santa Claus plays right into the hands of human weakness and desire: the tendency toward greed. Children are no exception to this weakness. The Santa Claus indoctrination in its present form is a powerful attitude influencer that works contrary to the meaning of Christ's coming. The comparison below is a serious effort at highlighting the differences in the two Advent-Christmas Gospels:

Gospel of Santa Claus

The good news of Santa Claus is for the affluent.

Santa's mission is mainly to the healthy and successful.

The Heralds of Santa Claus proclaim self-satisfaction.

Pleasure is a dominant theme of Santa Claus.

There is no room for self-denial and the cross.

To stimulate business, "Let [one] who has a coat, get another."

> Blessed are the wealthy...
> Blessed are the powerful...
> Blessed are the comfortable...
> Blessed are the satisfied...
> Love your own...
> Love your friends...
> Befriend the full,
>   the well-dressed,
>   the healthy,
>   the well-housed,
>   the respectable,
>   friends.

He comes that they may have things more abundantly.

– Reprinted from *Alternate Celebrations Catalogue, 4th Edition*

Christmas cards

The sending of greeting cards, whether for anniversary, birthday, Christmas or what-have-you constitutes a good example of a widespread practice in our society that wastes a lot of trees and paper products. I am not suggesting that you abandon your "card-sending habits" – just consider these ecological alternatives:

- If you must buy new cards, make sure they are printed only on recycled paper made from trash paper.

- Another way to send cards without destroying the environment is simply to save the cards people send you and reuse the picture by cutting the card at the fold. Then simply write your message on the blank surface on the back of the picture. You may want to add the word "Recycled" to your card.

- Many of my friends are already using "recycled" cards by the above method, so I get a third use out of them by letting the family cut up the pictures and then reassemble them to make creative cards. Remember, the anticipation of a holiday is usually as good if not better then the reality of the day. With Christmas just around the corner, get the kids to start "creating" cards for an ecological holiday. Keep saving those comics and old paper bags to use instead of wrapping paper, too.

Remember: if you must send cards – be sure they are recycled.

– Ron Ritz, Brookville, Ohio

New tradition

Here's another "new" tradition in card-giving. Members are asked to bring a homemade greeting (card or ornament) to hang on a tree in the hallway of the church instead of mailing individual cards to all their friends in the congregation. Then they are asked to give the money they would have spent on cards and postage to a specified project, such as the Heifer Project (an interfaith, nonprofit organization dedicated to alleviating hunger by helping low-income families around the world to produce food for themselves and for their communities). Most of the people give far more than the amount asked, and our church has had over $100 to send. And everyone loves to look at the greetings on the tree. It has contributed greatly to the fellowship before and after services.

– Karen Lull, Claremont, California

"Baby" tree ornaments

We don't buy costly ornaments for our Christmas tree. Since the time our children were born we saved their tiny baby rattles and small toys. They are the "decorations" on the tree, together with many small craft items the children made when they were little.

Now that our "children" are in their 20s and 30s, the tree is a great reminder

of the care and love in our family.

– Rose Lucey, Oakland, California

More alternative rituals shared by families

1. **Travel.** We leave the familiar environment. Sturbridge, Massachusetts celebrates Christmas as the settlers celebrated it – simply, non-commercially. A trip [there] at Christmas can be a helpful way to change a routine and gain perspective.

2. **Cards.** No one is allowed to give a commercial card. Each must make their own and compose their own verse.

3. **Eating tree.** Holiday cookies and other baking are made and decorated for use as tree decoration. On the afternoon of Christmas or some other holiday, open house is held for neighbors and friends to drop in and enjoy the fruits of the eating tree.

4. **Visits.** During supper on some particular day during the holiday season (such as Christmas Eve) we think about older people who have no families or whose families are away, or who might be a little happier at just the sight of us. (At this point we can't stand the sight of each other.) We let the dishes go, wrap up a few packages of cookies and go!

5. **Christmas Diorama.** A kind of diorama which replaces the crèche

has been developed. It includes the panorama of Jesus' life story and tries to convey the basic impression of Jesus as a teacher with some of his teaching evident.

6. **Drama.** Christmas can be celebrated with father (or mother) and children planning a drama of the birth of Jesus while mother (or father) prepares Christmas breakfast or Christmas dinner.

7. **Memory tree.** A tiny permanent tree, originally started by husband and wife on their first Christmas together, is decorated with mementos of hobbies, interests, etc. and added to each year. Each Christmas Eve, all lights are extinguished except two candles beside the little tree. The events represented by the "ornaments" are recalled.

8. **Good to the last...** When the tree is taken down, it is cut into lengths and used for a special wiener roast in the fireplace or it may be chipped for spring compost.

9. **Twelve Days of Christmas.**
   - In order not to swamp children with gifts all at once, we use the custom of receiving one gift on each of the 12 days before Christmas.
   - We have 12 candles on the fireplace mantel. We start lighting them on December 12 until all are lit on December 24. We sing

carols and read Christmas poems and stories for the 10-15 minutes the candles burn.

10. **Advent candles and wreath.** Light one of the four Advent candles on each Sunday before Christmas. Accompany with carols, poems, and stories.

11. **A gift for someone in need of a gift.** The family (or two families) gathers to make a gift for someone who might not have one at this season.

12. **Holiday blessings.** On Christmas night, all branches of the family get together with a covered-dish supper and a little service. Each member tells what they feel was their special blessing of the year.

13. **Doctor's prescription.** "Take one every four hours" is the prescription one doctor's family receives on Christmas. Beginning on the day before Christmas each member of the family opens a gift every four hours. This is done so that every gift may be cherished.

14. **Gift hunt.** Gifts are hidden and persons must follow a treasure map to find them. Pictures of where to look for the next clue are used for those too young to read.

15. **Preparing dinner.**
   - Everyone (including children) prepares their favorite dish – regardless of overall plan!
   - One parent and the kids take a

hike while another parent prepares the dinner. They bring treasures home to share.

- Invite a foreign student from a nearby school to spend the day. Invite them to share their own customs.
- Invite guests whose work takes them away from home on that day (such as truck drivers).

16. **Festive breakfast.** Instead of dinner.

17. **Piñata.** Make a piñata with the children. Fill it with sugarfree candy, nuts, fruits, little bags of popcorn, toasted soybeans, fancy crackers, etc. Invite the neighborhood (children) in on Christmas Eve to break the piñata. (Your library will have instructions for creating your version of this Spanish custom.)

18. **Christmas Day.** Plan alternate activities so that the center of the day is not gift-giving. (A skit, hike, visiting friends, having friends in, cooking.)

19. **Gift-giving party.** Invite children to wrap one of their own toys to give to another child. Or have them bring them wrapped to take to a family without many gifts.

20. **Send New Year's letters** (instead of holiday cards). If you are too busy during Advent, relax! Write out-of-town friends in the New Year.

21. **Family worship.** Write out songs, scripture, and poems for the holiday season on 25 pieces of paper. Each day, beginning December 1, a member of the family draws a slip from a bowl and reads it as a reminder of the forthcoming holiday.

Kids and Christmas

We have the kids go and pick out a new outfit of clothes to be given away. They enjoy it and realize that it's a season for giving. Maybe next year we'll be able to make the clothes instead of buy them. We also buy food to be given away, and give money to several organizations instead of buying gifts. For my parents one year, we all (10 children) wrote remembrances of growing up at home, and presented the booklet to them. Last year, we also cooked dinner for three neighbors plus another older woman who couldn't come to share a meal with us.

Last year for Christmas, the kids made napkins to give to their grandparents. We used the fabric crayons and ironed the kid's own drawings on the material. This way "Papps" and "Nanny" could see some art work and get a really personal gift that's ecologically friendly.

– Jeann Schaller, Midland, Michigan

God's idea of Christmas

If we Christians celebrate Christmas by consumptively spending more than we can afford on non-essential items, on non-nutritive foods – by, in other words, wasting our substance like prodigals – we can be sure that others, who can far less afford to do so, will imitate us. Christ warned us, after all, that we are to be the light of the world. How did God celebrate Christmas? God gave the gift of self. God came as a very small and precious baby. This idea of Christmas was simple, unexpected, and, paradoxically, also lavish. Can we begin to do likewise?

– Patti Sprinkle, St. Petersburg, Florida

Christmas open houses

In Flint, Michigan, members of the Unitarian Church annually hold a series of open houses during the Christmas Season. Individuals agree to open their homes to the church community for an afternoon or evening, beginning a day or so before Christmas. The final open house is held on New Year's Day.

The people hosting open houses are asked to provide coffee or tea for their guests, and possibly some Christmas cookies or munchies. They might also feature an activity: ornament-making, caroling, games. But the hosts are cautioned to avoid elaborate preparations, for the strength of this custom is its simplicity. The open houses provide occasions in which to relax with friends in an atmosphere of informality. For many people, these open houses constitute islands of calm and fellowship during an otherwise hectic season.

At one open house, only two or three people may visit during an afternoon or evening. At another, 15 or 20 assorted adults and children may squeeze into a small living room. But numbers aren't crucial. More to the point is the concrete message of openness, the presence of one or two or a few human beings with whom to share both the joys and the sadnesses of the season. For Christmas can be a hard time. Tucked among the messages of joy, people often discover feelings of sadness and loneliness.

The open houses of the Flint Unitarian Church are organized within an ongoing religious community. Yet the idea could be adapted by many groups: singles, social clubs, large extended families, neighborhoods, informal associations of friends. All it takes is a signup sheet with a list of available dates and a few people willing to offer the message of Christmas in a very personal form.

– Bruce Marshall, Flint, Michigan

The cooperative alternative

For the hundreds of thousands of people in North America who are members of cooperatives, the month of December is one of special meaning. It was December 21, 1844, that the first cooperative store opened in Rochdale, England. On that cold winter's night during a period called by historians the "hungry 40s," the poor and mostly-unemployed weavers of the town began their cooperative as a means to solving their suffering. They had in mind a cooperative system which would end poverty, hunger, and unemployment. Their vision was of a world of plenty, where machines produced for use, and where they could build communities which would represent the fulfillment of humanity.

Since that time, cooperatives have sprung up wherever people have needed to serve their aspirations for better living conditions. The growth of cooperatives in North America signifies the spiritual, social, and economic search for communal meaning.

At Co-Opportunity in Santa Monica, we celebrate "Rochdale Night" in early December. (Although we would love to celebrate on December 21, we have found that it is too late to sell crafts, and conflicts with too many other events.) We use it as a means of gathering co-op members together in a special evening of sharing and joy. When we first began three years ago there were 50 people. Last year there were 150. We suspect it will grow each year as the effect circulates among the membership. We plan for the evening to be one of entertainment with the members' own music-makers supplemented by inviting groups such as the Los Angeles Farm Workers' Choir to sing for us. The events are free, the co-op pays for the hall, etc., and we usually have a large, inviting potluck dinner.

In the December newsletter publicizing the event, we ask people to consider buying Christmas gifts from non-commercial sources, and to especially search for crafts from cooperatives in America and throughout the world. We also encourage our own members who make crafts to sell them in a parking lot holiday sale on the same day we have the party. The co-op itself sells many gifts from crafts people, displaying them throughout the co-op and bringing much beauty to our store. Because we have 1,300 families in our co-op and do $1 million in business a year, we have much potential for local impact.

As we develop the tradition of "Rochdale Night" and the crafts fair, we hope to guide our members' money into support for a more human and just lifestyle. We have the light of the Rochdale Pioneers of 1844 to keep us on the path. Our cooperatives can unite in this celebration to bring change, development, and liberation.

– David Thompson, Santa Monica, California

It's hard to be merry, sometimes

Lately, more and more people are

admitting that the Christmas Season, with all its jolliness blasted at us for weeks and weeks, makes us feel more, not less, miserable. Many of us grew up with the notion that if we weren't smiling all the time, we weren't acceptable. Now churches are recognizing this fact. At Scarboro United Church in Calgary, an annual candlelight "Hard to be Merry Christmas" service takes place one Sunday evening early in Advent.

Unemployment, death of a loved one, divorce, loneliness, and illness can all make us feel isolated and alone. In this service, the pain people experience is validated and people can remember that they are not alone.

The service is simple, quiet, nondenominational. It is advertised throughout the city. It is a gentle time to hear some reassuring scripture from both Testaments, to hear brief words of assurance and acceptance from the minister, to hear some meditative music. At one point during the service, the congregation is invited to come forward and light a candle. They may speak the name of someone, or of an event that makes them feel sad – or they may simply light a candle and return to their seats in silence.

In addition to the service, and a time for visiting afterwards, there are resource tables with books and information about bereavement, loss, divorce, and beginning again, and brochures and information from lo-cal self-help and counseling groups.

– Scarboro United Church, Calgary, Alberta

Advent promises

For your family's Advent celebration, make a Promise Tree. Put a branch in a sand-filled pot. Each day in Advent, write a promise to a family member and hang it on the tree. On Christmas Eve, decorate your Promise Tree with handmade symbols of Christ's birth.

– *Christmas Alternative Catalogue,*
Our Saviour's Lutheran Church, Tucson, Arizona

Peace notes at Advent

As a part of our Advent celebration, we send international Christmas cards. On Christmas stationery we write a short note wishing peace and justice for our world. Then we invite friends to sign their names. The cards are mailed to national and world leaders to let them know our concerns as we anticipate the coming of the Prince of Peace. It is moving to receive notes from all over the world acknowledging our greetings.

– Anne Broyles and Larry Peacock,
Norwalk, California

Advent workshop

In an effort to allow our small town of 2,000 to realize there are alternatives to Christmas gift-giving other than "shooting a wad" at K-Mart, we had an Advent workshop to encourage people to make some of their gifts.

We collected materials for making grapevine and pine cone wreaths, wooden candle holders, cutting boards, tree decorations, and for decorating Christmas gift-wrapping paper. We tried to plan something for everyone, young and old. With volunteer supervisors to help with the rudiments of structure and design, we were able to charge just enough to cover the cost of materials.

As the price of admission, participants brought a can of food to be used in food baskets distributed within our community at Christmas.

– Sandra Ellingsen, Ellendale, North Dakota

St. Nicholas Day

We give all our immediate family gifts on St. Nicholas Day. On St. Nicholas Eve we hang simple, homemade muslin stockings, to which we add an embroidered symbol each year. We remember the story of St. Nicholas and his gift of dowries to three young maidens. Then we play St. Nicholas for each other. We hang the stockings before bed, and everyone sneaks in to put gifts in each other's stockings. On St. Nicholas morning, my two-year-old was so excited about what he had wrapped to give to me that he walked right past the rocking horse we had set out for him to get my gifts and put them in my lap.

When possible, we share a common meal with others who also celebrate this way, followed by a visit from St. Nicholas himself.

Complete with festive (bor-rowed) bishop's garb, St. Nicholas talks to the children, particularly emphasizing that he and God and their parents love them whether they "cry" or "pout," whether they're "good" or "bad." He then gives each of them a gold coin chocolate.

In the remaining weeks before Christmas, we try to emphasize how nice it was to receive gifts. Now we do the same for others, for this is what God does at Christmas. So we bake, sew, glue, and paste for grandparents, aunts, uncles, and friends.

– Ed, Andrea, Nathanael and Rebekah Wills, Memphis, Tennessee

Greetings from the heart

For the past few years, we have printed our Christmas cards. Two families share a small silk screen along with a supply of colored inks.

Each family makes paper patterns and then we come together for an evening of designing cards. We use inexpensive colored paper for the cards and mail them in budget envelopes. Inside each card we write a personal message to family and friends. Our favorite designs are outlines of the three wise men and the dove of peace.

– Mary and Bill Merrill, Columbus, Ohio

Advent wreath

Braid a bread dough Advent wreath. Braid three rolled strands of dough and impress candle-sized holes before baking.

Christmas

Christmas in history: Mingling cultural traditions

Despite the fact that the Gospel of Luke links the date of Jesus' birth to a census in Palestine decreed by Caesar Augustus (Luke 2:1), nothing is known of the time of year of his birth. The first evidence of speculation about the date is in the third century when Clement of Alexandria suggested May 20. The earliest mention of observance on December 25 is in the Philocalian Calendar, representing Roman practice in the year 336. At about the same time, the Eastern church began to observe the Nativity on January 6, the feast of Epiphany. By the middle of the fifth century, however, most Eastern churches had adopted December 25.

As with other Christian holy days, the date of Christmas appears to have been set to provide an alternative to one or more popular pagan festivals. December 25 was originally the date of the feast to the sun god, Mithras. The cult of Mithras had spread from Persia into the Roman world in the first century, and by the third century was Christianity's main rival. December 25 also came at the end of the feast of Saturnalia, an ancient Roman festival commemorating the golden age of Saturn. Both of these festivals may well have been related to even earlier festivals marking the winter solstice.

Although Christmas was intended as an alternative to pagan festivals, the practices of those festivals were often simply incorporated into the Christian celebration. As Christianity spread through central and northern Europe, the accretions from local religions continued. As early as the fifth century, a small minority of Christian leaders expressed alarm at the growing pagan character of Christmas, a cause for concern that continued through the Middle Ages.

Christmas celebrations were not only enlarged by absorbing elements from local religions but from other Christian traditions as well, for example, St. Nicholas. The association of Christmas with St. Nicholas came about in the Middle Ages, especially in northern Europe. Little is known about his history except that he was Bishop of Myra in Asia Minor in the fourth century. Of the many stories about this saint, one of the most popular tells about his generosity in giving gifts anonymously to the poor. He became the patron saint of numerous countries, cities and groups, and especially of children. Because of this special relationship, tradition developed that he gave gifts to children on the eve of his feast day, December 6.

During the Reformation of the 16th century, many reformers wanted

Christmas dropped as a Christian celebration. In their view, not only was there no biblical sanction for Christmas, but its popular practices still looked too much like the old Saturnalia festivals. In their general resistance to things Catholic, they also wanted St. Nicholas banished. For a few years in 17th-century England, the Puritan-dominated parliament outlawed the feast of Christmas. At the same time, Puritans in Massachusetts passed similar legislation. Between the 16th and 18th centuries the widespread antipathy to Christmas as a holy day – especially by Puritans, Quakers, Baptists, and Presbyterians – had important consequences, consequences which those religious groups could not have imagined.

Resistance to attaching religious significance to Christmas encouraged its growth as a secular holiday. For example, St. Nicholas was replaced by a more secular figure known as Christmas Man, Father Christmas, and Papa Noël. The Dutch, reluctant to give up St. Nicholas, brought Sinterklass (St. Nicholas) with them when they came to America and honored him on December 6. In the 17th century, when the Dutch lost control of New Amsterdam to the English, Sinterklass was gradually anglicized into Santa Claus and acquired many of the accouterments of Christmas Man – the workshop at the North Pole and the sleigh with reindeer. By the 19th century, when the formerly-resistant Protestant groups began to celebrate Christmas, it was not only a religious holy day but a well-established secular holiday as well.

The 20th century: Commercializing Christmas

Through the 20th century in Europe and North America, the popular celebration of Christmas remains an amalgam of Christian and non-Christian traditions. The lack of clarity about the celebration's purpose has remained, accentuating a new factor in the 20th century: the commercialization of Christmas.

More than just a mixture of diverse traditions, Christmas is now big business. While the Christian calendar calls for a solemn four- or five-week preparation to celebrate the birth of Christ, the "Christmas economy" overshadows even Halloween, with Thanksgiving Day in the U.S. serving as little more than a prelude to the greatest shopping weekend of the year. In 1939, President Roosevelt moved the date of Thanksgiving back to the third Thursday of November to expand the Christmas shopping season. With the survival of many businesses dependent on Christmas profits and half of the annual advertising dollar spent on Christmas-related advertising, it is not surprising that for some shoppers Christmas spending is regarded as a patriotic duty.

The commercialization of Christmas did not occur in a social vacuum. It is part of our society in which consumption for its own sake – regardless of need – is legitimated and encouraged. Without reluctance, consumerism exploits religious beliefs and deep emotions to persuade people to buy. Advertising's behavior modification specialists demonstrate that the strains of "Joy to the World" trumpeting throughout the shopping malls in December produce greater profits, and that "Silent Night, Holy Night" is even better. Using Christmas as a religion-sanctioned occasion for extravagant spending, businesses hope that the practice of spending billions of dollars on Christmas gifts in North America is simply practice for greater spending throughout the rest of the year.

While it may be good for the economy in the short run, commercialized Christmas also has its costs. Preparations for observing the birth of one whose coming is "good news to the poor," are often displaced by the more financially attractive preparations to observe the coming of Santa Claus. Extravagant Christmas spending means fewer dollars available for those ministries and agencies addressing critical social and environmental problems. And the loss is more than dollars. The sense of exploitation that many feel at Christmas, the depression that comes when Christmas does

not deliver the happiness popular hype promises, and the guilt from being willing participants in a religious fraud, all rob Christmas of its power to renew the human spirit.

Perhaps the greatest cost of commercialization at Christmas is paid by the poor. In our society, the poor experience Christmas as a cruel hoax. Our pervasive cultural Christmas ideology is not Christology – celebrating Christ's coming as "good news to the poor" – but what we might call "Santology."

The creed of Santa Claus theology is the well-known song, "Santa Claus is Coming to Town." According to this creed, Santa is omniscient; like God, Santa knows all about us. There is also a day of judgment. It comes once a year when "good" children (and adults!) are rewarded with good things, while the "bad" (i.e., the poor) get coals and switches. The truth is, of course, that gifts are not distributed based on who has been "good or bad" or "naughty or nice," but on what people can afford or get credit to buy. But that's not what our culture teaches children.

What it teaches is bad for both poor and non-poor children. Poor children are told that they don't receive gifts because they are bad, while the non-poor are taught that they receive gifts because they are good. Both notions, equally reprehensible, are part of this culture's Santa Claus theology.

Commercial Christmas, its underpinnings of Santa Claus firmly in place, continues its spiraling growth. It seems evident that its cultural pervasiveness makes future change little less than a distant dream. It is also true that many Christians and congregations accept the distortion of their holy day without challenge. The reason, one suspects, is not so much an insensitivity to the issues, but rather a feeling of impotence – not knowing what to do or how to do it. Aware that slogans such as "putting Christ back in Christmas," and ideas about "Christmas basket charity" are simplistic, many Christians opt to do nothing. The commercialization of Christmas is something everybody talks about, but nobody does anything about.

Alternatives to the commercialized Christmas

What can you do to make Christmas a joyful celebration of Christ's birth? How can the meaning of Emmanuel, "God with us," be made real at Christmastime?

1. **Recognize** at the outset that there are no quick fixes for miraculously transforming our Christmas celebrations. Christmas commercialization is deeply ingrained in this society. You can save yourself a lot of frustration by realizing that patience and perseverance are virtues needed in good supply for this venture.

2. **Let** Advent be Advent! Use the Advent Season to develop a spirituality of cultural resistance to the commercialization of Christmas.

3. **Turn down** the volume of commercial Christmas hoopla. Long before Christmas arrives, the airwaves, print media, and shopping malls are saturated with messages to provide a "good" Christmas. Restrict exposure to this propaganda by watching television less frequently, making fewer trips to malls, and getting "Christmas" catalogues out of your house.

4. **Tune in** to activities that are less consumption-oriented. Set aside time in the weeks before Christmas for personal quiet time and reflection, time for family and/or friends, time to work through an Advent calendar or the Gospel Bible readings for Advent, time for making gifts at home, and time for household members to share in the pre-Christmas cleaning and cooking responsibilities.

5. **Expect** your religious community to provide resources and opportunities – through its church school, worship services, and outreach committees – for members looking for ways to resist the pressures of commercialization. Then, help out. Act to see that your expectation becomes reality. Con-

sider organizing a community-wide alternative Christmas festival.

6. **Take** Santa Claus theology seriously. Perpetuation of the Santa Claus myth is an issue on which people of good will can and do disagree. Many – especially young parents – struggle with this issue alone because some congregations actively perpetuate Santa Claus theology, while others say nothing. Consider recovering the St. Nicholas tradition, thereby creating new celebration traditions that do not detract from celebrating Christ's birth.

7. **Rediscover** creativity in gift-giving, both in what and where you buy. Recover the almost lost art of self-giving through gifts of time and skill, as well as presents made in the kitchen, workshop, or at the desk.

8. **Include** in your congregation and family celebrations, those who would otherwise be alone. Celebrate Christ's coming as "good news to the poor" by sharing the joy and intimacy of your Christmas with senior citizens living alone, foreign students, street people, refugees, or people who simply need hospitality.

9. **Give** to honor the birth of Christ. Do a cost analysis of your spending last Christmas. How much for presents? Decorations? Travel? Food? Covenant with members of your household to take 25 percent of what you spent last Christmas and make that a "birthday gift" this Christmas. Give it to those who are working with and on behalf of the really needy. ´

10. **Plan** for Christmas. Don't just be defensive. Find positive ways to react to society's idea of the "good" Christmas:

- During the summer, approach the appropriate committees in your church with ideas about how your congregation's celebrations might fully celebrate Christ's birth.
- Before Thanksgiving, write letters explaining your ideas about celebrating this year to family and friends with whom you ordinarily spend Christmas.
- Begin the gifts you want to make early enough to avoid being stampeded into buying at the last minute.
- Prepare your children early for an alternative Christmas. They need your help to resist the media's hard sell that begins right after Halloween.

– Reprinted from *To Celebrate: Reshaping Holidays & Rites of Passage*, 1987

Watch-dogging the media

In recent years there has been a growing movement against the barrage of television advertising aimed at children. Until more public outcry grows against the commercial domination of our airwaves, the big corporations and the media will continue money-making at our social, psychological, and financial expense.

What you may not realize is that you can work to combat this in your community. You may want to consider forming a special committee as a part of your community alternative Christmas campaign to begin work in this critical area. Consider organizing and sending delegations to talk with the management of local media about public concern over their advertising and program policies. You might:

- Ask them for public service time on the air to let people know about resources for decommercializing Christmas.
- Ask them to do a study and exposé on Christmas marketing and advertising practices as a community service. Suggest that TV shows or newspaper articles also cover community needs that could be met by diverting money at Christmas time.
- Ask for time on talk shows to discuss Christmas commercialism.
- Express concern about television advertising directed at children at Christmas. Since commercials promote a particular interpretation of Christmas to children, ask how the station intends to present other, alternative views of Christmas for young people.
- Go to any noncommercial community radio stations (college stations, NPR) and ask them to air a program on the commercial media's role in the yearly Christmas buy-a-thon.

Mission Mexico

Several years ago, our family felt the frustration of observing Christmas in ways that failed to celebrate what God did in that wondrous moment. So we deliberately planned a Christmas that would serve a need with no way for the gift receiver to give back anything of material value and no expectation of the giver to receive anything of monetary value in return.

What began as our family's alternative has become an expression of the miracle of Christmas for hundreds of people. It started with our "five fish" (our five children) and we estimate at least 10,000 people were the recipients of the food, clothes, toys, and other gifts we personally delivered into the desperately needy areas between Ciudad Acuña and Piedras Negras, Mexico's hill country.

Though most of the clothing and toys we take into these areas have been used before, we ask donors to make sure gifts are suitable and in good condition. Our criterion is to take only what we would feel good about giving. We also try to respond to community needs. One year we took gloves for street sweepers and policemen, along with gloves and rubber boots for firemen who, we had observed the year before, had to work without them in the coldest weather.

As a result of these efforts, our group now receives full support and cooperation from local officials. The first year they were very skeptical, but after our third year, border officials allowed us to cross without a search. Local police now escort us through the towns, our T-shirts communicating the message we bring more effectively than our halting Spanish: *Cristo Te Ama Y Yo Tambien*, which translated means, "Christ loves you and I do, also."

– Jerry L. Mash, Guthrie, Oklahoma

Las Posadas

Las Posadas, which literally means "the inns," highlights the plight of the refugees of Bethlehem. This custom was developed in the ancient Franciscan missions of Mexico and what is now the American Southwest.

One of the high points of Christmas festivities in San Antonio and other towns with a strong Hispanic tradition, *Las Posadas* is a procession led by Mary and Joseph looking for shelter. As they arrive at various places, they sing a song of entreaty, only to hear a song of rejection by those inside. Eventually, they are recognized by those in an "inn," and allowed to enter. Great rejoicing and feasting follows.

Reenactment of this festival might be used at a church supper where Mary and Joseph, looking bedraggled and dirty, seek shelter at different tables. When they are finally allowed in, all can join in singing the first stanza of "Gentle Mary Laid her Child." If possible, prepare traditional Mexican food for this occasion. The important point is for the congregation to see Mary and Joseph as unwelcome travelers whom "decent" people would not let in and how this wandering couple resembles homeless refugees in our midst.

The ecological cost of Christmas

Many people go around turning out lights to ease the energy crisis, then buy electric toothbrushes, hair dryers, toasters, and shoe kits for Christmas. Try making this a "low energy" Christmas by refraining from buying anything which uses electricity, by leaving the tree lights and spotlights in the attic and decorating with popcorn and cranberries.

Consider ideas for gifts and holiday preparations which focus on conserving, rather than consuming, so that these may be symbols of life and not death. Give to life-supporting organizations instead of buying that electric gadget that will only add to the pollution of our air and to the profit of war-supporting industries.

Make your own decorations. Set aside time for the whole family to make holiday decorations and ornaments: colorful wall-hangings, pine cone wreaths, Advent calendars, garlands of flowers or colored paper, dried nuts, seeds, or seashells. Lids to tin containers can be made into ornaments by fringing and cutting shapes with scissors and pliers (use gloves).

According to the Christmas Tree Growers Association over 30 million natural Christmas trees become a part of our throwaway society each year. An estimated 10 million artificial trees are bought each year. The natural trees are cut, sold, decorated, and discarded all within an eight-week period. It is a credit to some cities that the trees are collected, shredded into mulch and returned to the homeowner.

Buy a live tree. The Sierra Club or a local nursery can give you advice about using a live tree for Christmas.

Tons and tons of wrapping paper, much of it containing metal, goes through the same throwaway cycle. Reducing the number of presents bought will have a corresponding effect on wasted paper. Use homemade Christmas wrappings instead of commercial paper: decorate scrap paper or brown bags, or try potato printing on newspapers. Save and decorate shoe boxes, cookie and coffee cans to put gifts in, pieces of leftover material could be batiked, tiedyed, or embroidered and used for wrapping gifts.

For the birds!

One of the best ways of affirming the environment at Christmas is to care for the birds. One of our family's greatest delights is watching nuthatches, chickadees, titmice, juncos, and cardinals come to our feeder outside the kitchen door. If you don't have a bird book, get one for the whole family.

Bird feeders can be made by children from all sorts of recycled "junk." Check out your library for easy how-to instruction books. Bird feeders, bird books, and bird food all make wonderful gifts to another person and to the world.

Remember, too, when you plant such flowers as sunflowers, you provide more than wondrous beauty – you can feed the birds with the seeds during winter.

Different Season's Greetings

I was sick and tired of receiving Christmas cards from people I see all the time. It's wasteful and ecologically unsound. I asked the people at our local paper if they would print a "Community Season's Greetings Card" in the form of a full page ad at Christmastime, listing all the people who made a contribution to charity that year instead of sending cards to their friends in town. They agreed, leaving me to select the charity, stipulating only that it be local. After researching, I chose the Salvation Army because of their reputation for delivering the goods where they were most needed with a minimum of nonsense.

More than 270 families responded. We collected about $2,300, all of which went for food allowances, clothing, and for small gifts for deprived families, nursing home residents, and the homeless people who rely on the Army for shelter. Because regular advertisers in the *Times* contributed the space, our total overhead was $17, the price of the fliers.

– Paula Krongard, Upper Montclair, New Jersey

Perfection

When I was little, I got a perfect apple, a perfect orange and a narcissus bulb in my stocking.

– Eugenie Bradford, Alexandria, Virginia

Decorations

Hold an open house before Christmas with homemade food that everyone brings. Assemble supplies for making decorations – straw stars, snowflakes, popcorn and cranberries for stringing, pine cones, seed pods for ornaments, colored paper for chains.

Have lots of things for the children to do. This is a decoration workshop.

– Helen Brewer, Washington, D.C.

Simple Christmas meal

In lieu of a traditional Christmas dinner (turkey, ham) we had a simple meal consisting of beans, tortillas, and rice. We then gave a $25 contribution – representing what we would have spent on a traditional meal – to CROP, a hunger program of Church World Service.

– The Miodunski Family, Barnhart, Missouri

Checking out hunger

We kept a record of what we spent on our gifts, Christmas dinner, and tree. On Christmas Eve we wrote several checks to hunger appeals or other ministries equal to what we gave ourselves and our loved ones. That sum comes from our living budget.

– Carolyn Brown, Chapel Hill, North Carolina

Vacation

Why not devote the adult section of Vacation Bible School to the alternate Christmas idea?

– Mary Gray, Davidson, North Carolina

Stamp

Make a rubber stamp which reads "OPEN SOMEBODY'S MIND FOR CHRISTMAS" and stamp it on all your mail.

– Karen Zetit, Denver, Colorado

Real Christmas message

By going through our local Council of Churches, a very colorful yellow, green and red billboard was put up at the end of a large shopping mall. It said "Celebrate! with a creative alternative gift."... I was especially pleased with the spot they gave it; right beside "Season Ticket," the sign MasterCharge had put up for an entirely different direction in Christmas spending.

– June Barnwon, Chico, California

Richest Christmas

For Christmas last year we gave prayers to our friends and family. At the time, my husband and I worried that our gift might be misunderstood. Prayer, after all, doesn't sound like much. But it was given out of our need to make Christmas more meaningful. To our surprise it was received as a gift of great value, and it brought us, in return, the richest Christmas blessings we had known.

Our children took part in our prayers enthusiastically. Before the first devotion day arrived, our daughter noticed the craft supplies we had collected for illustrating the prayer cards. She volunteered to be in charge of crafts the first day, and thereafter she often planned that activity. Our son jealously guarded his role as acolyte and filled a basket with once-lit candles to send with prayer cards. We wrote prayers together, and even after the holiday season ended, the children did not tire of devotions.

Then our friends and relatives showed us the grace of Christmas in the way they received our prayers. For one couple, our prayers were the impetus for re-establishing a relationship. They came to our home to share their prayer day with us. Jewish friends invited us to join their Passover celebration in the new year. Several other friends planned special holiday dinners or concert trips with us. We were overwhelmed by the love and closeness of people.

Our alternative celebration permanently changed Christmas for us. It will always be a time when we remember that just as Jesus came as a gift to us, we are gifts to each other.

CoLaborer Magazine, Winter 1986.
Used by permission.

Whose Birthday Is It, Anyway?

In the Land of Puzzling Tales, there lived an eight-year-old boy by the name of Jason.

Now in this land and in the neighborhood where Jason lived, the unexpected always happened.

Instead of football they played kneeball; instead of the children "going to school" the teachers were busy "going to homes." In the summertime, it was not uncommon to see water freeze and in the wintertime to see leaves on trees. It was a funny, strange place.

One incident in the Land of Puzzling Tales stands out. When it was time for Jason's ninth birthday, as usual, the unusual happened.

Jason's grandparents came from their home across the country to help celebrate, but of course, when they got to Jason's neighborhood, they went immediately to the Browns' down the street and visited and stayed there.

When Jason's mother baked the birthday cake, she gave it to the letter carrier to eat.

And when all the neighborhood kids heard it was Jason's birthday, they exchanged gifts with one another and, of course, Jason got none.

There was a blizzard of birthday cards. The post office had to hire extra workers and work longer hours to handle the deluge of cards. Of course, in the Land of Puzzling Tales, the expected was the unexpected, and all the kids, the moms and dads, grandparents, and even a couple of dogs and a parakeet got cards, while poor Jason got none.

Finally, at about nine o'clock, in a fit of frustration and anger, Jason went out of his house, borrowed the school cheerleader's megaphone, rode up and down the street on his unicycle and shouted at the top of his lungs, *"Whose birthday is it, anyway?"*

And the night was so silent that all night long echoes bounced off the mountains. *"Whose birthday is it, anyway?" "Whose birthday is it, anyway?"*

The baby Jesus will be kidnapped again this year and held ransom for millions of dollars. This year North Americans will surrender billions of dollars to the stores to buy gifts to swap.

But it is Jesus' birthday! Jesus ought to receive the gifts. Jesus said, "Inasmuch as you have done it to the least of these my brothers and sisters, you have done it to me." We give to Jesus when we give to the poor, the weak, the hungry, the homeless, the refugees, the prisoners.

It will be a great birthday celebration when God's people begin in earnest to give once again to Jesus. For after all, it is his birthday, isn't it?

– Rev. Arley Fadness, Harrisburg, South Dakota

Alternative Christmas Campaign

Is it any of the church's business?

Although individuals and families can and must make their own decisions about changing the ways they celebrate, the church has a critical role in encouraging them. Indeed, if it is not the church's business to call for more responsible celebrations of Christmas, whose business is it?

What can the local church do?

1. Challenge commercialized celebrations and call for ways to observe Christmas which focus on the needs of others:

- Set aside a Sunday in October or early November to call the congregation to a new seriousness in the celebration of Christmas.
- Ask members to covenant to set aside 25 percent of what they spent on last year's Christmas and give it as a Christmas gift to denominational programs which minister to those in need.
- Consider initiating a community-wide alternative Christmas festival in which these concerns can extend beyond the local church into the community at large.

2. Encourage members who want to change by providing supportive programs and resources. Consider a mailing to members (or a special issue of the church newsletter), including the reasons for, and ideas about, an alternative Christmas.

- Offer study opportunities for all age groups on "Preparing to Celebrate the Birth of Christ."
- Provide guidelines for alternative giving, for example, buying from church-supported craft groups, giving of one's time and skills, or making contributions in a recipient's name.

3. Shape the worship life of the congregation to reflect the concerns about Christmas:

- Give particular attention to the worship service on a chosen Sunday in October or November.
- Use the "Whose Birthday Is It, Anyway?" (in this Christmas section) as a bulletin insert that reflects those concerns.
- Plan the Christmas worship service (on Christmas or Christmas Eve) to include a time when individuals and families can offer birthday gifts to the Christ child.

What gifts shall we bring?

1. Remember whose birthday it is. Christmas gift-giving begins with a recognition that Christmas is the day we celebrate the birth of Jesus Christ. He should be first, not last, on our Christmas list.

2. Give to those he came to serve – the poor, the homeless, the prisoner, the hungry, the oppressed, and the outcast. Is there a better way to honor him than to give of ourselves to these?

- Time: Commit time to participate in a group working with society's "devalued" persons. For example, you could participate in a senior citizens' lunch program, prison visitation program, or a refugee resettlement program.
- Skills: Volunteer to do cooking, bookkeeping, repair work, or to teach those skills to disadvantaged persons. Neither dollars nor bright wrapping paper can improve on these gifts.
- Money: Financial gifts to support ministries among society's "forgotten" people can make a difference. If 10,000 families re-distribute only $100 each this Christmas, that will be one million dollars.

3. **Plan your gift giving!** Make your gift list early. Discuss with your family your willingness to spend in time, skills, and money at least 25 percent of what you spent on last year's Christmas.

Warning: You probably do not have enough time or money to do everything you have done *before* and *add* this commitment, as well; this commitment must replace some of what you've done and spent before.

A Litany for Christmas

One: O Lord, as we prepare to celebrate the birth of Jesus, we give thanks for the light that has come into the world and given us hope. And we give thanks for those in every age who have been witnesses to the light.

All: The light shines in darkness, and the darkness has not overcome it.

One: In the darkness of the threat of nuclear disaster, we are thankful for the witness of those of all classes, races and nationalities who say, "It does not have to be."

All: The light shines in the darkness, and the darkness has not overcome it.

One: In the darkness of hunger and homelessness in a world that has enough for all, we are thankful for the witness of those who feed the hungry, welcome the stranger, clothe the naked, and struggle for them in the halls of government and corporate board rooms.

All: The light shines in darkness, and the darkness has not overcome it.

One: In the darkness from unsafe streets to death row cells, we give thanks for the witness of those who remember that justice is not served by violence.

All: The light shines in darkness, and the darkness has not overcome it.

One: In the darkness of greed that is a sickness in our souls, we give thanks for the witness of those who dispel the illusion that life consists of the accumulation of things.

All: The light shines in darkness, and the darkness has not overcome it.

One: O God, forgive us when we are content to live in the shadows. This Christmas, strengthen our faith and renew our hope that we may be witnesses to the Light.

All: Amen.

Organizing a Festival

Imagine how it would be to share and celebrate the true spirit of Christmas with your community in a well-planned and popular festival! Think how many, many more people might become involved in an alternative Christmas.

Festival goals

A Community Christmas Festival will contribute to:

- building a community base of understanding and support for alternative celebrations;
- learning how our celebrations can be both considerate of the needs of people and kind to Earth;
- diverting "Christmas" money to self-help groups and to community groups seeking to serve society's disenfranchised people;
- encouraging people to adopt more meaningful humane and personal gift-giving practices;
- challenging publicly the assumption that the birth of Christ is honored in commercialized Christmas celebrations;
- building a community base of understanding and support for other cooperative people- and Earth-oriented endeavors.

Planning the festival

1. **Plan early:** Plan your festival to be very early in the Christmas Season. September and October are ideal. This way you can expose the idea to many people who are unfamiliar with the alternative Christmas idea and leave time for them to participate this Christmas. This means getting the organizing and planning process underway much earlier.

   If it is October when you first read this and begin to think about a festival, don't despair! Adjust the scale of the festival to what you have time to organize, or use this as the time to begin organizing for next year.

2. **Planning committee:** An Alternative Christmas festival will involve many members of the community. Therefore, you should form a committee that represents all of the noncommercial interests of your community, such as people from other churches, schools, clubs, social change groups, and workers. People from all of these groups will have different and interesting ideas for the festival.

3. **Where to begin:** There is no one formula about where to begin organizing a festival. Since there are so few precedents for this kind of activity, you are really on your own! As you begin thinking about where to start, consider the following ideas:

- Enlist the support of your own local church for the effort first.
- You may find it useful to approach other churches in the community.
- Campus ministers often have the most interest, skills, and contacts for this kind of organizing. Don't hesitate to contact them.
- There are many ways to organize. What is needed most are a few persons willing to commit themselves to finding the best way, and then organizing.

4. **Logistics:** Once you have a planning committee together, set up the logistics of the festival with great care: where and when to have it, how to spread the word about it, what facilities and special skills you will need, who will be in charge of what, etc. Attention to detail will pay off in a more smoothly-run event and a greater sense of community self-confidence.

5. **Publicity committee:** Charged with obtaining widespread attention for this important event, this committee should be led by persons who believe in the festival and who are not timid in dealing with the media (see the section on dealing with the media below).

Ideas for the festival

1. Invite as many community social change groups (hunger coalitions, senior citizens groups, environmental protection groups) as possible to put up displays and information tables; ask them to make signs and posters relating their issue to a need for people to reorient themselves to more socially responsible lifestyles.

2. Invite all self-help crafts groups in your area to come and share their creations with the community. They can have crafts available for sale as alternative Christmas gifts. And, if possible, have representatives from the craft groups present to demonstrate their skill in their craft. Some of the groups will send a quantity of their goods on consignment to the festival.

3. You can also include booths with appropriate food items for sale (home-baked breads, nuts, fruits) alongside booths that educate about nutrition, food systems, hunger, and world food distribution. The hunger task force or lifestyle committee in local churches will probably be glad to work on these booths. Also contact local food co-ops for participation.

4. How about booths with people demonstrating how to make Christmas gifts? Perhaps a list of suggestions could also be made available at these booths. You might be surprised to find out how many persons in your community have skills they would be glad to demonstrate in a booth.

5. Every festival needs music and dancing. Arrange for local groups to play music and perhaps lead some folks to dancing. What about a sing-a-long for Advent carols? Someone might be able to rewrite some secular songs to fit the alternative Christmas.

6. You might have a video playing continuously which deals with hunger, Earth, or people issues. You may want to include celebratory films that fit the theme, too.

7. Invite a storyteller to perform a story about successfully celebrating Christmas in an alternative way.

8. You may want to have a book table where many of the books written on social justice issues, responsible lifestyles, and alternative celebration resources could be sold as gifts for friends and family.

9. You can have a table for making homemade decorations where people can either take their creation home, or hang it on a tree. The decorated tree (or the decorations) could be donated to a women's shelter or other suitable place.

A tree

The best way to obtain a tree is to find someone in your community who would be willing to give one from their own property. After the festival, the tree can be replanted where it came from, or maybe in a public park. If you can't find someone to donate a tree, then you might have to buy one from a nursery. Either way, make sure that the tree is replanted when the event is over.

You can decorate your tree with handmade decorations, such as strings of popcorn, chains made of paper (perhaps each link of chain could bear the name of one of the members of the community who cannot attend the festival due to illness or disability, or maybe each link could have a special "wish" of good intention printed on it), pine cones from the ground, cut-out pictures of people helping people, or any other decoration that would make your tree a real symbol of life. The rest of the hall could be decorated with such things as children's art or paper snowflakes made from recycled paper.

An alternative Santa Claus

Santa Claus is a very powerful cultural image in our society. An "alternative Santa Claus" could be an exciting, interesting, and attention-grabbing mechanism to call attention to the commercialization of Christmas. The alternative Santa might be the highlight of your festival, especially as the culmination of other activities.

What would an "alternative Santa" look like? Perhaps the traditional Santa outfit in a different color (say, green or blue in place of the red) would be appropriate. Or maybe just the white beard and cap with overalls or some other simple clothing. Whatever you decide, bear in mind that you want this Santa to be recognized as Santa Claus, but as one who is different.

What would an alternative Santa do? This Santa should personify the spirit of Christmas and at the same time protest the commercialization of Christmas. There is a lot of room for creativity.

Here are some suggestions:

1. Alternative Santas could show up, when appropriate, at public meetings, church functions, college campuses, and at shopping malls handing out announcements about the upcoming Alternative Christmas Festival, and talking with persons about commercialized Christmas celebrations.

2. Draft a letter to the local newspapers (signed "Santa Claus") asking why people have allowed Christmas to become so commercialized. Explain that Santa is changing his ways and so should they. You may want to arrange a press conference so that you could get coverage by local television and radio stations as well as the press.

3. If your city or town has any official Christmas festivities such as parades, fairs and the like, request that the alternative Santas be allowed to take part.

Warning: Unlike other activities in the alternative Christmas festival, this one is sure to arouse opposition as well as support. In 1980, in Chico, California, a green Santa who was handing out "Whose Birthday Is It, Anyway?" leaflets was run off the sidewalk, reprimanded for obstructing traffic, and ridiculed. Never mind. Change comes slowly!

Dealing with the media

Today's mass media play a central role in the commercialized Christmas celebration. Each November and December, billions of dollars worth of ads and commercials are bought by thousands of businesses, each vying for a piece of the Christmas take. "Television and radio stations," notes *Broadcasting* magazine, "are singing a happy tune during the Christmas advertising season."

If we hope to reach large numbers of people with the alternative Christmas message, it will be necessary to work with, or through, the media to whatever extent possible. While understanding the built-in limitations you will face, it is important to learn the following:

• how to approach the media with your message;
• what to do when they come to you;
• how to monitor and challenge their role in the commercial Christmas.

Feature coverage

In the fall, newspapers, television, and radio will all be hunting for interesting Christmas stories, and especially for those with a local angle. Try to arrange an appointment with the appropriate editors, producers, or journalists to present them with written material and information on the alternative Christmas idea, some basic facts about commercialization, and an outline of the local activities you are planning.

Public service announcements

Radio, television, and newspapers generally have free announcement times or space for community events or public service announcements (PSAs). Policies on these PSAs will vary greatly from station to station, or paper to paper. Check out each media outlet in your area on policies: time, space or word limits, content guidelines, deadlines.

When writing a PSA text, be brief, and end with the appropriate address or phone number. Repeat the phone number if possible.

For all publicity efforts, be sure to send copies of announcements to relevant community publications (church newsletters, college newspapers) and put posters or flyers on community and office bulletin boards.

News releases

A community alternative Christmas festival is "news." You will want to prepare a news release to send to all relevant media.

A news release should be written in a particular style. In the upper left hand corner, type in the words NEWS RELEASE. In the upper right hand corner, put your group's name and address (if it does not appear elsewhere on the stationery). In the same corner, put the contact person's name and phone number so reporters will know who and where to call for further information.

The release should include a "release date" indicating when the news item can be used or printed. In most cases, this will read "for immediate release."

A brief, interesting heading should be at the top of the release text. Remember that the person receiving your release may read over dozens of others that day, hunting for the most interesting item. Follow the headline with a summary of the "Who, What, Where, When, and Why" information. This should be followed by several paragraphs of background data, and possibly some quotes from people with insight into issues of commercialization and the commercialization of Christmas in particular. One or two pages should be the maximum length – a news release is an attention-getter, not an essay.

The releases should be mailed or hand-delivered to all television and radio stations and newspapers in your area. A release announcing your festival should reach the media a week ahead of time. If you can identify which reporters cover community news, religious affairs, and business news, send them a personal copy of the release. Then make follow-up phone calls. If the release is for the festival, ask if a reporter has been assigned to cover it. If the release was more informational in nature, call and ask if there are any more facts or figures that you can provide.

Finally, keep a file of all journalists and media contacts who cover your story or show a personal interest in the issue.

When the media comes

If your press release and public service announcements about the festival are successful and the media people show up at your festival – what then?

- Have press kits prepared that include copies of any relevant background materials for a journalist who will be filing the story. The press kits need not be elaborate, but they should be thoughtfully and interestingly prepared. Be sure to include any available art pieces, and perhaps a copy of "Whose Birthday Is It, Anyway?"
- Have a spokesperson chosen by your group to handle any questions and to make statements to the press. This person should decide in advance what you want to communicate through the media. Remember that you may have only 30 seconds in front of a camera to explain your issues.

One final reminder – have fun!

Kwanzaa

An Afro-American celebration

Kwanzaa (a Swahili word, in this context meaning "first fruits") is an Afro-American celebration that begins on December 26 and ends on New Year's Day. The festival was started in 1966 in California by Afro-American nationalist Maulana Ron Karenga. It is rooted in traditional harvest celebrations in Africa. The focus of the observance is on African and Afro-American history and culture, as well as on seven principles of Kwanzaa: unity, self-determination, collective work and responsibility, cooperative economics, purpose, creativity, and faith.

Each night, a ceremony is held which involves candle lighting by children, passing a unity cup, honoring ancestors, and discussion of one of the seven principles of Kwanzaa. Prayers of thanksgiving, songs, folk tales, and resolutions for the future are often part of the celebration. When the seventh principle has been discussed on the seventh day, the holiday ends with gift-giving, a feast, singing, and dancing. The emphasis for gifts is on small, handmade items with special meaning that will help the recipient get through the next year. Generally, gifts are played down while spiritual and social rejuvenation are emphasized.

Kwanzaa is celebrated in homes, and the celebration is shaped to suit each family. Kwanzaa symbols include: a straw mat (representing foundation), a seven-place candle holder (African origins), seven candles (principles), corn (children), and a bowl of gifts. Kwanzaa is a celebration for Afro-Americans of all religious and nonreligious persuasions. It was born of a desire to celebrate African roots, and is an alternative to the commercialized Christmas in the United States.

For more information, seek out books such as *Kwanzaa: A Family Affair*, by Mildred Pitts Walter.

Part 4

Rites of
Passage

Why Celebrate Passages?

Rites of passage are rituals or celebrations that mark the passage of a person through the life cycle, from one stage to another, from one role or social position to another. In the pre-modern world, these rites served at least four functions:

1. Safe passage

Rites of passage integrated biological reality (birth, reproduction, and death) with cultural and religious experience. Passages are anxiety-producing life crises. The rites not only "gave permission for" – or legitimated – the anxiety, but they allayed it by giving meaning to the experience. They made the "passage" from one life stage to another safe and clear.

2. Moments of learning

Although some rites of passage occurred at great moments of anxiety (life crisis), all provided an atmosphere in which learning could take place. By calling attention to the particular life change, rites of passage may have increased anxiety, but did so in a context where important learning occurred that assisted in the transition. For example, acknowledging the reality of death in a funeral or memorial service may increase anxieties already being experienced. But that ritual acknowledgment may also aid in accepting life without the one who has died.

3. Connection to community

Rites of passage celebrated the connecting of individuals to a community. The physiological fact is that one is born and dies alone, unique and separate. But each one is also a member of a community, a group that has particular values and understandings of life. Rites of passage connected the individual experience to the understandings of the group in such a way as to give meaning to that experience. While Christian rites of baptism, christening, and dedication are performed for different reasons, they have in common that they celebrate linking the individual to a group.

4. Transformation experiences

Not only did rites help to facilitate passage from one stage to another, but the rites actually shaped and manipulated biological imperatives as well. The message from ancient societies is that women and men are not simply born, nor do they merely procreate and die; what they are is in part what they are "made" through rites of passage. In some societies, girls "became" women when they went through puberty rites, whether or not they had begun to menstruate; and adolescent boys "became" men when they went on the hunt or were circumcised whether or not they had gone through puberty. As Mircea

Eliade has put it, one may become what one performs. Rites of passage were transformation experiences.

The place of rites in modern society

Some anthropologists have expressed doubt that rites of passage can have much meaning in a society so complex, so secular, and so fragmented. Gail Sheehy's best-seller, *Passages: Predictable Crises of Adult Life* called attention to the reality of life passages for adults and to the various cultural and psychological problems that result from them. She does not, however, consider the importance of "rites" to these junctures in life.

Few, however, doubt the need for such rites or the cost of not having them. In a society which so prizes individuality over community, many find it necessary to adjust to life's transitions alone. Increasingly, our lives are entrusted into the hands of experts and anonymous agencies or individuals who care for only a small part of our human needs. We are born, for the most part, in hospitals, and we usually die there. For many, the most profound events of their lives have become merely secular affairs left uncelebrated. Beyond the traditional passages, this society has numerous forms of crisis and transition: menopause, surgery, "empty nests," graduation, career change, divorce, retirement, leaving the family home

for a retirement home, etc. Traumatic, exciting and anxiety-provoking, these passages regularly go unobserved. As early as 1897, in his classic study on suicide, Emil Durkheim wrote that one of the consequences of the lack of social connection and unacknowledged existence in modern society was suicide. Others have since pointed to the relationship between mental illness and going through passages alone and uncelebrated.

Our consumer culture has also had its impact on the observance of rites of passage, especially by making them occasions for greater consumption. Under pressure to do "what society expects," some people spend beyond their means and end up resenting the occasion itself. Moreover, when the focus of the celebration is on consumption, the critical functions of safe passage, learning, connecting to community, and transformation become distorted or obscured altogether.

The absence of "community," in a traditional sense, makes observing the rites of passage in families, immediate communities, and religious communities all the more important. If you don't have suitable rites for the passages in your life, create them! But don't stop there. Resist the pressures of the consumer society and observe the rites in ways that enable you to recover the renewing and maturing power they are intended to have by focusing on the following:

- **People.** Focus on the people in passage, their anxieties, and the real issues they face in the new stage, instead of the gifts and other paraphenalia used to aid or celebrate the transition. In this way, those in passage can be brought "safely" through to a new stage of maturity.
- **Values and ideals.** Instead of mindlessly celebrating to anesthetize the person(s) to the trauma of transition, focusing on values and ideals needed for the next phase of life can make the occasion a critical moment for learning.
- **Community.** Instead of the consumer culture's narcissistic privatization of life transitions, focus the rites on the mystery and wonder of our place in community. These can be critical times to experience support from those relationships as well as times to mature in our understanding of the community which sustains us. While "fragmentation" rather than "community" may characterize 20th century society, we are more than ever part of a world community, dependent on one earth and a fragile ecosystem for survival.

  Just as the rites in ancient times moved those in passage toward their new responsibilities in the community, so today's rites of passage must celebrate our relationship to the larger community and to the ecosystem, and aid in moving us toward assuming the responsibilities incumbent on us because of those relationships.
- **Change.** By focusing on the life changes that are required in the particular passage, the rites can help make the passages transformation experiences. Rites help people visualize the desired outcome of the passage and to see themselves on the other side. As such, rites become occasions of transformation.

– Reprinted from *To Celebrate: Reshaping Holidays & Rites of Passage*

Creating our own rituals

Ever since the Industrial Revolution, much of Western society has shunned rituals. Many people believed that rituals, perhaps, were magic or superstitious nonsense, and that we could certainly live without them if we used logic, science, and common sense. But throwing so many of our rituals away has left us naked. Although some of life is logical, much of life is not. Even when we are young we come to understand that life is full of mystery. Without rituals and ceremonies within our communities and families, we feel adrift and cannot understand why.

One example of society's loss can be seen in how we have disengaged ourselves from the rituals surrounding death, dying, and grieving. Having given many of the meaningful rituals that humans need to hospitals and funerals homes, we find ourselves unable to adjust, or bewildered by feelings of denial. We suffer as a society.

As our millennium draws to a close, the hunger for meaningful ritual and spiritual practice only becomes more acute. The flood of recent books, articles, and essays in cyberspace attest to that.

There are rituals for menopause, retirement, puberty, mid-life, grieving, and so on. Joseph Campbell, author of *The Hero with a Thousand Faces*, and many other books, is one who helped till the soil for the rich harvest of searching currently underway. *Autumn Gospel: Women in the Second Half of Life*, by Kathleen Fischer, *The Magic of Ritual* by Tom F. Driver, and *Lights of Passage: Rituals and Rites of Passage* by Kathleen Wall and Gary Ferguson are just three of the books that can help us understand the need for, and creation of, rituals today.

Birth

From earliest times, birth has been regarded not only as a rite of passage for the baby, but for the parents and community as well. While modern science can explain in clinical detail the reproduction process, mystery and wonder still surround every pregnancy and birth. In ancient societies, this life transition required many different rites: taboos that related to pregnancy and birth; rites to ward off evil spirits and for protection; rites to make delivery easy and safe; rites to secure good fortune for the child; rites to admit the child to society; and rites to readmit the parents back into society in their changed state.

In today's world, many of the functions of the old rites have been dropped altogether or are performed by doctors and other health care professionals. The contribution of modern medical science and technology to the biology of the reproductive process has been incalculable.

It is lamentable, however, that our modern world has not been as successful in replacing those ancient rites relating to cultural traditions – those traditions which assured parents and children of acceptance and support by the larger community. The functions of those early rites are now provided by friends, parents, classes, and books. One birth rite that continues is the baby shower. A shower is more than an occasion to provide physical necessities for the new baby. It can be a time when friends gather around the parents-to-be in a ritual circle of support for the coming event, wonderful yet shrouded in mystery and uncertainty.

Like all other passages in the

consumer society, births present opportunities for excessive consumption. Baby industry promoters play on pride, insecurity, and ignorance to convince parents and their friends that the new baby must have a whole host of superfluous products. An ad for designer diaper covers maintains, "It's never too early for your child to learn the importance of class." Providing necessities for the new baby – clothes, blankets, diapers, etc. – is an important part of getting ready. There are also other ways to help prepare for this important passage. Consider giving more personal gifts of time and skill, such as painting the nursery, preparing some meals, or caring for other children in the family around the time of the birth. Gifts of books on baby care are common, especially if this is a first child. Equally appropriate is a book such as *Parenting for Peace and Justice* by Jim and Kathy McGinnis. If the family is adequately supplied and cared for, gifts made in the name of the family to projects which help less fortunate children are particularly appropriate.

Welcoming rites

Christening, dedication, and infant baptism are rites that celebrate the connecting of the child to a religious community. As these rites call attention to the responsibilities of the parents and the members of the community for the spiritual nurture of the child, they also recognize the new status of the parents in the community. In some families, baptism anniversaries are observed just like birthdays. Except in subsequent birthday celebrations, there are no generally-used rites to celebrate the entrance of the child into a family; however, you may want to create a rite to use with immediate family and close friends when mother and baby come home from the hospital.

It is unfortunate that the practice of naming godparents for a new baby is now largely symbolic. Traditionally, godparents not only had responsibility for the child in the event of the death of the parents, but they also had special responsibilities for the child's spiritual nurture. It was their responsibility to guide their godchild in the ways of faith by teaching the Ten Commandments, the Lord's Prayer, and the Apostles' Creed. In this time when grandparents may be far away, the traditional godparent role could provide active support and nurture to parents and children alike.

A naming ceremony is another way to welcome a new child into the community. Among the Cree people in northern Ontario, the baby is named at a gathering of family and friends. The baby is then passed around the circle. Each one offers a blessing, a wish, or a hope for the baby.

Roots for a new arrival

When my first grandson was born seven years ago, I gave considerable thought to what might be an appropriate gift for him. His other grandparents had generously supplied everything imaginable that would be needed for his care and entertainment. I found it rather frustrating that whatever I mentioned as a possible gift for him was something he already had.

What I came up with was something I did not have to shop for, except in the recesses of my memory and in a journal I had kept for many years. My gift took the form of a letter to our little Noah to be read to him at some suitable time in his growing-up years. This was the life story of certain family members with whom he would find his own identity.

In a radio interview, Alex Haley, author of *Roots*, made the following poetic statement. "Grandparents sprinkle stardust in the lives of their grandchildren." My "stardust" letter included our family's welcome to Noah, something of what we felt as he came into the world. There was some informal genealogical information, but quite a few special stories of his own father (our son Daniel), covering Danny's birth, position in the family, and early experiences related to such things as nature, prayer, family, and school.

Then came information about my husband and myself, our childhood and youth, experiences in school and church, and influences that led us into our life's work. Much of this section showed definite interest and involvement with moral or religious matters which were part of the formation of our faith.

The response to this letter was more than I had dreamed possible in terms of communication with my son, his wife, and her family. Danny said there were things in the letter which he had never known. His wife now had a better understanding of who we were and from where we came; her grandmother, with whom she shared Noah's letter, told me that it was one of the most beautiful things she had ever read. Yet this was not a pietistic, sentimental presentation. It was simply something I wanted to share with my grandson about some of the people in his life, and some of those who lived before us.

– Mary Lou McCrary, Atlanta, Georgia

The gift of natural childbirth

A time to be born. An exciting and busy time. A time when the forces of men and women unite to welcome a new life and celebrate the process of creation.

But wait. Why are we all closed out? Why are some professionals so anxious to make the process conform to time? Why has the woman often been removed from her body and sent away to dream? Is she not to greet her child? Is she not to feel the last movements within her body as the life of her child begins? Is birth too horrible for a mother to see who has already been with her child for months?

When our second child was expected, David and I decided medical professionals had not helped us enjoy our first baby's birth, and in all likelihood their attitudes were still professional, not personal. We didn't want a pep squad, but a few whoops and cheers for our team was not a lot to ask. Our doctors looked down their stethoscopes at us and refused to become involved beyond answering our questions and conducting regular checkups. They regarded our plans for unmedicated, unassisted labor as faddish and frivolous. They never encouraged or informed us in an open and caring way. They were happy, busy people with a modus operandi – and we were already taking up more time than the one-charge, set-fee plan permitted.

What were we to do?

Pregnancy is like going over the falls. You can't turn around halfway down and look for a better route. You can only reach out and grab on to the limbs. Fortunately, we found a support group already formed for prospective parents who wanted information and encouragement. We were not looking for answers so much as options. We wanted to be informed enough to recognize when we needed help and confident enough not to panic if I got hiccups during delivery.

So we began our preparation.

We began by getting to know our unborn child. We noted her turbulent days and what caused them. She was a person, not just a fetus. We enjoyed watching her grow, slowly shifting my center of gravity. She was gently touched and rubbed throughout the days and embraced, often upside down, by her sister. She moved, silently seeking us through her womb. She knew we were waiting to meet her. (Now, I miss that union without care for baths or feedings, that blind building going on inside me.)

Each day near the end brought the thought that "surely this is the day." And at that moment when Anna was ready, she began to enter our world. I told David we were into countdown and, in his own way, he prepared. He choked on his coffee and threw up several times. That is his way.

Stomach empty, he was ready to work. And work we did. To ensure our baby's health, we had decided to have her at a hospital, but we asked that we be left alone – alone to use the breathing and mutual support techniques we had learned in our childbirth education classes.

Like making a fine quilt, we had stitched each piece and, if it were possible, we wanted to finish up together without the ever-ready, speedy technology. We wanted to greet our child as she entered the world, with a smile on our faces, as you would greet a guest.

As David and I worked through each contraction, we talked for the last time of our constant, heartfelt hopes for a sister for Kirsten. We admired each other in our fears. We shared intimately. Neither of us expected birthing to be funny, exciting, sexual, or euphoric, but it was.

Then the hard work came. The self-doubt and anger crept in. The urge to run away – but how? Then, suddenly, we were alone, isolated from the bustle of the delivery room. My recollection is one of a slow motion, low-light film, like the shallow-breathed suspense of Blind Man's Bluff just before being touched. Then the push.

My body knew what to do! Amazed at my own strength and consumed by my excitement, I finally began to see my passenger's head. Then quickly, easily, her shoulders and body. She looked at once both dark and shiny. Her body was long and slippery. She was warm on my tummy and heavier there than she had been inside.

She was not mad or frantic, but peaceful and alert. David and I cried together. We had worked more closely that day than we had dreamed possible, and we would never forget that intimacy.

I think how easily we could have turned the entire process over to a doctor and waited to get our baby, and I understand why medical professionals have taken charge in so many cases. They have cleaned up the act and anticipated the complications. They have sterilized the process, and they have tried to do it better each time. But they don't make the babies, and they don't raise the children, and they don't recall the snatches of confused consciousness from drugged labors. They don't join you each year to celebrate the birth or to laugh with you at the funny memories. They walk away and forget which day you came in or what sex your child was. They take their fees and do a good job on you. But why give this beautiful part of your life away? Why not share it with those who will still be around to nurture and love that new life?

By involving ourselves, we take on the work and responsibility of giving birth, but we also enjoy a sharing and satisfying period of life that prepares us to face raising our children ourselves. We earn the privilege of joining in a celebration of life. And we learn to appreciate miracles.

– Hank Ingebretsen, Jackson, Mississippi

Recipes

In order to greet the new arrival, have a shower after the baby is born. Have guests bring an index card with their "recipe" for a happy childhood to give to the mother. Other items might include "recipes" for a happy motherhood/fatherhood with guests sharing their experiences and wisdom on parenting.

– Mary Ann Sloan, Jonesboro, Arkansas

Gifts

For years I have been conditioned to feel the necessity of sending a gift whenever friends have a baby. I have recently found that there are ways of showing your love and joy without sending a blanket or silver spoon or cup – many of which never get used. I first learned about alternative "baby gift" ideas from Nancy Gilbert, who sends checks to UNICEF or similar organizations which help children. Recently, we have started sharing our "retired" baby clothes with close friends when they have a child. Naturally, this alternative soon runs out. Another idea is to send $10 to the Easter Seal Society, the Cerebral Palsy Association or the local school for retarded children.

Alternate baby shower

One very successful idea was to give an "alternate baby shower," at which the mother-to-be received promises of help, time, meals for her family, a poem, and so on.

– Paul and Marie Crosso, Washington, D.C.

In Sarah's name

On the occasion of the birth of our daughter, our congregation wanted to give us a shower to mark her birth. I agreed on the condition that the guests bring children's or babies' clothing to be given to Church World Services in Sarah's name. Everyone had a great time, and left the party feeling a closer tie with the less fortunate of the world.

– Connie Hansen, Malden, Massachusetts

Channeling gifts

We sent the money given to our new child to support a nonprofit day care center which serves the local community. We notified our friends as to where the money would be going, and asked them to let us know if they preferred another channel for their gift.

– Mrs. Paul Rothfusz, Atlantic, Iowa

Two children

Think about the idea of godparents "adopting" a child overseas on the occasion of their godchild's baptism. There are many organizations that will accept monthly contributions to support a needy child overseas.

– Rev. Susan Thistlethwarte,
Durham, North Carolina

Showers: A community affair

Frustrated by the typical ladies-only-sweet-dessert-type showers, our church hosts family-oriented wedding and baby showers. We usually hold these following the Sunday morning worship service when most family members are together. We share a potluck meal and have some songs and games to involve every-one. Helpful hints, words of wisdom, or a favorite Bible verse may be written on an index card and read aloud as part of the shower program, as well as given to the honored couple. We emphasize practical and humorous gifts. For parents-to-be we might include books and magazines about parenting, coupons for babysitting or for a meal to be brought to the home soon after the baby's birth, cloth diapers, and recycled baby clothes.

– Anne Hall Shields,
Cooperstown, North Dakota

Homemade frozen dinners make fantastic gifts

I belong to a group that has shared Monday dinners together for more than four years. During that time there have been three births among our members. For each birth our eating group hosted a shower, including the couple's other friends. For our collective gift, each adult member prepares a one-dish meal which is frozen and delivered around the day of the birth. Given the size of our group, this provides the family with dinners for about two weeks.

As a recipient as well as a preparer, I know this is a fantastic gift.

– Kathie Klein, Atlanta, Georgia

Siblings are proud, too

New babies can be announced with homemade cards featuring artwork by older siblings proudly announc-ing the arrival of their new baby brother or sister.

– Meryl A. Butler, Virginia Beach, Virginia

Tree planting commemorates birth

"It is with [people] as it is with trees – one must grow slowly to last long."

– Henry David Thoreau

This inscription accompanies a small Japanese red maple tribute tree. It was planted in August of 1982 in commemoration of the christening of our son Benjamin Blair, and grows in the Dawe's Arboretum in Newark, Ohio. We wished to emphasize, to our son and our family and friends attending his christening, our connection with Mother Earth and the many blessings and responsibilities which are a part of that connection. This concept of a life token, found among folklores and legends of many countries and cultures, is not new. For instance, it was formerly a Jewish custom to plant a tree at the birth of a child, a cedar for a son and a pine for a daughter. When a couple married, their respective trees were then cut down to make their *huppab*, or bridal bower.

As loving family and friends encircled Benjamin (and Dr. Pete who helped deliver Benjamin into the world) and his tree, the baptism waters nourished the young sapling.

Water is what God uses to wash and nourish Earth. It is what we use to wash and nourish ourselves. God uses water to cleanse us spiritually and to initiate us as Christians.

In addition to scriptures, selections from an anthology of Native American spiritual thought and Thoreau's writings were read.

– Jennifer Kinsley, Baltimore, Ohio

Prayer of blessing

At our church, it is important to welcome new babies into our community and to assure parents of the community's support. A tradition for doing this developed around a symbol reintroduced to this country by the televised rendition of *Roots.*

On the first Sunday the mother and baby are able to come to service – often on the way home from the hospital – the parents bring the baby to the front of the church as deacons present the collected offering. A minister in our congregation prays a prayer of thanksgiving for the child and the parents. He then lifts the baby high, as if in offering to God, asking God's blessing on the new life and God's guidance for the parents and church community as we accept our shared responsibility for nurturing the child in the faith.

The "Prayer of Blessing by Jim Brooks," as it has come to be called, is an important birth rite, a rite that surrounds the family with our love and support and enables us to share in their joy.

– Rachel G. Gill, Stone Mountain, Georgia

Baptism day stoles

Each member of our family has a homemade baptismal stole with the person's name, a baptism symbol, and whatever else has special meaning for that person embroidered or appliquéd on white material. On the anniversary of each baptism day, the celebrant chooses a special food for dinner. Then we all put on our stoles, light the baptism candle and have a prayer of thanksgiving. We remember the symbols of baptism on our stoles and talk about what baptism means.

Our oldest child will soon make her first communion so a Eucharist symbol will be added to her stole at that time. We have also made and given baptism stoles to our godchildren.

– Rodger and Mary Beth Routh, Ankeny, Iowa

Prayers for Sarah

Sarah, our first daughter, had been showered with gifts since the day we announced her coming! We wanted her baptism to be a celebration of prayerful presence (not presents!). The invitations invited family and friends to write a short prayer for Sarah and bring it as a gift for the occasion. We asked that prayer be the only gift to celebrate this holy time in her life. We provided the prayer sheet, simple paper decorated with her name and the date of her baptism. It was marvelous when we realized that most people did exactly that – there were no gifts other than the gift of prayer. We prayed the prayer-gifts during the ceremony. We celebrate the day of Sarah's baptism each year by sharing dinner with her godparents and the priest who baptized her, and by reading a short selection of those prayers.

– Nancy Parker Clancy, Troy, Michigan

Naming ceremony celebration

Within a few minutes after our daughter's birth in an alternative birth center, we shared in a celebration for her birth with two close friends. Using the service we had prepared earlier, we gave thanks, sang, spoke her name out loud for the first time, and prayed. We four "worship professionals" (all United Methodist ministers) were teary-eyed and could barely sing because of the deep emotions this service called forth.

Prayer of Thanksgiving:
Sing to our God, all the earth,
Break forth and sing for joy.
Sing praises to God with the harp,
and with voices full of joyous melody.
With trumpets and the sound of
the horn,
Sing out to God.

Antiphon:
Thank you God for the gift of birth,
For love made flesh to refresh the earth.
For life and strength and length of days,
We give you thanks and praise.

Prayer of Thanksgiving:
Let the sea roar in all its fullness,
the whole world and all its inhabitants.
Let the floods clap their hands,
and the mountains sing for joy
Before God and the nations.
(Psalm 98)

Repeat Antiphon

Hymn: "Now Thank We All Our God"

Prayer:
O God, like a mother who comforts her children, you strengthen us in our solitude, sustain and provide for us. We come before you with gratitude for the gift of this child, for the joy which you have brought into this family, and the grace with which you surround them and all of us. As a father cares for his children, so continually look upon us with compassion and goodness. Pour out your spirit. Enable your servants to abound in love and establish our homes in holiness. Amen.

Naming:
A name has power. It distinguishes us from another, yet it connects us with our Christian roots and our family heritage. "Fear not, for I have redeemed you. I have called you by name. You are mine. When you pass through deep waters I will be with you, your troubles will not overwhelm you. Fear not, I am with you.

I have called you by name." (Taken from Isaiah 43)

Giving of the Name

Prayer:
Loving God, sustain this child with your strong and gentle care. May the life of (child's name) be one of happiness, goodness and wisdom.

Grant that (child's name) may seek after peace and justice, compassion and joy, for all of creation. Amen.

– Anne Broyles & Larry Peacock,
Norwalk, California

Adoption Day

Our special time

Our family (father, mother, two daughters, and one son) loves celebrating birthdays. For our children, whose birthdays are all in the first 20 days of December, this causes a lot of rushing around with other seasonal activities.

The fact that our oldest daughter and our son are adopted gave us a perfect reason to create a celebration that has become special to us. For years now, we have observed a day in March or April, a less hectic time of year, as our family's Adoption Day. This lets us all celebrate an occasion that we appreciate and talk about freely in our family.

Actual arrival for our adopted children was in March, so it is appropriate to observe our day then.

All of us are involved in planning and preparing for the occasion, which we celebrate in a variety of ways: having a romp in the park and eating at a fancy restaurant; picnicking at a state park, visiting a new town, and going to a movie.

Whatever our plans or activities, we always spend time talking about each child's "special story" – what the children looked like, where we first saw them, what we did the first day, etc. As the children get older the stories are repeated over and over and we add details of the "first mother" as they are appropriate and as the children are ready to hear them. Sometimes we laugh so much over past incidents that we can hardly continue. It's a very happy time for our family.

– Larry Miller, Macon, Mississippi

Birthdays

Observing birthdays, especially for children, is a relatively new phenomenon. The practice of marking an individual's exact date of birth came into existence only with the reckoning of time by a fixed calendar. Even then, birthday observances were usually reserved only for gods, kings, and nobles. Some societies did not note the day of birth at all, fearing that such knowledge in the hands of evil spirits was dangerous.

Others were careful to mark the hour of birth as well as the day, especially those societies where astrology and horoscopes were thought to reveal special influences on the infant because of the particular planetary configuration at the hour of birth.

Birthdays celebrate entry and continuing place in the family, a time to recall the birth and significant events of an individual's life, and a way to highlight the honored one's uniqueness.

While each birthday may be considered a rite of passage, some are clearly more universally important than others. For many years, the first significant life transition happened at the age of six when a child left home to go to school for the first time. Today, with the preponderance of working mothers and the increase of preschool care and kindergarten, this is less true. At age 13, Jewish children are ushered into adulthood with a formal celebration of bar/bat mitzvah. At age 16, children in most places are considered old enough to become licensed drivers – a first step into adult responsibilities for many. At 18, young women and men become eligible to vote and may register for the armed forces. Throughout adulthood, the decade birthdays (30, 40, 50) are important passages for many people. The 65th birthday – the standard retirement age – is another of the more universal passages in this culture. While all of these are usually happily-celebrated occasions, they may also be anxiety-producing passages. These life transitions need to be celebrated with a focus on whatever makes them special, including new responsibilities to be undertaken.

– Reprinted from *To Celebrate: Reshaping Holidays & Rites of Passage*

Seventh was best

Our family prefers outings for birthday celebrations. Some were memorable occasions, but the very best birthday party we ever had was in honor of our daughter's seventh birthday. I gave her the choice of an outing with one or two of her friends, or a backyard barbecue with anyone she liked. She chose the barbecue and invited her family, a few friends her own age, several neighbors including adults, and at least two infants. In addition, she asked if she could invite the young man who taught her swimming class at the local pool.

I felt sure she would be disappointed, but that charming young man accepted her invitation, appeared at the party, ate a hamburger, and gave her his second-best lifeguard whistle as an absolutely memorable gift for a seven-year-old.

We made hand-cranked ice cream and had bowls of soap suds for blowing bubbles. There were no games. The children ate and ran about and watched the stars come out. Everyone enjoyed it.

– Carolyn K. Willett, Larchmont, New York

Forty more years

The 40th birthday party for a friend of mine was depressing. His pride was his physical strength, and he thought of this birthday as a milestone to physical deterioration. He cried, his wife was miserable, and a pall settled over all of us.

My 40th birthday came soon afterward, and I was determined to celebrate in a positive way, forestalling any thoughts or feelings I might otherwise develop about my declining physical prowess. The theme I came up with was "40 More Years," and I used the occasion to assure both my friends and myself that I planned to be vigorously involved in the things I loved for many years to come. This celebration brought optimism about my place in the world and the feeling that I can accomplish some things that are very important to me during the rest of my lifetime.

– Brian Sherman, Decatur, Georgia

Picture-perfect birthday

My brother and I no longer live close enough to spend birthdays together. I wanted to let him know I was thinking of him, so for his birthday I sorted through family photographs and had copies made of some of my favorite ones with my brother in them. I put together a scrapbook of his growing-up years and added favorite quotes. It is something he will always cherish, and I relived some wonderful memories creating it.

– Patti Wilson Marcum, Oxford, Mississippi

A triple celebration

The invitation read, *Can you join the Olsens and Santos on Sunday afternoon, August 17 from 3–7 p.m. at Mark Keirs Kids 'N Stuff Nursery School? We're honoring two birthdays: Granddaughter Cristina's 13th, Elmer's 80th, and Kate's and Elmer's 50th anniversary as partners and pals. No presents, please, except the pleasure of your presence. Bring a dish for a potluck meal (A–I: dessert, J–Q: casserole, R–Z: salad) and folding chairs, beach blankets, balls, games, photo albums, and slides. It will be a do-it-yourself fun afternoon, an instant celebration.*

The nursery school, with its fenced, tree-filled yard, was a wonderful place for our intergenerational affair. Two local folk singers led a singalong after the meal, aided by song booklets illustrated by Cristina and her eight-year-old brother. We used banners with a "Good Luck" message on which guests pinned colored slips of paper with messages for each honoree.

– Kate Olsen, Martinez, California

New twist on family trivia

Each year, my family tries to think up something creative and fun for our birthday celebrations. For my Aunt Catherine's surprise party, to which non-family members were invited, we decided to make our own trivia game. A friend and I agreed to do the necessary research. This included going to the library to read microfiche newspaper articles on the date of my aunt's birth and for each decade birthday. We also looked up references to "Catherine" in encyclopedias, history books, and maps.

We devised questions relating to important events on her birthdays. We also had questions on "Catherines" in history and geography. Cards with one question on each were given to the guests. Then they took turns asking the questions on their cards. The participants would try to guess the answers. If no one else knew the answer, my aunt was allowed to guess. It was great fun! Everyone learned something they didn't know about the life and times of my aunt. For Catherine, the effort that went into preparing the game was an affirmation of her importance to us.

– Ondina Gonzalez, Decatur, Georgia

At 75, she's the talk of the post office!

For my mother's 75th birthday, my sister and I gave her a card shower. We felt that "things" were unnecessary and cumbersome at that point in her life, but renewing old associations and friendships would be truly joyful for her.

With this in mind, I heisted her address book (a tricky deal!) and copied down every single name and address. Since she has a penchant for saving addresses, we had a wealth of information. We printed a letter bringing friends up-to-date on her activities and asked them to share in the celebration of her birthday by sending a card to arrive on her special day.

At a family birthday dinner a few days before her birthday, we announced the surprise by reading the letter that had gone out. Then the mail began to arrive – 170 birthday cards from all over the country and from people she had not seen in years! Her postman said she was the talk of the post office.

This gift gave her hours of fond remembrance and it was satisfying for

my sister and me, as well, for I don't think anything else could have given her as much pleasure and happiness.
– Ronice E. Branding, Florissant, Missouri

Birthday parties

The birthday party is one of the best training grounds for conditioning children to expect to receive presents. It should be a time for a child to develop a deep appreciation for life and people, to celebrate another year of growing.

The best way to break this pattern is to establish a family tradition of birthday parties without presents. (At some time prior to the party, the family may wish to give its gift to the person being honored, preferably gifts handmade or "recirculated.") Let the party be a time for celebrating the joy of being a child, not a time for counting the loot.

Encourage your friends to do the same. If your child is invited to a party where you know presents will be brought, discuss with your child the giving of a check to some charity which helps children. Let your child write a personal note explaining that this is a family tradition.

Or invite the birthday child on a camping trip to experience the beauty of nature, discuss the need to preserve wilderness areas from developers, and to nurture relationships outside the nuclear family. Such an experience can also build peer relationships and teach children how to be cooperative rather than competitive, and foster team spirit rather than individualism. As an alternative to camping, invite the child to a concert, a baseball game, or the circus.

If you decide to send a gift, consider several packages of seeds, a terrarium, or a green plant. Growing plants teaches children an appreciation for life. The Third Day plant shop in Washington, D.C., has a special corner for children to buy plants at children's prices. Wouldn't it be great if every plant shop had the same? Consider a good book which says something about life, cooperation, and the gifts of different cultures. If you are close friends with the other family, you may want to "circulate" a toy or book which is still in good condition.

An alternative birthday party

So how do you plan an alternative birthday party? Suggestions include asking guests not to bring gifts, and taking children on an outing such as a camping trip, museum, circus, or ball game. Try handmade gifts, or "recirculated" toys, books, and sports equipment in good condition. Starting with these alternatives at an early age is easier than a transition after peer pressure has made the celebrant rigid.

Ask party guests to bring one of their own toys or books, gift-wrapped, then have a draw where everyone gets one gift. Have the birthday child plan and make favors and decorations for his or her own party.

Take a beady-eyed look at birthday party food. If your meals don't normally run to hot dogs and chocolate icing, why cave in because it is a birthday? Cakes can be made with honey and whole wheat pastry flour. Whipped cream can substitute for icing. Ice cream is available made with honey only. Hot dogs can be found without additives. Or natural peanut butter can be substituted. Raisins, peanuts, and popcorn can take the place of candy, and unsweetened fruit juice the place of soda.

Children are direct and will ask you why you don't have "regular" food. Tell them you used to have "regular" food until you discovered this "new" food makes everyone stronger, slimmer, and more beautiful. Don't say "healthy" and "good-for-you"!

Celebrating with creations

For our daughter's fifth birthday, we struggled with the traditional party to which kids bring presents for a girl who already has enough. So we sent a note to the families asking that they not buy a gift, but that the children create something on their own as a gift of themselves to Tracy. The response was great. All the children made "creations" – painted rocks, pictures, artificial flowers out of pipe-cleaners potted together in an English Leather bottle cap, etc. And our daughter greatly appreciated and enjoyed receiving "a part of her friends" instead of a commercial gift. The parents liked it too! We have taken the idea a step further this Christmas and have suggested to our family relations that we use our talents and create rather than buy something for each other.

– Jan and Ed Spence, Aztec, New Mexico

Birthright (rite)

My siblings and I, and now our children, have what we consider our "birthright" (rite) – our favorite menu and release from our daily chores for one special day. When my sisters and brother and I were growing up in the 1930s and 1940s, my parents would never have dreamed of indulging us in an orgy of parties and presents. Even if they could have afforded it, they would have felt it wasn't good for us. But our special menu for the day was really special. Whatever we wanted (within reason, of course) we could order for breakfast, lunch, and supper.

Being released from chores made us feel like a king or queen. With my own children, we've continued this custom and they love it. Another thing I've done with my children is to buy each one a nice book on their birthday, and over the years they've accumulated a pretty good library.

– Mrs. Charles Jackson, Madison, New Jersey

From me to you

Our daughter will take a gift to present to her class (something everyone can use and enjoy) in honor of her birthday rather than bring in a candy treat. If everyone did this individually, or the class got together and decided on something they could get for their room or the school, they could contribute something plus cut out the sweets.

– Jeann Schaller, Midland, Michigan

Twelve birthdays each year

Our house is a commune, a collective, an extended family of 12 folks. As you would expect, one of the main sources of celebration is each person's birthday. The birthday celebrations take various forms, some very much planned, some not, but all having the same creative caring as well as casual informality. They usually focus on particular aspects or interests of the person.

When a drama instructor recently had her birthday, we put on a scene from one of her favorite plays. The scene was exaggerated, and hilarious adaptations alluding to special events in her life were added. When a pancake and strawberry fanatic had his birthday, you know what we had for dinner. When the founder of our house had his birthday, we covered the dining table with a roll of shelving paper and each person drew a representation (symbolic or otherwise) of some special event that took place between them.

– Reprinted from *The Alternate Celebrations Catalogue*, 1982

Favorites

Some of our favorite birthday gifts include a concert for Dad's birthday (I arranged a song so that each of the children could play an instrument, then we practiced it and performed it for my husband for his birthday) and a promise to the children for lessons in riding, gymnastics, etc. My brother-in-law, my husband and myself "share" a birthday card. It's about five years old now, and we are able to send it back and forth because our birthdays alternate.

– Frances M. Hraster, Wheaton, Maryland

Mysterious celebration

We hold a "mystery night" for each other or for other couples on birthdays. They are asked to reserve a particular evening on or around their birthday, with only a suggestion of how to dress for the evening. We make plans to do something unusual – always a surprise!

– Paul and Linda Hartman, Mesa, California

Birthday honor

We recently celebrated my father's 80th birthday and invited many of his friends. One of the guests played the piano, and all sang songs, most of which were 70 or 80 years old. The older people there were encouraged to tell tales of their lives as we all sat in a big circle. Our 11-year-old daughter gave a gift to her grandfather by learning to play "Happy Birthday" on her flute and then playing it at the party. Our eight-year-old made his grandfather a crown and a birthday flag. I wrote my father a poem which covered events in his life and the feelings that I have for him.

– Katie Barker, Lake Oswego, Oregon

Ongoing birthday wrap

To eliminate wrapping paper and create a personalized gift wrapper, use large scraps of cloth cut into the proper shape, or sew smaller pieces together. Make these gift cloths for each member of the family and use them over and over again. Some of the history of the person could be recorded on the cloth by embroidering birthday and holiday events such as "First Bicycle," etc.

– Reprinted from *The Alternate Celebrations Catalogue*, 1982

Early Passages

Tooth rites

When a child loses the first tooth, the event is usually noted with a ritual visit from the tooth fairy. This stage of development is symbolic of leaving babyhood behind. Planting a tree or bush with the child to symbolize new life and growth and giving the child new privileges and responsibilities are ways that this time might be made more meaningful.

Starting school

Entering the first grade at the age of six is no longer the universal passage it once was in this society. Now many parents place their children in day care as early as their first year and many children attend preschool and kindergarten. Whenever a child

first leaves home, it is an important passage. It may be a time of joy for the new level of maturity reached by the child, but it also may be a time of great anxiety for the parents and the child. The child experiences anxiety at being left alone for significant periods without the family support system, and the parents worry about whether or not the child will make the passage successfully and about the quality of care the child will receive. For the parents, there is also great concern about the values and ideals to which the child will be exposed outside the home. This is such an important life passage that it ought to be observed in the family, both for the sake of the child and the parents.

Puberty

This period of rapid growth marks the end of childhood and the beginning of physical and sexual maturity. The bodies of boys and girls change noticeably, as do many of their feelings. While in pre-modern societies puberty was often marked by elaborate celebration, there are no commonly-used rites for this passage in our culture. With many parents reluctant to discuss – let alone celebrate! – this development, boys and girls often make this passage with only advice from peers and information gained from television and sex education classes at school.

Naming what we do

Many parents take their children and their friends camping; many help their children host pajama parties or dinners. At puberty, these events can be turned into rites of passage by including other significant adults, by discussion, and by focusing on symbols of the childhood being left, and the new stage of life being entered. Whether serious and/or humorous, if this event is named as a rite of passage and some thought is given by the parent as to what they would have liked for themselves, the evening can be one to be cherished for years to come.

Not a curse, but a blessing!

One of my fondest memories of time spent with a warm, creative family occurred several years ago. Their eldest daughter had experienced her first menstrual period, and her mother and I were particularly concerned that this be greeted with a positive attitude. For us, as well as for many generations of women who preceded us, menstruation was regarded as a curse – certainly not a blessing. We wanted to help this young woman avoid that experience and also set a pattern for her two younger sisters.

Like women's rites held so sacred in earlier times, all the females gathered: her mother, myself, another unofficial "aunt" and the two younger sisters. We presented the "initiate" with a bouquet of rosebuds with which we wished to express budding womanhood. At a special dinner that evening, her father made a short speech acknowledging this new stage of development, a life passage, of which many more would follow.

The same ritual has been observed for each of the sisters and all have spoken warmly of the importance of that occasion in their lives.

– Kathleen Timberlake,
Ann Arbor, Michigan

In the Faith Community

Bar mitzvah ("son of the command-ment") is a special confirmation cer-emony for Jewish boys; for Jewish girls it is bat mitzvah ("daughter of the com-mandment"). Conducted in the syna-gogue, usually around age 13, the cel-ebration signals the young person's assumption of adult religious duties.

Confirmation is a rite observed in many Christian traditions that also signifies a spiritual coming-of-age. Usually for teenagers who were bap-tized as infants, the rite celebrates the assumption of adult responsibili-ties in the Christian community. In some traditions this may also mean taking an additional name, a name of a favored saint with whom the child chooses to identify.

Bar/bat mitzvah in kibbutz

A creative joint bar/bat mitzvah took place in an Israeli kibbutz.

During their 13th year, the boys and girls engage in 13 creative projects (field trips, directing a play, writing poems). The year-long pro-cess of creativity instead of a crash event symbolizes the rite of passage into responsible adulthood.

– Art Waskow, Washington, D.C.

Belated bar/bat mitzvah

I believe that bar/bat mitzvah ceremo-nies for 13-year-olds are premature and would be far more meaningful at an older age. A senior at Brandeis Uni-versity had his bar mitzvah as a part of the Sabbath morning *havurah*. Thirty friends joined in the singing, *davening* and Torah reading, and the young man's *derasha* (preaching) on the covenant highlighted the event. The Kiddush was catered by his friends.

Other alternative ways of celebrat-ing bar/bat mitzvah include designing and making invitations at home; serv-ing homemade food or sharing the task of food preparation with the congre-gation; having joint services with other families to share expenses and joy; creating decorations at home; and us-ing puzzles, games, and rented mov-ies for entertainment.

A growing number of rabbis are setting spending limits on weddings and bar/bat mitzvahs for the sake of simplicity and religious integrity. An alternative is to give money to wor-thy causes in honor of these obser-vances and celebrants.

– Rabbi Albert Axelrad, Boston, Massachusetts

Graduations

From kindergarten to graduate school, graduations are important passages that recognize the graduate's growth and accomplishment and acknowledge the role others played in making the graduate's educational experience possible. For the graduate, this is a time to accept responsibility for making a positive contribution to society. Although graduation ceremonies bring joy at achievement and accomplishment, they may also bring anxiety about the future: Can I get a job? Can I get into graduate school? Am I ready to assume responsibility for my life?

It is not enough to leave these important passages to commencement rituals nor to treat them as new occasions for needless consumption. Observances at home, with friends and in one's religious community can give these passages the attention they merit and aid the graduate to move on to life's next stage.

Marriage

In every known society, marriage is the culturally-prescribed way of expressing adult love and establishing a family. Marriage gives both permanence and responsibility to the relationship, as well as responsibilities for the children of this relationship.

More than the socialization of reproduction, marriage is a relationship that offers the possibility of respect between equals, deep experiences of fidelity, trust in another person, self-acceptance, growth in intimacy and nurturing new life. It is belief in a relationship with these profound ideals which moves two single people to join in a covenant of marriage.

Marriage as an institution into which two people enter voluntarily as equals – both in the sight of law and the faith they hold – is relatively new in Western civilization. As in most other civilizations, marriage in Western tradition has historically been an institution which rationalizes and enforces the subordination of women through its religious and legal systems. Neither the emphasis of the Hebrew Scriptures on justice in human relationships, nor the New Testament emphasis on mutual love for both husband and wife was sufficient to transcend the culture's prevailing belief that women should be subordinate to men.

Marriage was considered a sacrament in the medieval period, but negative views of women and sexuality made celibate life in a religious order morally superior to marriage. The Protestant Reformation brought about basic changes in the church's way of viewing women and marriage. When Martin Luther, an ex-monk, forsook his vows of celibacy and married Katy, a former nun, he made a dramatic statement about the sanctity of marriage. He accepted marriage as the normal life intended by God and rejected the notion that it was not morally inferior to celibacy. He saw women and sex as fundamentally good, a radical change from the tradition that viewed women and sex as evil. Despite religion's attitudinal change, tradition and vested political and economic interests continued to treat women as less than equals in marriage. A strong current of public opinion that the wife's place is in the home as the primary care provider, and the husband's place – with less parental responsibility – is outside the home as primary breadwinner, continues to pressure couples to fit into these traditional roles. Unfortunately, in this society, when two people determine to enter a covenant of marriage based on respect for each other as equals, it is still a countercultural commitment.

While the issue of equality is an old one, there are new realities that affect marriage. Many assume that social conditions now exist for a new intimacy between women and men. Freeing sex from procreation made it possible for people to value the erotic life for its own sake; the shrinking family size made it possible for women and men to respond more easily to each other's needs; and the loss of the binding character of the marriage contract makes it possible to ground sexual relations in something more than legal compulsion. The "new intimacy" may be an illusion, and the eagerness for it may be the symptom of a serious sickness in our culture.

In his classic work, *The Culture of Narcissism: American Life in an Age of Diminishing Expectations*, Christopher Lasch argued that one of the key characteristics of the narcissistic culture is the inability "to take an interest in anything after one's own death." The need for close personal encounters in the present, the avoidance of self-investment in a life-long covenant, and the demand for instant gratification have undermined genuine intimacy between men and women and also between parents and children. In this culture, women and men who enter a covenant of marriage based on a life commitment, the equality of both partners, self-giving and sacrifice, are taking a truly radical stance. Our culture pays lip service to the institution of marriage, but prevailing cultural values with stress on the primacy of self-gratification, novelty, and excitement work to undermine it.

Legitimate anxieties which accompany such an important life passage are exacerbated by consumer society's definition of the value of the wedding and related rites by the quantity of consumption. Wedding costs can be astronomical. "It's an ego-building thing," said a consultant who plans weddings from New York to Texas. "If we are going to spend $150,000 on baby sister's wedding, we do it to build egos and to show that we have good taste. And secretly, I think they love to have people discuss how much they spent on it."

Marketing people in the industry speak of "bride-generated" purchases. To understand what this means, you need only pick up a copy of one of the bridal magazines to find page after page of ads for china, crystal, and silver – to say nothing of vacuum cleaners, luggage, electric cookware, photographers, tuxedos, and bridal gowns. The travel industry is also there with "Days You'll Always Remember." While brides-to-be represent only three percent of the population, they account for a disproportionate share of household purchases in many categories: sterling silver flatware, crystal, small kitchen appliances, etc. A promotions director for *Modern Bride* magazine explained, "They don't want to wait anymore to get things. In effect, these new brides have become upscale."

It is sad that such expenditures bring little happiness on the wedding day or after, nor do they offer any assurance for the success of the marriage. Sadder yet is the fact that the consumptive aspects of the celebration often overshadow the religious and personal significance of the rite itself. The good news is that some can and do reject this tradition and create alternatives that better express their values, ideals, and commitments.

Alternatives

How do you plan an alternative wedding? There are no formulas, because there is no one "right" way to do it. A good way to begin your planning is to talk about the kind of lifestyle you expect to lead, your mutual goals, and your priorities. Think about how your engagement and wedding ceremony can reflect these values. Talk with friends, clergy or other advisors. Be sensitive to the wishes of your parents or relatives, but don't let them decide for you. And if you are serious about being equal partners in marriage, don't assume that it is the bride's prerogative to decide what kind of wedding it will be, or that her family will pay for it.

Engagement. The engagement period is historically one in which the couple has time to prepare for marriage – getting to know one another and their respective families better. It is an important time to discuss in-depth the shape you expect your lives to take, the priorities each of you has, and the goals you want to work for. Don't let preparation for the wedding ceremony get in the way of preparing for the marriage. Many couples take time to enroll in a marriage preparation course offered through pastoral institutes, religious institutions, or personal awareness groups.

Rings. The custom of giving an engagement ring may have originated at a time when marriages were arranged – as they still are in some cultures – and a groom gave a ring as a down payment on the agreement. Neither the engagement ring nor the wedding ring is a requirement. If rings are important to you, there are alternatives to the traditional diamond. You may wish to exchange family rings or rings found at auctions or antique jewelry stores. You may have a local craftsperson make a ring that is less expensive than a diamond and has special meaning. You may choose to exchange pendants, make an ongoing commitment to a foster child, buy a piece of art, or plant and tend a tree together.

Parties and showers. These social occasions are good opportunities for couples to feel the support of their friends and families. They serve the useful function of helping supply a couple's household needs, but they can also create an unnecessary financial burden for friends and relatives who may feel obligated to give a wedding gift as well. The new couple needs more than things. Consider giving ideas: recipes, information and hints can be cleverly packaged and shared. You might give an I.O.U. for a dinner or some other service you will provide for the couple later.

If the bridal couple hosts a party, they may ask that the gift be advice or help with a potential problem, or the issue of how to live simply. They may ask for a storytelling party in which couples come and tell them stories of living in partnership that are helpful, meaningful, or funny.

Invitations. According to bridal magazines, invitations are key status indicators. Consider making your own invitations or simply use handwritten notes. You might use silk-screening, photographs, or woodcuts. Inviting friends by phone may be the most personal way. For larger numbers of guests, consider inexpensive methods of duplicating such as quick-copy. Whatever way you choose, be sure to give your guests an idea of appropriate gifts and attire. The more information they have, the more comfortable they will be, and the more festive your celebration.

Gifts. It is perfectly all right to suggest the kinds of gifts you would like. Your friends usually want to give something you will find useful or beautiful. If you have enough things and would like donations made to a favorite group, give them the name and address of the organization.

Rehearsal dinner. Consider carefully whether you want – or are able to afford – an expensive dinner at a restaurant. Friends may be delighted to help prepare such a meal as a wedding gift.

The wedding day. Like any other event, a wedding should be carefully planned or it may turn into a catastrophe for everyone concerned. That does not mean you have to hire a wedding consultant. A friend or two is usually available to help with the required organizing. Take the time several weeks – or months! – ahead of the wedding to sit down and talk about the day with the person you choose to help you. Then you'll be able to relax and enjoy the celebration, too.

Place. Wedding ceremonies and receptions can be held just about anywhere – from a great hall to a barnyard – provided arrangements are thought out and made well in advance. The high costs of receptions have more to do with status projection than with the discovery of a place that has special meaning for you, your family and friends. If the church family is the major support community for your marriage, then the wedding should be in the church. Wherever you decide to have the wedding and reception, be sure that your guests know how to get there.

Dress. Some brides wouldn't feel they were married without the traditional bridal dress and veil. If owning a new wedding dress is not important to you, you may want to use your mother's or a friend's dress. Consider buying a dress that can be used on other occasions. You may even want to consider renting a dress. What is true for bridal dresses is also true for attire for grooms and attendants. Men don't have to wear matched tuxedos; in fact, they don't even have to wear suits. Nor do the bride's attendants have to wear matching dresses. Decide what you really want. Dress does make a statement. What kind of statement do you want to make?

Decorations. It is possible to have a wedding without decorations, but just as a lifestyle of responsibility would be drab without celebrations, so celebrations would be drab without decorations. That doesn't mean that "more is better." Simple, carefully thought-out decorations can convey the spirit of the occasion. Mixed flowers from your neighbor's, your grandmother's, or your own garden (or wild flowers from a field) are every bit as beautiful as purchased bouquets. Candles are simple but always elegant.

The ceremony. This is an area that couples seem to think about after they've planned photographers, clothes, and food – yet it is the most important part of the celebration! Your wedding ceremony should say what you want it to say. Work with the person you choose to perform the service. There may be fewer legal requirements than you think. Most denominations have certain requirements for the service, but most clergy will work with you to make the service meaningful for you.

Consider the music most meaningful to you. If it isn't a soloist singing "O Promise Me," what is it? Could a family member or friend provide music for you? Would you consider writing a song yourselves? What scripture speaks to your heart? What poetry or prose is your favorite? What is it, exactly, that you want to promise one another?

The reception. This most expensive item in the average wedding cries out for rational thought. How much of your parents' or your own money are you prepared to spend for this occasion? It does not have to be expensive to be fun and for you to receive congratulations and good wishes from friends and family. If you want to keep it simple, light refreshments or a covered-dish dinner will not lessen the joy and fun of the occasion. Music can often be provided by friends who want to make their music a special gift to you.

– Reprinted from *To Celebrate: Reshaping Holidays & Rites of Passage*

An inclusive wedding shower

My daughter wanted to have a non-sexist wedding celebration. Her efforts to that effect began when a friend suggested a bridal shower. After finessing an invitation for her fiancé, she was asked to provide a list of her friends she would like to invite. On this list she included both male and female names. A couple of her male friends were taken aback when they received a standard shower invitation. A more serious problem was when one of the hostesses panicked on hearing the bride wanted to invite men. "What will they eat?" she worried. "We are only having finger food." As it turned out, the men who came enjoyed the finger food immensely... using their fingers to stuff it into their mouths.

– Sara Lee Schoenmaker, Iowa City, Iowa

Alternative wedding registry

As we thought about the wedding gifts we would receive, we decided to keep the "things" and to give away the money we received to three nonprofit organizations. We knew a number of relatives who hadn't met us would want to give gifts but didn't know our tastes. To help them, we commissioned a set of dishes from our favorite potter. It was like a wedding registry at a store: people ordered place settings or serving dishes, and the potter, not a store, made the profit. Our wedding date is inscribed on the backs of all our dishes – a great memory when cleaning up after supper.

– Kathie Klein, Atlanta, Georgia

It's all in the family

At the home of an older friend, I recently saw a beautiful friendship quilt. When she became engaged, each female relative embroidered one white muslin square with her own name in the middle along with birds, flowers, or any design she chose. An elderly aunt who was blind wrote her name in pencil and her daughter embroidered it for her.

The squares were assembled into a quilt top and quilted by her mother and sisters. It made a beautiful, lasting, practical and inexpensive gift, although it took some effort. Each member of her family had one as it was always their gift to one another.

– Sheryl Craig,
Warrensburg, Missouri

A variety of special gifts

Some special monetary gifts for our wedding were made to the Heifer Project (dedicated to alleviating hunger by helping low-income families around the world to produce food for themselves and for their communities), and to a "Christmas angel" program which supplies gifts to poor children at Christmas. Our organist donated music for the ceremony; a woman loaned her lovely silver trays for our reception; my aunt and uncle made the mints for our wedding reception; and Russ's brother made a clock for us. And we made a gift of our wedding flowers to another couple who were married the day after our wedding.

– Karen Greenwaldt, Nashville, Tennessee

When wedding plans don't go smoothly

Harsh words, tension-filled moments, and decisions that were seen as selfish all stood in the way of our wedding being a grace-filled moment.

In order not to make a mockery of the love we were about to celebrate, we decided to have a service of reconciliation.

Family and wedding party were invited to the church for rehearsal. After the traditional practice, we invited everyone to take part in a short prayer time focusing on the theme of reconciliation. We prayed a common prayer asking for forgiveness and spoke a greeting of peace to each other. Finally, we joined hands and prayed together the Lord's Prayer. This experience was a necessary and prayerful part of our marriage.

– Nancy Parker Clancy, Troy, Michigan

Back porch elegance

At our son's wedding, we decided to extend the rehearsal dinner to include family members who were coming to Georgia from as far away as California and Oregon. Having the dinner in a local restaurant was rejected because it was too expensive for our values and budget, and because we wanted this occasion to be a personal expression of our family.

As their wedding gift, close friends of our family made their large, screened back porch available for our party and agreed to serve the dinner and clean up. Our nutritionist hostess helped us plan a meal that was both reasonably priced and delicious. We did all the food preparation the night before. Four of us gathered in her small kitchen and wrapped marinated chicken breast in phyllo dough for hours! We were very tired at the end of the evening, but we had a good time as we did it. We agreed that a less-complicated recipe would have been more practical, but the chicken was delicious and elegant. The rest of the menu was quite simple: garden salad, steamed broccoli, whole wheat rolls baked by another friend, and sherbet. On the day of the dinner, a neighbor cooked some of the chicken in her oven, so at dinner time it arrived hot and steaming.

We borrowed tables and chairs from our church, but since this was to be a family party we used our own china, silver, and linens. A friend brought colorful flowers from her yard, and our hostess made beautiful arrangements for each table. Carefully planned seating helped members from the two family groups get to know each other. The relaxed atmosphere afforded by our host family helped the tired feelings from all the preparation slip away. The gratitude of our son and new daughter, and the support we felt from our gathered families, made this a highlight of our celebrations.

– Rachel G. Gill, Stone Mountain, Georgia

International dinner

Since Dennis and I were both seminary students and we felt that the seminary was our community at that point in our lives, we decided to be married on campus. Since we had both served as short-term mission volunteers – he in Nigeria and I in Paraguay – and several of our friends and professors had also worked overseas, we decided to have an international dinner with costumes. Friends made West African stew, a festive meal served on African tablecloths at the home of one of our professors. As table decoration we bought several variegated plants which doubled as gifts for members of the wedding party.

– Paula Meador Testerman,
Wake Forest, North Carolina

Remember my name

When I got married, I kept my own

name. I wanted to communicate this decision to our relatives. Our friends' experiences with either not specifically announcing it or being subtle and understated had not met with success – many relatives ignored the women's use of their own names. We didn't expect such a reaction from close family but wanted to inform more distant relatives. We decided to use the invitation/announcement to let people know.

With my choice of words I wanted to address several points. I wanted to make it sound as unsurprising for me to keep my name as for my husband to keep his. It was not my purpose to be strident, aggressive, or alienating in tone nor to seem critical of any who made a different choice. I did want to indicate some expectation that others would honor our decision.

As the folded invitation was opened, the wedding information was on the right-hand side. On the left side at the bottom we put: We will continue to be known by our own names. Your cooperation will be appreciated.

– Kathie Klein, Atlanta, Georgia

Wedding fiesta in Taos

We wanted to help my daughter make every aspect of her wedding significant. She began by choosing to have the wedding in the place where she had grown up rather than the place where she or the family was currently living. The date of the wedding coincided with local fiestas and Pueblo Indian dances.

Following the wedding, a supper party and dance were held at our little adobe house. After the festivities were over, many of the guests camped out in the beautiful field by the river – some in sleeping bags under the stars, some in tents.

As a part of our larger celebration, we planted a tree in memory of her father who had died two summers earlier. The children presented a romantic play, *The Owl and The Pussycat*, and had fun swinging at a homemade piñata. Candles and a big bonfire of piñon logs gave soft light to the house and added beauty and warmth to an unforgettable occasion.

– Virginia McConnell, Boulder, Colorado

Incorporating different perspectives and potluck

A major issue in planning our wedding was to create a common and congenial form from two very different perspectives – Cliff and his family are militantly secular and my family and I are rooted in faith. We scrutinized each element of the ceremony to determine how to shape it to express our particular meaning, and to respect the integrity of our differences.

In our planning with Mike, my colleague and our wedding celebrant, we imagined the ceremony as concentric circles with ourselves in the middle. The inner circle was family, spreading out to friends and the larger community. In the church, to bridge the space between the straight rows of seats and where we stood facing those seats, we placed a semicircle of chairs for our immediate families.

Our parents were involved in the ceremony at two different points. We arranged it to make sure each parent had a role. After Mike and I welcomed everyone, my mother welcomed Cliff into our family and Cliff's father welcomed me. They wrote their own greetings – my mother's included a prayer and Cliff's father's was a story – each standing on its own terms. Later, my father and Cliff's mother brought us the rings to exchange.

For the reception, we organized a gigantic potluck dinner (there were over 100 guests). One close friend's gift to us was to coordinate it. We provided hams and a core group made particular items at our request. The rest was potluck. Since it was spring and since there was no stove in the church basement, we asked only for salad-type dishes or ones that required no heating.

– Kathie Klein, Atlanta, Georgia

A blessing for Hannah

Because the wedding was "out-of-town" for everyone but a few, the bride and groom reserved rooms for most wedding guests in a hotel. The night before the wedding, a group of seven wedding guests, all women, were gathered with the bride. We ranged in age from the teens to the 50s. At first, we chatted. Then one by one, we all offered the bride a word of encouragement, or something we had learned from married life. When we had finished, I asked the bride if there was anything she wanted to ask of us. She replied, "A blessing." She sat on a stool as we gathered around her and placed a hand on her head or her shoulder. Spontaneously, and simply, we asked that she and Bob be blessed in their life together. It was a beautiful moment.

– Carolyn Pogue, Calgary, Alberta

An Alternative Service

If there are parts of the traditional wedding ceremony that mean little or nothing to you and thoughts you'd like to include that say more about your own marriage, feel free to explore this with the person you choose to perform the service. Various denominations also make certain portions of the vows a required part of the service, though one mainline Protestant minister in San Francisco makes it a practice to ask a couple into his office and talk with them about their feelings and plans. If they appear ready for marriage, he informs them at the end of the interview that they are married and, except for civil requirements, they need do no more.

But for most couples who choose a nontraditional wedding, the ceremony is the heart of the matter because it is here that you can express your most cherished thoughts. The traditions of some faiths or officials may limit your choices, but most will work with you to make the celebration meaningful for you.

Since the prelude and the processional are the first elements of a traditional ceremony, it makes sense to talk about music first. Its association with weddings dates back to the days when noise was thought to keep evil spirits away, but whatever the reasons for its use, its effect is to evoke emotion. In other words, it can get people into whatever mood you want to create, which should be reflected in the other elements of the ceremony.

If you want a feeling of community, a processional hymn is a good choice. One couple chose to begin with the joyful old Shaker song "Tis the Gift to be Simple," as sung and danced by talented friends. Other couples prefer the tranquility of classical selections or the informal notes of jazz. And one couple, as they turned from the altar for the recessional, asked their guests to join them in a rousing rendition of "I've Got That Joy, Joy, Joy, Joy Down in My Heart." Church musicians are good people to contact first. Even if they're not eager to discuss possibilities with you, they'll usually direct you to other musicians in the community who will be able to explore new ideas with you. One note of caution: music is marvelous as a part of the ceremony, but too much of it may change the wedding to a concert and overshadow what you want your wedding to say.

Other introductions to the ceremony generally include some explanation of the reason for the gathering together, such as the following three examples:

Example one

Reading by minister:

Julie and Kevin have honored us by inviting us to be with them during this time that will make them husband and wife. They wish to dedicate themselves to each other publicly today. The wedding they perform will not join them; only they can do that through an awareness of the spiritual bond which already exists between them. The ceremony is only proclaiming that fact.

It is fitting and appropriate that you, families and friends of Julie and Kevin, be here to witness and participate in their wedding, for the ideals, the understanding, and mutual respect which they bring to their marriage have their roots in the love you have given them.

What Julie and Kevin mean to each other is obvious in their lives, but not easily expressed in the language of a ceremony. To convey the sense of what they wish their marriage to mean, they have asked their good friend Marty to read from Kahlil Gibran's *The Prophet*. (At this point in the service, the chapter "On Marriage" was read from *The Prophet*.)

Example two

This reading was used in a Jewish/ Christian service:

We are gathered together today as family and friends of Earl and Ellen. They have honored us by choosing us to be with them, and we rejoice with them in making this important commitment, which will make them husband and wife.

The essence of this commitment is the taking of another person in his or her entirety, as lover, companion, and friend. It is therefore a decision which is not made lightly, but rather undertaken with great consideration and respect for both the other person and oneself.

A marriage that lasts is one which is continually developing and one in which both persons grow in their understanding of each other. Deep knowledge of another person is not something that can be achieved in a short time, and real understanding of another's feelings can fully develop only through years of intimacy.

While marriage is the intimate sharing of two lives, it can enhance the differences and individuality of each partner. We must give ourselves in love, but we must not give ourselves away. A good and balanced relationship is one in which neither person is overpowered or absorbed by the other.

We are here today, then, to celebrate the love which Earl and Ellen have for each other, and to give recognition to their decision to accept each other totally and permanently. Into this state of marriage these two persons come now to be united.

Example three

This greeting was used in a Protestant/Catholic service:

Dearly beloved, we are gathered together here in the sight of God, and in the presence of these witnesses, to join together Patrick and Janet in holy matrimony; which is an honorable estate, instituted of God and signifying between Christ and his Church; which holy estate Christ adorned and beautified with his presence in Cana of Galilee. It is therefore not to be entered into unadvisedly, but reverently, discreetly, and in the fear of God. Into this holy estate Patrick and Janet come now to be joined.

– Rev. Edward J. Wynne Jr.,
Caldwell, New Jersey

Charge to the couple

A charge to the couple, and sometimes to the congregation, is common. Involving your friends in the ceremony usually makes the occasion meaningful for all of you, as in the following dedication made before the exchange of vows.

Pastor: This couple comes together out of a community of friends and relatives. They ask our support as they together begin the adventure of married life. We come today to join in marriage _____ and _____. It is our fondest hope that their separate lives may together explore new dimensions of love.

Congregation: We dedicate ourselves to the continuing task of helping them in all ways possible to build a deep and abiding love.

Pastor: We ask for them the excitement of new discoveries and new creations, that their lives may be an adventure together wherever they may go.

Congregation: We dedicate ourselves to the continuing task of helping them in all ways possible to live the most fully human life.

Pastor: We know that love is not a state-of-being easily achieved. We ask that _____ and _____ find the courage and the patience to overcome any obstacle to a profound communication – the very cornerstone of all relationships of love.

Congregation: We dedicate ourselves to the continuing task of helping them in all ways possible to meet the challenge of a marriage pledged to honest struggle, open words, and shared lives.

Pastor: And finally, we recognize that love is not limited nor can it be contained. We ask that the love _____ and _____ feel for each other reaches out beyond themselves, to their family and to the world in which they live.

Congregation: We dedicate ourselves to the continuing task of helping them in all ways possible to let their love so shine that it touches all who know them; and may their lives be lived not only for themselves but for all humanity.

Vows

Personalization of vows has become a common practice, even in the most traditional ceremonies.

The suggested Lutheran vow, for instance, is open to one stipulation being that the "as long as we live" sentiment remains. The two obvious ground rules for writing original vows are that they be a sincere expression of your feelings for each other and that they be worthy of the occasion. They need not be identical. In fact, if you're taking a standard vow and adding your own touches, why don't you both try making the changes without consulting the other? The vow each of you develops could be the one you use as your promise.

Some vows are quite short, like the examples shown below. Others take the form of a contract specifying the understanding and expectations each partner has about the marriage. Some have included agreements on finances, child-rearing, in-law relations, careers, even provisions for separation – though that seems to insert a defeatist attitude about the marriage from the start.

Others have been short, general statements of purpose – often lettered and illustrated by an artist friend, designed to be read and/or signed at the ceremony.

We think of contracts as a modern innovation, but in ancient times the Ketubah, a legal contract, was used in Jewish marriages to set forth in writing the terms of the marriage agreement, thereby protecting the woman by discouraging the man from divorcing her. Today it is still used in Jewish ceremonies, but in most cases it has become wholly symbolic.

I take you...

I take you as my wife (husband) and equal. I pledge to share my life openly with you, to speak the truth to you in love. I promise to honor and tenderly care for you, to cherish and encourage your own fulfilment as an individual through all the changes of our lives.

(Groom's attendant – Groom's A; Bride's attendant – Bride's A)

Bride's A: Love is a growing thing...

Groom's A: ...a growing awareness of the meaning of "otherness." Another self who stands outside your self, whose life is a mystery and a challenge, a vexation and a thing of wonder.

Bride's A: It comes from involvement, and grows in living with a person, sharing with him, and building something with him. It requires energy and imagination.

Groom's A: It is impossible for superiors and inferiors to love, since the superior can only condescend and the inferior only admire. Love means recognition between two equals, not exploiting each other's strengths or weaknesses, but rejoicing in each other's presence.

Bride's A: Love must be a bond and yet not binding, else our freedom is stifled in the name of love, and with our freedom, our humanity is lost.

Groom's A: It is a relationship of greater possibility and greater risk, for the power to create is the power to destroy.

Bride's A: Marriage, then, is not a bond made of words or promises or the clauses of a contract.

Groom's A: For no set of rules or promises can possibly exhaust the demands love may come to make on you.

Bride's A: It is a special spirit or style of life between two people. And if it is there, no possible words will make it more sacred or worthwhile.

Groom's A: If it is not, no special phrases will make it exist. The words are an affirmation of that spirit, not a substitute for it.

Bride's A: Marriage is an affirmation of the possibility and power of forgiveness.

Groom's A: It must have permanence. It should be something to depend on, a rock to anchor against the storm, a place to come home to.

Bride's A: Yet its permanence is not that of a wall which shuts things out or seals something in. It should be free and open to the winds of God.

Groom's A: It is a stage on the road of friendship and love and discovery.

Bride's A: It means opening yourself a little more to the possibilities of another self and life itself.

Groom's A: Finally, it was meant to be a continuing celebration of the gift of life and love. For it is in sharing and in joy that it is fulfilled.

Groom: I, _____, having full confidence that our abiding faith in each other as human beings will last our lifetime, take you, _____, to be my wedded wife. I promise to be your loving and faithful husband, in prosperity and in need, in joy and in sorrow, in sickness and in health, and to respect your privileges as an individual as long as we both shall live.

Bride: I, _____, having full confidence that our abiding faith in each other as human beings will last our lifetime, take you, _____, to be my wedded husband. I promise to be your loving and faithful wife, in prosperity and in need, in joy and in sorrow, in sickness and in health, and to respect your privileges as an individual as long as we both shall live.

All that I have I offer you. Wherever you go I will go. What you have to give I gladly receive. I pray God will grant us lifelong faithfulness, and so I take you for my husband (wife).

Officiant: _____ and _____, if it is your intention to share with each other your laughter and your tears and all the work and pleasure the years will bring, by your promises bind yourselves now to each other as husband and wife. (The couple faces each other, joins hands and repeats:)

I take you (name) to be my (wife/husband) and I promise these things: I will be faithful to you and honest with you;

I will respect you, trust you, help you, listen to you and care for you. I will share my life with you in plenty and in want;

I will forgive you as we have been forgiven; and I will try with you better to understand ourselves, the world, and God;

so that together we may serve God and others forever.

Finally...

In some weddings, there is an opportunity for each person present to reaffirm his or her own marriage vows. Some include a time for each person present to turn to one another with the greeting, "Peace be with you," and the response, "and also with you."

For more information on alternative weddings, see *The Alternative Wedding Book*, Northstone Publishing Inc., 1995.

Whatever you plan, remember that the focus is on the act of joining together. All your plans need to leave you feeling excited, but not overwhelmed. It is important, above all, that the bride and groom savor each moment of this day.

Anniversaries

Happy anniversary to you!

On our 25th wedding anniversary, we sent out the following card to friends and family: *In celebration of God's providential care through 25 years of marriage and in honor of your friendship, we have made Edmarc Children's Hospice, Suffolk, Virginia, the recipient of a gift in your name.*

– Virginia and Dick Bethune, Pulaski, Virginia

A family affair

Wedding anniversaries are a family affair, especially if children were part of the wedding (not rare anymore in this age of blended families). This can be a special time of celebrating the birth of the family unit with family-oriented activities or gifts. Candles from each family member's birthday cake can be melted down into one big candle for this occasion.

– Meryl A. Buder, Virginia Beach, Virginia

Food bank shares in anniversary celebration

A couple in our church celebrated their 50th wedding anniversary with an open house in the church fellowship hall. They asked that no gifts be given to them. Instead, they asked their friends and neighbors to remember the poor and needy.

Some of their friends took this a step further. The friends asked everyone who came to the open house to bring a can of food to share with the needy through the local city rescue mission food bank, the favorite charity of the anniversary couple.

The response was overwhelming. More than 30 bags of food were collected. This food was greatly needed since we live in an area that has been hard hit by plant and steel mill closings. The opportunity to share a little of their blessings was a thrill for the couple and the church.

– Jacquelyn S. Thompson, Pulaski, Pennsylvania

Friends tell all

When my parents celebrated their 50th wedding anniversary, my family and I wanted to give them some special remembrances of their life together. On a formal anniversary celebration announcement, friends were asked to bring stories instead of gifts. The invitation read, *If you would like to present a gift other than your presence, we suggest a written account of a special time spent with our parents as a reminder of the richness each of you has added to their life together.*

– Kay Goodman, Lexington, Virginia

The Second Time

Pledges to the children, too

It was the second marriage for both of us. Between us, we had five children. Before we made our wedding vows to each other, we each made vows to our own children, and to our soon-to-be stepchildren. We pledged to our own children that our love and care for them would never change. To our partner's children, we pledged friendship and love. We made it clear that we would always consider our home to be their home, too. My youngest daughter honored us by reading scripture during the service.

Our honeymoon was a camping trip across the country. We invited all of them to join us – and all but one did. "Amazing" doesn't cover it!

– Carolyn Pogue,
Calgary, Alberta

Children participate

Milton and I wanted to share our expressions of love and commitment with our children, our families, and friends. Since this was a second marriage for both of us, it was important for our children – who through our wedding were becoming part of a blended family – to feel as much a part of the service as we did.

Unlike our first traditional weddings, we were determined to have a ceremony that was an expression of ourselves. We chose an open-air stage in a local park with benches in the shade of oak trees. We decorated the stage area with borrowed hanging baskets of begonias and ferns. A small table covered with a white linen cloth and adorned with candles and daisies served as an altar, and hanging on the wall behind the altar was a rustic cross made by our friend who officiated at the wedding. Other friends made paper cranes and hung them as mobiles on each side of the stage.

It was a casual wedding. A friend played the recorder as everyone gathered for the ceremony. Accompanied by our children, each of us walked to the altar where each child declared his support of the marriage. Family members from both sides and friends also pledged their support and lighted candles as a symbol of their promises. After we said our vows to one another, we marched out to an old fiddle tune played by a musician friend.

Dinner on the grounds followed. We supplied barbecue and punch bowls with iced tea and lemonade while guests brought their favorite dishes. Wedding cakes were gifts from friends. After dinner we had an old-fashioned barn dance. Our casual dress (I chose a peasant dress and Milton wore dress slacks with a knit shirt), and that of our guests, enabled everyone to dance until their feet ached.

As we had hoped, it was a wonderful, fun-filled day and uniquely our own. We will always cherish those memories, including the pack of dogs that roared through the park and helped themselves to one of the pans of barbecue.

– Janie Howell, Ellenwood, Georgia

Retirement

In many pre-modern societies, aging was regarded as a natural part of life, and the elderly were treated with respect, if not reverence. The high esteem accorded the elderly was based both on the fact that they had survived to be old, as well as the wisdom accumulated from many years of living. Moreover, the sense of interdependence within the community made respect and care for the elderly a natural expression of gratitude for their earlier contributions.

In modern Western society, the passage from middle age to old age is generally perceived to be at retirement. The idea of retiring at a particular age – whether at 65, 70 or some other age – is new. It is an outgrowth of industrialization when machines began to produce a surplus of products and, combined with increased longevity, created a surplus of laborers. At the turn of the century, only 39 percent of the people in the U.S. could expect to reach the age of 65. Now more than 70 percent can expect to reach that age. Of course, people retired before the Industrial Revolution, but there were no standard ages at which retirement began. In earlier times, the age for retirement had more to do with an individual's health or financial status than with chronological age.

Some people eagerly anticipate retirement. For them, it offers a break from heavy work schedules and time to focus on other priorities: spend more time with family, travel, hobbies, etc. Others dread retirement. Some see it as a symbolic inauguration of deteriorating health. For others it means an unwanted change in routine, the loss of job satisfaction, too much leisure time, decrease in social contacts, and reduced income.

While the consumer culture offers many comforts and conveniences to the aging, its prevailing values undermine respect for older people. In an aging society, the consumer culture idolizes youth. To people living on reduced and fixed incomes, having money to spend is touted as the source of happiness and satisfaction. For those most in need of community, individualism is prized above the common good.

As is the case in all passages, more than the individual is involved. Births are passages not only for the baby, but for the parents. Getting married is a passage not only for the bride and groom, but for parents and friends. Death is not only a passage for the deceased, but for the survivors. Retirement and other later passages – selling the family home, entering a nursing home, etc. – are not only passages for the individual, but for the surrounding family and community as well.

Most retirement ceremonies point to the accomplishments of the honoree and look forward to the positive side of retirement. Recognition of the community's indebtedness to the retiree should be coupled with recognition of the community's new responsibility to and for the person. Somewhere – in the family and/or in the religious community – there need to be rites that anticipate the joys and the sorrow of the next phase of life. Rites are needed, not unlike a wedding, that celebrate the new relationship with the rest of the family and community and call attention to family and community responsibilities in this new relationship.

– Reprinted from *To Celebrate: Reshaping Holidays & Rites of Passage*

Time to get deeper into the fray

What is coming up for me is not retirement from anything, as I see it. It is advancing. When you live in an industrialized country where the majority of the poor are little children, you have to think about moving deeper into the fray. For dozens of years, I've made my living consulting with a smorgasbord of anti-poverty groups. When I stop consulting, I intend to keep right on working with some of these groups as a volunteer.

– Gene Sylvestre, Minneapolis, Minnesota

Retirees make hospital possible

In the small North Carolina town in which I grew up, there was a desperate need for a new hospital. With the complexity of federal regulations about funding, the necessity to raise a large amount of money locally, and the demands to find suitable administrative personnel and additional medical personnel, the job was mammoth and time-consuming. I watched from a distance as two men and a woman, all retired, took on the job and succeeded. Only retired people could have given so much time, combined with their wisdom and experience. One of the men was my father. I flew there for the grand celebration of the hospital opening and his 80th birthday.

– Julia T. Gary, Decatur, Georgia

Rite to retire

One: Retirement is a perfect time for taking a serious look at this gift we call life. It is also a time to examine our relationship to our Creator. With retirement, there is time to think, to study and to pray; there is time to see life in a new perspective, to be thankful. And most of all, there is time to live!

For many of the significant transitions in our lives, there is a ceremony – a ritual, a rite of passage – in which we cast off an old status and assume a new one. In the presence of family and friends we take on new responsibilities. From birth we go through personal, educational, and professional changes that indicate beginnings. Baptism, confirmation, and marriage are religious rites in our church. Jews celebrate bar and bat mitzvah, marking the passage of boys and girls into manhood and womanhood and adult religious responsibilities.

Today, we shall begin a new rite in our church, a service that I hope will become an annual event. Those in the congregation who are 65 years of age or more and who wish to redirect their lives to renewed growth and service may come to the altar for a time of celebration and dedication. The congregation is invited to join in a litany of support for their redirection.

In this community of faith, love, and service, we come to celebrate a time of passage for some of our members – a passage through retirement to redirection.

Congregation: We believe that we are created in the image of God; that we are intended for a special relationship with God through Jesus Christ and, thereby, for service to all humankind. At this moment we, of all ages, reaffirm this statement of the purpose and meaning of our lives.

Minister: Retirement is a gift, a wonderful gift of increased personal freedom and time. Our friends at the altar come now to ask for God's guidance and help in redirecting their lives.

Seniors: We pray that we may be open to new direction, new insights, and new opportunities for service.

One: This congregation challenges you as mature and experienced elders among us to use your gift of time and freedom to increase your understanding of a life lived for God and in close relationship with God.

Seniors: We pledge ourselves to increased study of scripture, to regular times of meditation, and to prayer.

Minister: We recognize your accomplishments and contributions as members of this congregation and affirm your experience and knowledge. We need your continued involvement in this fellowship and actively seek your wise counsel.

Congregation: As a congregation, we applaud the accomplishments of our senior members and are grateful for their contributions to this community of faith. We celebrate their passage into a new phase of life and offer our support.

Minister: Let us pray. Dear God, you are mother and father to all; you defend, nurture, and support us as we seek to serve you. We thank you for our friends and loved ones standing here, for their past service to you in their business, professional, and family lives. We celebrate their entry into this new phase of life, a time for renewal in the faith, for growth and service.

For the new challenges and opportunities that will come to them and for the new roles that they will assume, we seek your nurture and support. As a congregation, we pledge our help in this time of passage, knowing that your divine guidance is always there. Let this be a time when our congregation, your church, will grow in its mission as we work together, all ages, in keeping with your will and to your glory. In the name of Jesus Christ our Lord, we pray. Amen.

– Julia T. Gary, Decatur, Georgia

The gift of a lifetime

The Gift of a Lifetime program is the Presbyterian Church's response to the growing numbers of older adults among its members and in the communities where its congregations are located. This program gives older adults an opportunity to serve as full-time volunteers, sharing with others the gift of growing faith, commitment, experience and skill.

The program has two specific goals: to help congregations develop new approaches to older adult ministry, and to demonstrate the importance of older people's faith, experience, leadership, and commitment. Volunteers are placed for two-year periods and begin their ministry as-signments with a two-week orientation and training conference.

– Presbyterian Office on Aging, Atlanta, Georgia

Grandpa's room

Great-grandpa was too old to live alone and was coming to live with us. We fixed up his room with comfortable, used furniture and a clock; we selected our best pictures for the walls and made new curtains. We put lace doilies and fresh flowers on all the tables so the room wouldn't look empty when he came, but we left room for the things he would bring with him.

He arrived with two suitcases and his violin. In the suitcases he brought his clothes, some pictures, and his Bible. He put his things away and we had supper. It was a special meal to welcome him, but it was just his family.

It was clear from that first day that this, like a good marriage, was a "till death do us part" arrangement. He was immediately part of the decision-making process and was made privy to all household and family matters. Everything was done beforehand to make him feel he had just come home. I think the simplicity of the occasion and the homey, readied room – which we were already calling Grandpa's room – made it easy for him to slip into the family.

– Sheryl Craig, Warrensburg, Missouri

Divorce

Next to death, divorce is probably the most traumatic life passage. That it is now so commonplace does little to alleviate the pain, suffering, and sense of failure often felt by the wife and husband, their children, and other family and friends. The reasons for divorce are as many and complex as the people involved, but prevailing values in the consumer culture could contribute to a high rate of divorce.

There are numerous rites with which to move through the passage into marriage – engagement, showers, wedding – but, apart from legal proceedings, there are almost no rites to move individuals and their families through the passage of divorce. Perhaps one of the reasons for the absence of divorce rites is the assumption that to provide such rites would be to encourage the incidence of divorce. Moreover, newly-divorced people often find themselves isolated from former friends, especially couples. Sometimes the isolation is self-imposed, perhaps out of shame. Sometimes it is because friends are not able to cope with the experience themselves. The reality is that many people are left to pass through this nightmare alone. Not only the former spouses suffer, but their children as well.

Although there are few existing rites for the divorce passage, couples and individuals are expressing a need for them, and many are creating their own rituals. As in marriage ceremonies, there is a need for expressions of joy as well as sadness at changing relationships. There is a need for the divorced person to recognize the death of a particular relationship and the sadness that brings, as well as to celebrate the joy and excitement of entering a new life. Like funerals, such rites provide a medium for family and friends to grieve and to offer support when words are inadequate.

Adapted from *To Celebrate: Reshaping Holidays & Rites of Passage*

Divorce: A service of ending and beginning

Leader: It is Christian tradition for the community to gather and to surround major events in the lives of its members with worship, with songs and prayers and expressions of mutual support in the presence of God. We observe marriage with weddings, birth with baptism and blessing, and death with funerals.

Divorce is a major event, similar in many ways to death. We are only beginning to learn to put it into a public worship setting – much like a funeral – in which we can deal with our guilt and our grief, our gratitude and our hope, in the healing fellowship of the Christian community.

There is no long tradition here, no established guidelines, but with reverence toward God and with kindled affections and tender hearts toward those who have suffered a grievous loss, let us worship God.

Hymn: "Be Still My Soul"

Call to confession: In his time on earth our Savior encountered many people whose relationships were tangled and who suffered from a sense of failure and guilt. He invited them: "Whoever comes to me I will in no way cast out." He forgave them: "I do not condemn you. Your sins are forgiven." Let us bring our tangled relationships, our failures and our guilt to him.

Dear Lord, we all start out with high hopes and good intentions, especially in our marriages. When we take our vows we mean them sincerely. But sometimes communication breaks down. Sometimes we are betrayed, and sometimes we ourselves betray.

Love can be so wounded that it dies, and a loveless marriage becomes a living lie and a source of endless pain, blocking any meaningful future. And in the friction between adults, children are hurt. Have mercy on us, O God, in the shame and guilt and failure that we feel. We do not ask that you approve of us, but only that you forgive us. Forgive us all, for when a marriage fails in the Christian community, we are all involved. Amen.

Silent personal confession

Assurance of pardon: Hear the comforting words of our Savior: "Whoever comes to me I will in no way cast out...Your sins, which are many, are forgiven. Go and sin no more." Amen.

Response: You are the Lord, giver of mercy.

A Prayer of Thanksgiving: Great God, giver of every good gift, we thank you for all that was good about _____ and _____'s marriage. For their first love, for years of faithfulness through good times and bad, for the wonderful children, _____, who came to bless their home, for the way each furthered the work of the other, for joys and sorrows shared that are too numerous to name, we give you thanks. As we value the lives of loved ones who have died, help us to value all that was good in this marriage that is ending. You are the giver of all good things, and we praise your name. Amen.

Hymn: "If Thou but Suffer God to Guide Thee"

Unison prayer of grieving: God of all comfort and mercy, hear our grief.

Something very precious has died and we want to cry, to wail, to mourn, perhaps to scream in our anguish. You know our pain and sorrow and you hear our anger and distress. Our brother Jesus wept, and we know that weeping is a part of our humanity. So we offer you our tears and beg for your comfort. Comfort us, O God. In Jesus' name. Amen.

Hebrew Scripture lesson: Psalm 46

Unison prayer of hope: Creator God, you make all things new. And you can give to _____ and _____, their children, and to all of us a new future, a time full of hope and of unforeseen possibilities. We pray that in your wisdom you will prepare us and lead us into that future one day at a time, one step at a time. Your love is in our hearts. And we rest assured that if our hope comes from you, we will live in your light. Praise be to you. Amen.

The New Testament lesson: 2 Corinthians 5:16–19

Expressions of concern and support: We now invite the friends of _____ and _____ and their children to stand and speak simply from the heart your concerns and your support.

Hymn : "Blest Be the Tie that Binds"

Benediction: May the God of hope fill you with all joy and peace in believing, so that by the power of the Holy Spirit you may abound in hope. Amen.

– North Decatur Presbyterian Church, Decatur, Georgia

Children need support from both parents

When my parents divorced, I was only 11 years old. The divorce was hard on my mother, and I spent a lot of time at home trying to console her. My reaction to my situation at home was to cause trouble at school. My mother had the foresight to know this might happen, so she spoke with my teachers letting them know about the divorce and the tough time I was having at home. This simple alerting process helped my teachers respond to me in positive ways. They helped me at school by allowing me to do things alone so I would not make trouble with the other students. This enabled me to deal with the divorce without spending a lot of time in trouble.

Divorce has many implications for children, but one I have become aware of is the loss of the parent without custody. The child might spend time with this parent, but it is not the same relationship the two once had. In my case, my father moved out of our house. He saw my brothers and me on weekends, but he could no longer discipline us the way he once had. He talked with us, but he did not reprimand us for fear we would not want to see him.

My mother was busy with work and her night classes so she had little time to spend with us. My dad could spend time only on the week- end, so he became more like a friend than a parent. Though I love him, we will never be able to have the same relationship we once had as parent and child.

– Joe Hayes, Morrow, Georgia

Death

Pregnancy loss

Modern medical technology has made it possible for the bonding process, that series of interactions through which we humans come to know one another, to begin much earlier in preg- nancy than ever before in human his- tory. It is, for example, possible to know one is pregnant within days of conception, to know the sex of the baby before mother "begins to show," and to see fetal responses to the moth- ers voice and activity even before she can feel movement. These dramatic yet commonplace developments and today's drastically reduced childhood mortality give the impression that pre- natal and infant death are relatively rare. Unfortunately, the common per- ception is illusory. Far from being an infrequent event, perhaps as many as one-fourth of all pregnancies end in death before birth.

The death of a child before birth is a crisis of unrealized magnitude; it remains a frequent family crisis in modern life. These deaths can be very lonely times for the bereaved parents. In these lonely and painful circum- stances, the opportunity to worship is an opportunity to challenge God for answers, to forgive and be forgiven, to share one's grief with others, to re- member and celebrate special mo- ments, and to hear a word of hope.

– Marilyn Washburn, M.D., M.Div.,
Avondale Estates, Georgia

Those babies were real

It is strange that an infant, wanted or unwanted, planned or unplanned, an infant not even properly born, let alone named, can affect a person. It has been almost 20 years since my five-day-old daughter died, and almost 25 years since a miscarriage, but those babies still affect the way I see love and life, children, the world, and myself.

I know now it is a mistake not to properly grieve infants or even fetuses who die. Somewhere inside (and from society) we hear the mes- sage that "we didn't know them – it's not as if they were real." And so we "buck up"; we "get on with life."

But they were real. They changed my marriage, my faith, my outlook on life, my other children's lives. If I had to do it over again, I would have a funeral, or make up a ritual of loss. I would gather together the people who loved me and ask them to weep and wail with me. I would forget about being brave until all my tears had fallen.

I am sure that no one outside my immediate family remembers those babies. But I do. They changed me.

Today, organizations for bereaved parents allow parents to grieve in community with others who have been down the same sad road. Their names are listed with funeral homes, social service agencies, YMCA and YWCA, and mental health groups.

Death of a child

Learning to live with the death of a child is best done in the presence of other bereaved parents. In small or large groups, you will likely discover that what the rest of society might call strange or bizarre is very much normal. You will likely hear about personal rituals that help people readjust to life. To the uninitiated, some rituals may appear unusual, but they seem to maintain a necessary connection with the deceased and to offer creative and personal expressions of a grief that has no equal. These rituals are expressed most of-

ten on the anniversary of the child's death, on the child's birthday, on the first day of school, and during "regular" celebrations such as Christmas, Hanukkah, Halloween, Easter, Mother's Day, and Father's Day.

Rituals include writing periodic letters to the child, visiting the gravesite, giving a gift to a library or school on the birthday in memory of the child, hanging the child's Christmas stocking and having members of the family write notes to the child to place in it, burning special candles during the holidays or on some special date, decorating a small Christmas tree and placing it on the gravesite, making a quilt in memory of or with the clothing from the deceased, and so on. Most bereaved parents agree that the most difficult time of year is December; perhaps this is why rituals are more important then.

In December, nondenominational candlelight services are held annually by chapters of the Compassionate Friends, an international organization of bereaved parents and siblings. At this service, the children are remembered with candles and flowers, and their photographs are displayed.

Ritualized customs are also important within the context of the family's religious or cultural practices. During grieving, some people let their hair grow, or cut it off. Some cultures encourage wearing black for the period of a year. In some traditions, family members bathe the body before the funeral; in others, a funeral director does this. It is important to give these rituals careful consideration. Skipping them in order to try to "hurry" grief is usually fruitless.

It is important, too, to remember that when a child dies, you don't "get over it." You need to learn to say good-bye again and again and again, sometimes alone, sometimes with others. You need to learn to live with the loss. You need to repeatedly re-create yourself in order to learn to live a new way.

"Build a relationship;
Do a good deed;
Suffer as well as you are able."
– Victor Frankl, Holocaust survivor

Living with loss

When Todd died I wondered if I'd ever be happy again. The absence of our vibrant 15-year-old son left a hole in my heart and in my life. A deep, dark vast hole. Today, a few years later, I'm glad to be alive once again. The drag in my step has given over to a skip. The tight rope around my chest has dropped away, allowing free and easy breathing. The iron hand squeezing my heart has released its grip. Facial lines of worry and fatigue have softened to make room for the crow's feet of crinkled smiles. Once

again I respond to people and things. Life is good!

What made the difference? How does one move from the devastation of loss to a rich and full life? When we experience loss we have a choice. We can choose to be hateful and bitter or to grow and develop and become contributing members of society. In examining my personal loss and in conducting workshops where I've observed and counseled others going through grief, the following insights for constructive coping have emerged.

- Loss occurs frequently – learn from it.
- Loss drains the spirit – seek solitude and sociality.
- Loss can be put to work – help others.
- Life is short – get on with your goals.
- Life is now – enjoy this moment.

These insights don't erase a loss, but they do assist us in using loss for good. However, they're mere words unless they're woven throughout by a common thread – that of hope. When hope is present one can face loss. For Christians, that hope lies in knowing God is with us. My favorite symbol of hope is that of the caterpillar. In his furry coat, he crawls over Earth's hills and valleys, constantly facing obstacles, but trudging on. His hope lies in someday soaring over the obstacles in his new-found freedom as a butterfly. My prayer is that in our losses we may experience such hope: the hope of a caterpillar waiting to become a butterfly.

– Vivian Elaine Johnson, Minneapolis, Minnesota
(Adapted from "Living With Loss," *Faith at Work*, April 1979)

A daughter's funeral

The young daughter (25) of a friend of ours died of cancer. Instead of a funeral they had an open house and potluck one afternoon between 1:00 and 4:00. People came together out of love for this girl, to talk and share their feelings. They were encouraged to speak to the group about their memories and feelings. Some of her friends sang songs that she had enjoyed.

The ashes of her body were later scattered in a beautiful wooded area in a private ceremony.

– Beth Brownfield, Golden Valley, Minnesota

Ancient rite helps grieving process: Death of a spouse

My husband died very suddenly of a heart attack on the summit of Torrey's Peak, one of Colorado's highest mountains. He died in our youngest daughter's arms, although our son and members of a rescue squad tried several hours to revive him.

When our family went to the mortuary, I asked for a pan of water and a cloth to bathe my husband's body before cremation. I had just read about an ancient rite where the person nearest to the deceased bathes the body, a custom that is still practiced in many cultures. Although we had never had this kind of experience before, it felt right. It was an important part of a grieving and healing process for me and a very special way to say good-bye.

– Virginia McConnell, Boulder, Colorado

Open house memorial

Several months after my wife died, our family decided to have an open house as a memorial to my wife. Guests were invited to bring finger food and a recollection or comment for a memory book. We showed family slides and, with the warm comments and memories shared by friends, it was a true celebration of her life.

– Robert K Marsh, Berkeley, California

Grandmother's quilt

An Ontario quiltmaker made an unusual tribute to her grandmother by making a quilt in her memory. She used pieces of tatting, crochet, and embroidery that her grandmother had made, photographs that had been transferred to fabric, and excerpts from her grandmother's diaries (hand-lettered with indelible ink on fabric). To bring it all together, she used flowered fabric similar to fabrics she remembered from her grandmother's home. Making the quilt was a productive and beautiful way to grieve her own loss, and to celebrate her grandmother's life.

Sugar cookies make wonderful memories of grandmother

After the memorial service for my grandmother, who had died several months earlier, a number of people came back to our house for a meal and conversation. My sister had baked two of my grandmother's most often-used recipes – one was her legendary sugar cookies and the other a loaf-style chocolate cake. It was a lovely way to remember, as everyone there had at one time or another tasted these special goodies from Grandma's kitchen.

– Jane Ander, Rock Island, Illinois

Hospice Care

Dying with dignity

The hospice movement in the United States grew out of several concerns of the 1960s and early 1970s. The hospital environment was no longer one of "hospitality," but of impersonal technology; the cost of care began the skyrocketing course on which it continues; and many people sensed an absence of any control over their own lives once they entered the foreign territory of hospital rules and regulations.

In an effort to reclaim an opportunity for intimate personal relationships, reduce the costs, and once again make dying a significant life passage, especially at the point past which medical technology has little to offer, dying people simply went home. In many situations, however, nursing, pastoral, social, and to a lesser extent, medical support were needed for the comfort of dying persons as well as their family members. So, the home-based hospice was born.

Studies revealed that hospice patients lived longer, and with more comfort and dignity, while their care cost far less than that of hospitalized patients. There remained, however, many of the terminally ill whose family members could not care for them at home, so only a couple of years after the beginning of its home-based program, the first "freestanding" hospice was built by Connecticut Hospice. As more patients began to choose hospice care, and as health care workers grew increasingly familiar with its benefits, hospitals began to develop hospice units or wards – islands of alternative care within traditional hospital settings. This movement back into the hospital has resulted in the diffusion of hospice learnings and philosophies. Now health care providers themselves are wondering why people have to be dying to get hospice care.

And the learnings are many. We have proven that family-given care is more intense as well as loving; that the opportunity to care for a loved one can be healing to the family as well as to the dying person; and that families can almost always learn to manage necessary "high-tech" equipment, including ventilators and intravenous pain medications. The costs are lower and pain is better controlled. Health care professionals have worked together as interdisciplinary teams, establishing new relationships and new respect for one another's contributions. All these developments and more offer a great deal to health care delivery in many situations.

But, there are concerns as well. Because of the cost efficiency of hospice care, federal legislation made hospice care Medicare-reimbursable, and many "third party" insurance companies have followed suit. While this has made hospice care available to many persons who could not otherwise afford it, this development has also opened the door to the possibility of "for-profit" care for the dying, and threatens to divorce the hospice concept from its very personalized, grassroots origins. Only a great deal of vigilance will protect the fledgling institution of intimate personal care from commercialization.

– Marilyn Washburn, M.D., M.Div.,
Avondale Estates, Georgia

Hospice: Stewardship of the rites of passage

The most devastating reality of terminal illness is the continued loss of control over daily life. Accordingly, the goal of hospice care is to give dying persons and their loved ones as much agency over, and autonomy in the midst of, their situation as possible.

Hospice, then, is spiritual care inasmuch as caregivers explore what gives meaning and order to the living, dying, and grieving of those they serve. Hospice structures this meaning and order by supporting rites of passage which will enable them to journey along an uncharted path; rites fashioned from their family tradition, cultural milieu, and religious heritage.

Consequently, hospice doesn't *do* things for those who suffer. Rather, hospice allows persons to continue to *be*, in the midst of their suffering.

– William E. Wallace, Director of Hospice,
Grady Memorial Hospital, Atlanta, Georgia

Memorial Societies

Memorial societies are cooperative, nonprofit, democratically-run consumer organizations that help members get simplicity, dignity, and economy in funeral arrangements through advance planning. They are not run by funeral directors.

These societies act in an advisory capacity and often have contracts or agreements with funeral directors, helping members get exactly the services they want at reasonable cost. Although a few of the large societies have paid secretaries, the work of the societies is usually done by unpaid volunteers. Memorial societies do collectively what few individual families are prepared to do – they inquire around, compare services and prices, then share this information with their members. They do not collect payment for funeral services.

There are memorial societies in some 200 cities in North America with a combined membership of more than one million people. Most societies charge a nominal one-time membership fee, and some have a small "records charge," which they collect from the family at the time of death, via the funeral director. Families moving to another city can transfer their membership at little or no charge. Likewise, when a death occurs away from home, the society in the host city and its cooperating funeral director will assist the family.

Memorial society members commonly save 50 to 75 percent of usual funeral costs. The savings are in part due to collective bargaining by the societies, but more from the simplicity that members are encouraged to practice.

The success and popularity of memorial societies has led to imitations. Private companies calling themselves societies have entered the funeral service business. If someone from a "society" tries to sell you something or offers you a prepayment plan, investigate carefully. Memorial societies have no commercial interests and rarely charge membership fees over $25. The societies are an outstanding example of how consumers, by democratic group effort, can empower themselves at the grassroots level.

Nearly all bona fide societies in the United States and Canada are members of their respective national organizations. If you have doubts about a society, check to see if it is a member of the national association. For more information about memorial societies, where the nearest one is to you, or how to organize one, contact one of the two national associations (see Appendix).

– Adapted from *Dealing Creatively with Death: A Manual of Death Education and Simple Burial* by Ernest Morgan

Bequeathal

How the dead can help the living

There are many ways in which socially-concerned people can arrange to serve the needs of their fellow men and women after they have died. Many lives can be saved, and health and sight can be restored to thousands through the intelligent "salvaging" of organs and tissues from persons who have died. Medical and dental training requires thousands of bodies each year, for anatomical study. Medical research, too, needs our cooperation, in the form of permission for autopsies (not permissible if the body is left to a medical school) and the bequeathal of special parts, such as the ear bones of people with hearing difficulties.

If we truly accept our own mortality and genuinely identify ourselves with humanity, we will gladly help in every way we can. These ways are steadily increasing through the bequeathal of organs.

Although many driver's licenses have a form which gives permission for organ bequeathal, these permissions may be overturned by the family at the time of death. It is most important that family discussions are held before there is a death, to ensure that everyone understands the donor's desires and understands exactly what is involved. Discussion with the family and exploration of the issue with a doctor should be carried out before there is a crisis.

The dead helping the living: Anatomical gifts

The day will come when my body will lie upon a white sheet tucked neatly under the four corners of a mattress, located in a hospital busily occupied with the living and the dying. At a certain moment a doctor will determine that my brain has ceased to function and that for all intents and purposes, my life has stopped.

When that happens, do not attempt to instill artificial life into my body by use of a machine, and don't call this my deathbed. Let it be called the bed of life and let my body be taken from it to help others lead fuller lives.

Give my sight to the man who has never seen a sunrise, a baby's face or love in the eyes of a woman. Give my heart to the person who has nothing but endless days of pain. Give my blood to the teenager who was pulled from the wreckage of his car so that he may live to see his grandchildren play. Give my kidneys to a person who depends upon a machine to exist from week to week. Take my bones, every muscle fiber, every nerve, and try to find a way to make a crippled child walk. Explore every corner of my brain, take my cells, if necessary, and let them grow so that some day a speechless boy will shout at the crack of a bat or a deaf girl will hear the sound of rain against her window.

Burn the rest and scatter the ashes to the wind to help the flowers grow.

If you must bury something, bury my faults, my weaknesses, and my prejudices against my fellows. Give my sins to the devil, give my soul to God.

If by chance you wish to remember me, do it with a kind deed or a word to someone who needs you. If you do all I have asked, I will live forever.

– Robert Noel Test; reprinted from *The Bank Account,* January 1987, with permission from The Living Bank, Houston, Texas.

Appendix

The following is a list of agencies you may wish to contact for more information on a specific area of concern, for the purpose of making a charitable donation, or for finding the branch nearest you.

Central America Week

Inter-American Task Force on Central America
475 Riverside Drive, Room 563
New York, NY 10115
212–870–3383

Inter-Church Committee for Human Rights in
    Latin America
129 St. Clair Ave. W.
Toronto, ON M5V 1N5
416–921–0801

Children

Cooperative Disaster Child Care Program
P.O. Box 188, 500 Main St.
New Windsor, MD 21776

Crafts and Trade Goods

The Desert Homestead
c/o The Family McCardel
3175 State Rt. 3
Loudonville, OH 44842

Friends of the Third World
National Resource Center
611 West Wayne Street
Fort Wayne, IN 46802

Crafts and Trade Goods (cont.)

MCC Self-Help Crafts - USA
Department A
704 Main St.
Akron, PA 17501
717–859–8100

MCC Self-Help Crafts - Canada
Box 869, 65 Heritage Drive
New Hamburg, ON N0B 2G0
519–662–1879

Mountain Maid
Box 1386
Port-au-Prince, HAITI
U.S. Forwarding Address:
Box 15650
West Palm Beach, FL 33416

Pueblo to People,
A Non-profit Organization
1616 Montrose
Houston, TX 77006
713–523–1197
1–800–842–5220
1–800–843–5257

SERRV
Self-Help Handcrafts
500 Main Street
P.O. Box 365
New Windsor, MD 21776-0365
301–635–8748

Crafts and Trade Goods (cont.)

Third World Handarts
4151 La Linda Way
Sierra Vista, AZ 85635

Death- and Bereavement-
Related Services

The Compassionate Friends
Canadian National Office
685 William Ave.
Winnipeg, MB R3E 0Z2

The Compassionate Friends
P.O. Box 3696
Oak Brook, IL 60522-3696

Continental Association of Funeral and
    Memorial Societies
(includes Canadian Memorial Societies)
2001 "S" St. NW, Suite 530
Washington, DC 20009
202–745–0634
(or check your phone book for your local
Memorial Society listing)

National Hospice Organization
1901 N. Fort Myer Dr., Suite 402
Arlington, VA 22209

Economic Development and
Alternatives

Co-op America
2100 M Street, NW
Suite 310
Washington, DC 20063
202–872–5307, 1–800–424–2667

Evergreen Society
Box 222
Grand Rapids, MI 46588

Federation of Southern Cooperatives/
    Land Assistance Fund
P.O. Box 95
Epes, AL 35460
Or: 100 Edgewood Ave., NW
Suite 1228
Atlanta, GA 30303

Economic Development and
Alternatives (cont.)

Heifer Project International Headquarters
P.O. Box 808
Little Rock, AR 72203
501–376–6836

Interfaith Center on Corporate Responsibility
475 Riverside Drive, Room 566
New York, NY 10115
212–870–2295

Peace Corps Partnership Program
806 Connecticut Ave., NW
Washington, DC 20526

Environment

Heschel Memorial Forest Fund
211 Florida Ave, NW
Washington, DC 20036

Jewish National Fund of Canada
National Headquarters
1980 Sherbrooke St. W., Ste 500
Montreal, QC H3H 1E8

Save the Redwoods League
114 Sansome Street, Room 605
San Francisco, CA 94104

Scoutrees for Canada
Scouts Canada
P.O. Box 5151, Station LCD-Merrivale
Ottawa, ON K2C 3G7

Sierra Club
730 Polk Street
San Francisco, CA 94109

Hostels and Elderhostels

Elderhostel
75 Federal St.
Boston, MA 02110

Elderhostel Canada
Bajus Building
308 Wellington St.
Kingston, ON K7K 7A7

Hostels and Elderhostels (cont.)

Hostelling International Canada
400–205 Catherine St.
Ottawa, ON K2P 1C3

Hostelling International USA
American Youth Hostels
733–15th St., NW
Washington, DC 20005

Housing

Habitat for Humanity International
121 Habitat Street
Americus, GA 31709

Hunger Programs

Bread for the World
802 Rhode Island Ave., NE
Washington, DC 20018

ELCA Hunger Appeal
Evangelical Lutheran Church in America
8765 W. Higgins Rd.
Chicago, IL 60631
312–380–2700

Hunger Action
United Church of Christ
3rd floor,
700 Prospect Ave.
Cleveland, OH 44115
216–736–3290

Oxfam America
26 West Street
Boston, MA 02111

Presbyterian Hunger Program
100 Witherspoon St.
Louisville, KY
40202–1396
502–569–5832

Society of St. Andrew
P.O. Box 329
Big Island, VA
24526
804–299–5956

Hunger Programs (cont.)

United Methodist Committee on Relief
General Board of Global Ministries
World Program Division
475 Riverside Drive, Room 1307
New York, NY 10115

Overseas Development

Church World Service
28606 Phillips Street
219–264–3102

Pax World Foundation
4400 East-West Hwy.
Suite 130
Bethesda, MD 20814

Reformed Church World Service
475 Riverside Drive
New York, NY 10115

United Methodist Church
General Board of Global Ministries
World Program Division
475 Riverside Drive, Room 1516
New York, NY 10115

Political and Social Justice

Agricultural Missions, Inc.
475 Riverside Drive, Room 624
New York, NY 10115
212–870–2553

Amnesty International
214 Montreal St., Ste. 401
Vanier, ON K1L 1A4
613–744–7667

Center for Global Education
Augsburg College
2211 Riverside Ave.
Minneapolis, MN 55454

Commission on Religion in Appalachia
P.O. Box 10867
864 Weisgarber Road, NW
Knoxville, TN 37919
615–584–6133

Political and Social Justice (cont.)

Fellowship of Reconciliation
523 N. Broadway
Box 271
Nyack, NY
10960-0271

The Gray Panthers
3700 Chestnut St.
Philadelphia, PA 19104

Institute for Peace and Justice
4144 Lindell #122
St. Louis, MO 63108
314–533–4445

Koinonia Partners
Americus, GA 31709

National Farm Worker Ministry
1337 West Ohio
Chicago, IL 60622
312–829–6436

Rural Advancement Fund (RAF)
National Sharecroppers Fund (NSF)
2124 Commonwealth Ave.
Charlotte, NC 28205
704–334–3051

Rural Crisis Issue Team
Domestic Hunger and Poverty Project
National Council of Churches of Christ
Division of Church and Society
475 Riverside Dr., Rm. 572
New York, NY 10115
212–870–2307/2308

United Farm Workers
La Paz
Keene, CA 93570

Tourism

The Center for Responsible Tourism
2 Kensington Road
San Anselmo, CA 94960

Contours
P.O. Box 11–357
Bangkok 10110
Thailand